The New Official LSAT
TriplePrep
Volume 4™

A Publication of the Law School Admission Council,
Newtown, PA

From the Editor

Although these PrepTests are presented to you in paper form, the LSAT® is now delivered electronically. Please visit LSAC.org for the most up-to-date information about these tests.

The Law School Admission Council's mission is to advance law and justice by encouraging diverse and talented individuals to study law and by supporting their enrollment and learning journeys from prelaw through practice. See https://www.lsac.org/about.

ISBN-13: 978-1-7334330-6-8

Print number
5 4 3 2 1

Table of Contents

Introduction to the LSAT

The Law School Admission Test (LSAT) is designed to measure skills considered essential for success in law school: the reading and comprehension of complex texts with accuracy and insight; the ability to think critically; and the analysis and evaluation of the reasoning and arguments of others.

The LSAT provides a standard measure of acquired reading and verbal reasoning skills that law schools can use as one of several factors in assessing applicants.

For up-to-date information about LSAC's services, go to our website, LSAC.org.

Scoring

Your LSAT score is based on the number of questions you answered correctly. This is called your "raw score." All test questions are weighted exactly the same. The total number of questions you get right, not which particular questions you get right or wrong, is what matters for your score. There is no deduction for incorrect answers.

To make it easier to compare scores earned across different LSAT administrations, your raw score is converted to an LSAT scale. The LSAT scale ranges from 120 to 180, with 120 being the lowest possible score and 180 being the highest possible score.

The LSAT Multiple-Choice Question Types

The multiple-choice questions on the LSAT reflect a broad range of academic disciplines and are intended to give no advantage to candidates from a particular academic background.

The following material presents a general discussion of the nature of each question type and some strategies that can be used in answering them.

Logical Reasoning Questions

Arguments are a fundamental part of the law, and analyzing arguments is a key element of legal analysis. Training in the law builds on a foundation of basic reasoning skills. Law students must draw on the skills of analyzing, evaluating, constructing, and refuting arguments. They need to be able to identify what information is relevant to an issue or argument and what impact further evidence might have. They need to be able to reconcile opposing positions and use arguments to persuade others.

Logical Reasoning questions evaluate the ability to analyze, critically evaluate, and complete arguments as they occur in ordinary language. The questions are based on short arguments drawn from a wide variety of sources, including newspapers, general interest magazines, scholarly publications, advertisements, and informal discourse. These arguments mirror legal reasoning in the types of arguments presented and in their complexity, though few of the arguments actually have law as a subject matter.

Each Logical Reasoning question requires you to read and comprehend a short passage, then answer one question (or, rarely, two questions) about it. The questions are designed to assess a wide range of skills involved in thinking critically, with an emphasis on skills that are central to legal reasoning.

These skills include:

- Recognizing the parts of an argument and their relationships

- Recognizing similarities and differences between patterns of reasoning

- Drawing well-supported conclusions

- Reasoning by analogy

- Recognizing misunderstandings or points of disagreement

- Determining how additional evidence affects an argument

- Detecting assumptions made by particular arguments

- Identifying and applying principles or rules

- Identifying flaws in arguments

- Identifying explanations

The questions do not presuppose specialized knowledge of logical terminology. For example, you will not be expected to know the meaning of specialized terms such as "ad hominem" or "syllogism." On the other hand, you will be expected to understand and critique the reasoning contained in arguments. This requires that you possess a university-level understanding of widely used concepts such as argument, premise, assumption, and conclusion.

Suggested Approach

Read each question carefully. Make sure that you understand the meaning of each part of the question. Make sure that you understand the meaning of each answer choice and the ways in which it may or may not relate to the question posed.

Do not pick a response simply because it is a true statement. Although true, it may not answer the question posed.

Answer each question on the basis of the information that is given, even if you do not agree with it. Work within the context provided by the passage. LSAT questions do not involve any tricks or hidden meanings.

Reading Comprehension Questions

Both law school and the practice of law revolve around extensive reading of highly varied, dense, argumentative, and expository texts (for example, cases, codes, contracts, briefs, decisions, evidence). This reading must be exacting, distinguishing precisely what is said from what is not said. It involves comparison, analysis, synthesis, and application (for example, of principles and rules). It involves drawing appropriate inferences and applying ideas and arguments to new contexts. Law school reading also requires the ability to grasp unfamiliar subject matter and the ability to penetrate difficult and challenging material.

The purpose of LSAT Reading Comprehension questions is to measure the ability to read, with understanding and insight, examples of lengthy and complex materials similar to those commonly encountered in law school. The Reading Comprehension section of the LSAT contains four sets of reading questions, each set consisting of a selection of reading material followed by five to eight questions. The reading selection in three of the four sets consists of a single reading passage; the other set contains two related shorter passages. Sets with two passages are a variant of Reading Comprehension called Comparative Reading, which was introduced in June 2007.

Comparative Reading questions concern the relationships between the two passages, such as those of generalization/ instance, principle/application, or point/counterpoint. Law school work often requires reading two or more texts in conjunction with each other and understanding their relationships. For example, a law student may read a trial court decision together with an appellate court decision that overturns it, or identify the fact pattern from a hypothetical suit together with the potentially controlling case law.

Reading selections for LSAT Reading Comprehension questions are drawn from a wide range of subjects in the humanities, the social sciences, the biological and physical sciences, and areas related to the law. Generally, the selections are densely written, use high-level vocabulary, and contain sophisticated argument or complex rhetorical structure (for example, multiple points of view). Reading Comprehension questions require you to read carefully and accurately, to determine the relationships among the various parts of the reading selection, and to draw reasonable inferences from the material in the selection. The questions may ask about the following characteristics of a passage or pair of passages:

- The main idea or primary purpose

- Information that is explicitly stated

- Information or ideas that can be inferred

- The meaning or purpose of words or phrases as used in context

- The organization or structure

- The application of information in the selection to a new context

- Principles that function in the selection

- Analogies to claims or arguments in the selection

- An author's attitude as revealed in the tone of a passage or the language used

- The impact of new information on claims or arguments in the selection

Suggested Approach

Since reading selections are drawn from many different disciplines and sources, you should not be discouraged if you encounter material with which you are not familiar. It is important to remember that questions are to be answered exclusively on the basis of the information provided in the selection. There is no particular knowledge that you are expected to bring to the test, and you should not make inferences based on any prior knowledge of a subject that you may have. You may, however, wish to defer working on a set of questions that seems particularly difficult or unfamiliar until after you have dealt with sets you find easier.

Strategies. One question that often arises in connection with Reading Comprehension has to do with the most effective and efficient order in which to read the selections and questions. Possible approaches include:

- reading the selection very closely and then answering the questions;

- reading the questions first, reading the selection closely, and then returning to the questions; or

- skimming the selection and questions very quickly, then rereading the selection closely and answering the questions.

Test takers are different, and the best strategy for one might not be the best strategy for another. In preparing for the test, therefore, you might want to experiment with the different strategies and decide what works most effectively for you. Remember that your strategy must be effective under timed conditions. For this reason, the first strategy— reading the selection very closely and then answering the questions—may be the most effective for you. Nonetheless, if you believe that one of the other strategies might be more effective for you, you should try it out and assess your performance using it.

Reading the selection. Whatever strategy you choose, you should give the passage or pair of passages at least one careful reading before answering the questions. Try to distinguish main ideas from supporting ideas, and opinions or attitudes from factual, objective information. Note transitions from one idea to the next and identify the relationships among the different ideas or parts of a passage, or between the two passages in Comparative Reading sets. Consider how and why an author makes points and draws conclusions. Be sensitive to implications of what the passages say.

You may find it helpful to mark key parts of passages. For example, you might underline main ideas or important arguments, and you might circle transitional words—"although," "nevertheless," "correspondingly," and the like—that will help you map the structure of a passage. Also, you might note descriptive words that will help you identify an author's attitude toward a particular idea or person.

Answering the Questions

- Always read all the answer choices before selecting the best answer. The best answer choice is the one that most accurately and completely answers the question being posed.

- Respond to the specific question being asked. Do not pick an answer choice simply because it is a true statement. For example, picking a true statement might yield an incorrect answer to a question in which you are asked to identify an author's position on an issue, since you are not being asked to evaluate the truth of the author's position but only to correctly identify what that position is.

- Answer the questions only on the basis of the information provided in the selection. Your own views, interpretations, or opinions, and those you have heard from others, may sometimes conflict with those expressed in a reading selection; however, you are expected to work within the context provided by the reading selection. You should not expect to agree with everything you encounter in Reading Comprehension passages.

Taking the PrepTests Under Simulated LSAT Conditions

One important way to prepare for the LSAT is to simulate the day of the test by taking a practice test under actual time constraints. Taking a practice test under timed conditions helps you to estimate the amount of time you can afford to spend on each question in a section and to determine the question types on which you may need additional practice.

Since the LSAT is a timed test, it is important to use your allotted time wisely. During the test, you may work only on the section designated by the test supervisor. You cannot devote extra time to a difficult section and make up that time on a section you find easier. In pacing yourself, and checking your answers, you should think of each section of the test as a separate minitest.

Be sure that you answer every question on the test. When you do not know the correct answer to a question, first eliminate the responses that you know are incorrect, then make your best guess among the remaining choices. Do not be afraid to guess as there is no penalty for incorrect answers.

When you take a practice test, abide by all the requirements specified in the directions and keep strictly within the specified time limits. Work without a rest period. When you take an actual test, you will have a short break between two of the sections.

When taken under conditions as much like actual testing conditions as possible, a practice test provides very useful preparation for taking the LSAT.

Official directions for the four multiple-choice sections are included in these PrepTests so that you can approximate actual testing conditions as you practice.

To take the test:

- Set a timer for 35 minutes. Answer all the questions in Section I. Stop working on that section when the 35 minutes have elapsed.

- Repeat, allowing yourself 35 minutes each for Sections II, III, and IV.

- Refer to the "Computing Your Score" section at the end of each PrepTest for instruction on evaluating your performance. An answer key is provided for that purpose.

PrepTest 149

1

SECTION I
Time—35 minutes
25 Questions

Directions: Each question in this section is based on the reasoning presented in a brief passage. In answering the questions, you should not make assumptions that are by commonsense standards implausible, superfluous, or incompatible with the passage. For some questions, more than one of the choices could conceivably answer the question. However, you are to choose the **best** answer; that is, choose the response that most accurately and completely answers the question and mark that response on your answer sheet.

1. The mayoral race in Bensburg is a choice between Chu, a prodevelopment candidate, and Lewis, who favors placing greater limits on development. Prodevelopment candidates have won in the last six mayoral elections. Thus, Chu will probably defeat Lewis.

   Which one of the following statements, if true, most weakens the argument?

   (A) Lewis has extensive experience in national politics, but not in city politics.
   (B) Prodevelopment mayoral candidates in Bensburg generally attract more financial backing for their campaigns.
   (C) Bensburg is facing serious new problems that most voters attribute to overdevelopment.
   (D) Lewis once worked as an aide to a prodevelopment mayor of Bensburg.
   (E) Chu was not thought of as a prodevelopment politician before this election.

2. Rose: Let's not see the movie *Winter Fields*. I caught a review of it in the local paper and it was the worst review I've read in years.

   Chester: I don't understand why that might make you not want to see the movie. And besides, nothing in that paper is particularly well written.

   Chester's response suggests that he misinterpreted which one of the following expressions used by Rose?

   (A) see the movie
   (B) caught a review
   (C) local paper
   (D) worst review
   (E) in years

3. Enrique: The city's transit authority does not have enough money to operate for the next twelve months without cutting service or increasing fares, and the federal government has so far failed to provide additional funding. Nonetheless, the transit authority should continue operating without service cuts or fare increases until it has exhausted its funds. At that point, the federal government will be willing to provide funding to save the authority.

   Cynthia: If the transit authority tries that maneuver, the federal government will probably just let the authority go out of business. The transit authority cannot risk allowing that to happen.

   The dialogue most strongly supports the claim that Enrique and Cynthia disagree over whether

   (A) the transit authority should continue operating without cutting service or increasing fares until it has exhausted its funds
   (B) the federal government should provide additional funding to the transit authority
   (C) it would be better for the transit authority to cut services than it would be to raise fares
   (D) the federal government is willing to provide additional funding to the transit authority now
   (E) the transit authority can afford to operate for the next twelve months without cutting service even if it does not receive additional funding

GO ON TO THE NEXT PAGE.

4. A survey published in a leading medical journal in the early 1970s found that the more frequently people engaged in aerobic exercise, the lower their risk of lung disease tended to be. Since other surveys have confirmed these results, it must be the case that aerobic exercise has a significant beneficial effect on people's health.

The reasoning above is questionable because the argument

(A) ignores anecdotal evidence and bases its conclusion entirely on scientific research
(B) considers only surveys published in one particular medical journal
(C) concludes merely from the fact that two things are correlated that one causes the other
(D) presumes, without providing justification, that anyone who does not have lung disease is in good health
(E) fails to consider that even infrequent aerobic exercise may have some beneficial effect on people's health

5. Researchers examined 100 people suffering from herniated disks in their backs. Five of them were found to have a defect in a particular gene. The researchers also examined 100 people who had no problems with the disks in their backs; none had the genetic defect. They concluded that the genetic defect increases the likelihood of herniated disks.

Which one of the following, if true, most strengthens the researchers' reasoning?

(A) The researchers also examined a group of 100 people who did not have the defective gene; 80 were found to have herniated disks in their backs.
(B) When the researchers examined a group of 100 people with the defective gene, they found that 2 of them had herniated disks in their backs.
(C) When the researchers examined the families of the 5 subjects who had the defective gene, they found that 30 family members also had the defective gene, and each of them suffered from herniated disks.
(D) Another team of researchers examined a different group of 100 people who suffered from herniated disks, and they found that none of them had the defective gene.
(E) When the researchers examined the family of one of the subjects who did not suffer from herniated disks, they found 30 family members who did not have the defective gene, and 20 of them suffered from herniated disks.

6. The only vehicles that have high resale values are those that are well maintained. Thus any well-maintained vehicle has a high resale value.

The flawed nature of the argument can most effectively be demonstrated by noting that, by parallel reasoning, we could argue that

(A) since none of the plants in this garden have been pruned before, no plant in this garden needs pruning
(B) since the best mediators have the longest track records, the worst mediators have the shortest track records
(C) since only those who desire to become astronauts actually become astronauts, that desire must be the most important factor involved in determining who will become an astronaut
(D) since all city dwellers prefer waterfalls to traffic jams, anyone who prefers waterfalls to traffic jams is a city dweller
(E) since one's need for medical care decreases as one's health improves, a person who is in an excellent state of health has no need of medical care

7. Rita: No matter how you look at them, your survey results are misleading. Since people generally lie on such surveys, the numbers you collected are serious underestimates.

Hiro: I have no doubt that people lie on surveys of this type. The question is whether some people lie more than others. While the raw numbers surely underestimate what I'm trying to measure, the relative rates those numbers represent are probably close to being accurate.

Rita and Hiro disagree over whether

(A) the survey results are misleading regardless of how they are interpreted
(B) people tend to lie on certain kinds of surveys
(C) a different type of measure than a survey would produce results that are less misleading
(D) the raw numbers collected are serious underestimates
(E) the number of people surveyed was adequate for the survey's purpose

GO ON TO THE NEXT PAGE.

8. Lopez: Our university is not committed to liberal arts, as evidenced by its decision to close the classics department. The study of classical antiquity is crucial to the liberal arts, and it has been so since the Renaissance.

   Warrington: Although the study of classical works is essential to the liberal arts, a classics department isn't, since other departments often engage in that study.

   Warrington's argument proceeds by

   (A) offering additional reasons in favor of the conclusion of Lopez's argument
   (B) claiming that the reasoning in Lopez's argument rests on an illicit appeal to tradition
   (C) mounting a direct challenge to the conclusion of Lopez's argument
   (D) responding to a possible objection to the reasoning in Lopez's argument
   (E) presenting a consideration in order to undermine the reasoning in Lopez's argument

9. Ted, a senior employee, believes he is underpaid and attempts to compensate by routinely keeping short hours, though it is obvious to everyone that he still makes some valuable, unique, and perhaps irreplaceable contributions. Tatiana, Ted's supervisor, is aware of the deficit in Ted's performance, and realizes other workers work harder than they should to make up for it. Nevertheless, Tatiana decides that she should not request that Ted be replaced.

   Which one of the following principles, if valid, would most help to justify Tatiana's decision?

   (A) Supervisors should request that an employee be replaced only if they know that all the work done by that employee can be performed equally well by another employee.
   (B) Employers should compensate all their employees in a way that is adequate in relation to the value of the contributions they make.
   (C) Only someone with greater authority than a particular employee's supervisor is entitled to decide whether that employee should be replaced.
   (D) Workers in a work setting should regard themselves as jointly responsible for the work to be performed.
   (E) An employee's contributions in the workplace are not always a function of the amount of time spent on the job.

10. One adaptation that enables an animal species to survive despite predation by other species is effective camouflage. Yet some prey species with few or no other adaptations to counteract predation have endured for a long time with black-and-white coloration that seems unlikely to provide effective camouflage.

    Which one of the following, if true, most contributes to a resolution of the apparent discrepancy mentioned above?

    (A) Most species with black-and-white coloration are more populous than the species that prey upon them.
    (B) No form of camouflage is completely effective against all kinds of predators.
    (C) Animals of many predatory species do not perceive color or pattern in the same manner as humans do.
    (D) Conspicuous black-and-white areas help animals of the same species avoid encounters with one another.
    (E) Black-and-white coloration is not as great a liability against predators at night as it is during the day.

11. Lecturer: If I say, "I tried to get my work done on time," the meanings of my words do not indicate that I didn't get it done on time. But usually you would correctly understand me to be saying that I didn't. After all, if I had gotten my work done on time, I would instead just say, "I got my work done on time." And this example is typical of how conversation works.

    The lecturer's statements, if true, most strongly support which one of the following statements?

    (A) Understanding what people say often requires more than just understanding the meanings of the words they use.
    (B) It is unusual for English words to function in communication in the way that "tried" does.
    (C) Understanding what people use a word to mean often requires detecting their nonverbal cues.
    (D) Speakers often convey more information in conversation than they intend to convey.
    (E) Listeners cannot reasonably be expected to have the knowledge typically required for successful communication.

GO ON TO THE NEXT PAGE.

12. Legislator: The recently passed highway bill is clearly very unpopular with voters. After all, polls predict that the majority party, which supported the bill's passage, will lose more than a dozen seats in the upcoming election.

The reasoning in the legislator's argument is most vulnerable to criticism on the grounds that the argument

(A) gives no reason to think that the predicted election outcome would be different if the majority party had not supported the bill

(B) focuses on the popularity of the bill to the exclusion of its merit

(C) infers that the bill is unpopular from a claim that presupposes its unpopularity

(D) takes for granted that the bill is unpopular just because the legislator wishes it to be unpopular

(E) bases its conclusion on the views of voters without establishing their relevant expertise on the issues involved

13. Songwriters get much of the money they earn from their songs from radio airplay. A hit song is played thousands of times, and the songwriter is paid for each play. Only a fraction of songwriters actually achieve a hit, however, and even fewer manage to write several. Writers of hit songs are often asked to write songs for movie sound tracks, but they sometimes decline, because although such songs frequently become hits, their writers receive single up-front payments rather than continued revenues from radio airplay.

If the statements above are true, which one of the following must be true?

(A) Any songwriter who receives revenue from radio airplay has written a hit song.

(B) All songwriters who write songs for movie sound tracks have had their songs played on the radio thousands of times.

(C) Some songs written for movie sound tracks are played on the radio thousands of times.

(D) Most songwriters prefer the possibility of continued income to single up-front payments for their songs.

(E) Some songwriters earn money solely from the radio airplay of their songs.

14. Debate coach: Britta's command of the historical facts was better than Robert's, and that led to the distinct impression that Britta won the debate. But it's also important to evaluate how reasonable the debaters' arguments were, regardless of their ability to bring the facts to bear in those arguments. When you take that into consideration, Robert's debate performance was as good as Britta's.

The debate coach's argument depends on the assumption that

(A) Britta's arguments were quite unreasonable

(B) Robert's arguments were more reasonable than Britta's

(C) good debate performances require very reasonable arguments

(D) neither Britta nor Robert was in full command of the facts

(E) winning a debate requires having a good command of the facts

GO ON TO THE NEXT PAGE.

15. Physicists attempting to create new kinds of atoms often do so by fusing together two existing atoms. For such fusion to occur, the two atoms must collide with enough energy—that is, at high enough speeds—to overcome the electromagnetic force by which atoms repel each other. But if the energy with which two atoms collide greatly exceeds the minimum required for the fusion to take place, the excess energy will be converted into heat, making the resulting new atom very hot. And the hotter the atom is, the greater the chance that it will immediately split apart again.

Which one of the following is most strongly supported by the information above?

(A) When physicists create new kinds of atoms by fusing together two existing atoms, the new atoms usually split apart again immediately.

(B) If a new atom produced by the collision of two other atoms immediately splits apart again, then the collision did not produce enough energy to overcome the electromagnetic force by which atoms repel each other.

(C) The stronger the electromagnetic force by which two atoms repel each other, the hotter any new atom will be that is created by the fusion of those two atoms.

(D) Whenever two existing atoms are made to collide and fuse together into a new atom, little energy is produced in the collision unless the new atom immediately splits apart.

(E) If two atoms collide with considerably more energy than is needed for fusion to take place, the new atom will be likely to immediately split apart again.

16. Fremont: Simpson is not a viable candidate for chief executive of Pod Oil because he has no background in the oil industry.

Galindo: I disagree. An oil industry background is no guarantee of success. Look no further than Pod Oil's last chief executive, who had decades of oil industry experience but steered the company to the brink of bankruptcy.

Galindo's argument is flawed in that it

(A) fails to justify its presumption that Fremont's objection is based on personal bias

(B) fails to distinguish between relevant experience and irrelevant experience

(C) rests on a confusion between whether an attribute is necessary for success and whether that attribute is sufficient for success

(D) bases a conclusion that an attribute is always irrelevant to success on evidence that it is sometimes irrelevant to success

(E) presents only one instance of a phenomenon as the basis for a broad generalization about that phenomenon

17. Discharges of lightning from a volcanic ash cloud occur only when the cloud's highest point exceeds an altitude of 5 kilometers. Those discharges become progressively more frequent as the ash cloud moves higher still. Weather radar can measure the altitude of ash clouds, but it is not available in all parts of the world. Hence lightning discharge data can sometimes be our only reliable indicator of the altitude of ash clouds.

Which one of the following is an assumption required by the argument?

(A) The highest point of any volcanic ash cloud will eventually exceed an altitude of 5 kilometers.

(B) Lightning discharges can be detected in some regions in which weather radar is unavailable.

(C) Weather radar is no less accurate in determining the altitude of volcanic ash clouds than it is in determining the altitude of regular clouds.

(D) A volcanic ash cloud whose highest point exceeds an altitude of 5 kilometers is likely to be at least partly beyond the reach of weather radar.

(E) Lightning discharges are no more frequent for large volcanic ash clouds than for small volcanic ash clouds.

GO ON TO THE NEXT PAGE.

18. If the standards committee has a quorum, then the general assembly will begin at 6:00 P.M. today. If the awards committee has a quorum, then the general assembly will begin at 7:00 P.M. today.

Which one of the following statements follows logically from the statements above?

(A) If the general assembly does not begin at 6:00 P.M. today, then the awards committee has a quorum.

(B) If the standards committee does not have a quorum, then the awards committee has a quorum.

(C) If the general assembly begins at 6:00 P.M. today, then the standards committee has a quorum.

(D) If the general assembly does not begin at 7:00 P.M. today, then the standards committee has a quorum.

(E) If the standards committee has a quorum, then the awards committee does not have a quorum.

19. One of the things lenders do in evaluating the risk of a potential borrower defaulting on a loan is to consider the potential borrower's credit score. In general, the higher the credit score, the less the risk of default. Yet for mortgage loans, the proportion of defaults is much higher for borrowers with the highest credit scores than for other borrowers.

Which one of the following, if true, most helps to resolve the apparent discrepancy in the statements above?

(A) Mortgage lenders are much less likely to consider risk factors other than credit score when evaluating borrowers with the highest credit scores.

(B) Credit scores reported to mortgage lenders are based on collections of data that sometimes include errors or omit relevant information.

(C) A potential borrower's credit score is based in part on the potential borrower's past history in paying off debts in full and on time.

(D) For most consumers, a mortgage is a much larger loan than any other loan the consumer obtains.

(E) Most potential borrowers have credit scores that are neither very low nor very high.

20. Computer modeling of reasoning tasks is far easier than computer modeling of other cognitive tasks, such as the processing of sense images. Computers can defeat chess champions, but cannot see. So, it appears that we understand the analytical capabilities of our minds much better than we understand our senses.

Which one of the following principles, if valid, most helps to justify the reasoning above?

(A) The degree of difficulty of constructing computer models of cognitive tasks is a good index of the degree of difficulty of performing those tasks.

(B) The better we understand a computer's ability to perform a type of task, the better we will understand our own ability to perform it.

(C) A computer's defeat of a chess champion should count as an indication that the computer possesses true intelligence.

(D) The less difficult it is to construct a computer model of a process the better understood is that process.

(E) We should not underestimate the usefulness of computer modeling to the study of human cognition.

GO ON TO THE NEXT PAGE.

21. Archaeologist: Our team discovered 5,000-year-old copper tools near a Canadian river, in a spot that offered easy access to the raw materials for birchbark canoes—birch, cedar, and spruce trees. The tools are of a sort used by the region's Aboriginal people in making birchbark canoes in more recent times. It is likely therefore that Aboriginal people in Canada built birchbark canoes 5,000 years ago.

The archaeologist's argument depends on the assumption that the copper tools that were found

(A) had no trade value 5,000 years ago
(B) were present in the region 5,000 years ago
(C) were designed to be used on material from birch, cedar, and spruce trees only
(D) were the only kind of tool that would have been used for canoe making 5,000 years ago
(E) are not known to have been used by the region's Aboriginal people for any task other than canoe making

22. Advertisement: Hypnosis videos work to alter behavior by subliminally directing the subconscious to act in certain ways. Directions to the subconscious must, however, be repeated many times in order to be effective. Hypnosis videos from Mesmosis, Inc. induce a hypnotic state and then issue an initial command to the subject's subconscious to experience each subsequent instruction as if it had been repeated 1,000 times. Because of the initial instruction, the subsequent instructions on Mesmosis videos are extremely effective—it is as if they had actually been repeated 1,000 times!

The advertisement's reasoning is most vulnerable to criticism on the grounds that the advertisement

(A) overlooks a requirement that it states for the effectiveness of directions to the subconscious
(B) takes for granted that the effectiveness of a direction to the subconscious is always directly proportional to the number of times the direction is repeated
(C) concludes that hypnosis is the most effective technique for altering behavior without considering evidence supporting other techniques
(D) draws a conclusion that simply restates a claim presented in support of that conclusion
(E) concludes that hypnosis videos will be effective simply because they have never been proven to be ineffective

23. The traditional view of the Roman emperor Caligula as a cruel and insane tyrant has been challenged by some modern historians. They point out that little documentation of Caligula's alleged cruelty or outrageous behavior survives from the time of his reign and that the histories that have come down to us were written by his enemies.

Which one of the following, if true, adds the most support for the challenge from the modern historians?

(A) There is less documentation of any sort from Caligula's reign than from the reigns of most other Roman emperors of Caligula's era.
(B) People who have lived under someone regarded as a cruel tyrant are more likely to view that person unfavorably than favorably.
(C) The specific outrageous acts attributed to Caligula in Roman documentation are very similar to acts attributed in earlier writings to other rulers alleged to be cruel tyrants.
(D) The little documentation that survives from Caligula's reign indicates that the Roman people believed Caligula to be crueler than other emperors who were widely thought to be tyrants.
(E) There is ample documentation of modern tyrants being responsible for outrageous acts worse than those attributed to Caligula.

GO ON TO THE NEXT PAGE.

24. Critics of a plan to create new building sites from land that currently lies under only 5 meters of water claim that it will reduce the habitat area available to a local subpopulation of dolphins. It is true that the dolphins never enter water more than 30 meters deep, and the current area of habitation is bounded on one side by land and everywhere else by water that is considerably deeper than that. Nevertheless, the critics are mistaken, because _____.

Which one of the following most logically completes the argument?

(A) the dolphins' current habitat area is large enough to support a dolphin population several times the size of the current one
(B) the dolphins do not inhabit water that is less than 10 meters deep
(C) the most serious threat to the dolphin subpopulation is not habitat reduction but disease and ocean pollution
(D) the average depth of water in the dolphins' habitat area is 25 meters
(E) a short distance from the dolphins' habitat area, the ocean floor drops to a depth of 100 meters

25. Any popular television series that is groundbreaking is critically acclaimed. But not all popular television series are critically acclaimed. Thus, not all popular television series are groundbreaking.

The pattern of reasoning in the argument above is most similar to that in which one of the following arguments?

(A) If articles use specialized technical terminology, they are not widely read. So, since all academic works use specialized technical terminology, articles are not widely read if they are academic works.
(B) Professor Attah gives students high grades if she thinks their work is greatly improved. So, since she gives some of her students high grades, she thinks those students' work is greatly improved.
(C) If a biography is unbiased, it contains embarrassing facts about its subject. So, since not all biographies contain embarrassing facts about their subjects, not all biographies are unbiased.
(D) Mr. Schwartz is polite to anyone who is polite to him. So, since all of his colleagues are polite to him, it must be that he is polite to all his colleagues.
(E) If a book is worth reading, it is worth buying. So, since not all books are worth reading, not all books are worth buying.

S T O P

IF YOU FINISH BEFORE TIME IS CALLED, YOU MAY CHECK YOUR WORK ON THIS SECTION ONLY.
DO NOT WORK ON ANY OTHER SECTION IN THE TEST.

SECTION II
Time—35 minutes
27 Questions

Directions: Each set of questions in this section is based on a single passage or a pair of passages. The questions are to be answered on the basis of what is **stated** or **implied** in the passage or pair of passages. For some questions, more than one of the choices could conceivably answer the question. However, you are to choose the **best** answer; that is, choose the response that most accurately and completely answers the question and mark that response on your answer sheet.

The following passage is adapted from an article published in 1981.

Chinese is a language of many distinct dialects that are often mutually unintelligible. Some linguists have argued that a new dialect of Chinese has evolved in the United States, which is commonly used in the Chinatown section of San Francisco. The characterization of this "Chinatown Chinese" as a distinct dialect is based primarily on two claims: first, that it is so different from any other dialect used in China that a person newly arrived from that country might have a difficult time communicating with a Chinese American in San Francisco who speaks nominally the same language as the newcomer, and, second, that no matter which of the traditional Chinese dialects one speaks, one can communicate effectively with other Chinese Americans in San Francisco so long as one is proficient in the uniquely Chinese-American terminologies.

Regarding the first claim, much of the distinctive vocabulary of Chinatown Chinese consists of proper names of geographical places and terms for things that some people, especially those born and raised in villages, had never encountered in China. Some are transliterated terms, such as *dang-tang* for "downtown." Others are direct translations from American English, such as *gong-ngihn ngiht* ("labor" plus "day") for "Labor Day." However, the core of the language brought to the U.S. by Chinese people has remained intact. Thus, the new vocabulary has supplemented, but not supplanted, the traditional language in the traditional dialects. In fact, normal conversations can be conducted fairly readily between Chinese-speaking Chinese Americans and new arrivals from China, provided that they speak the same traditional Chinese dialect as each other. Terms not familiar to the newcomer, most of which would name objects, places, and events that are part of the local experience, can easily be avoided or explained by the speaker, or their meaning can be inferred from the context. The supposed language barrier is, therefore, mostly imaginary.

The second claim—that the sharing of a uniquely Chinese-American vocabulary makes possible communication among Chinese Americans no matter what their basic dialect of Chinese may be—is a misleading oversimplification. While many Chinese-American speakers of other Chinese dialects have become familiar with Cantonese, now the most common dialect of Chinese spoken in the U.S., through watching Cantonese movies and by hearing that dialect in Hong Kong, Guandong, or the U.S., this is not the same thing as sharing a single unique dialect. Moreover, the dialects of Chinese can differ markedly in their systems of sounds and, to some extent, in grammar and vocabulary, and these differences persist among Chinese-American speakers of these various dialects. Hence, even a common vocabulary for such things as names of U.S. cities, street names, and non-Chinese items does not guarantee mutual intelligibility because these words constitute only a minute percentage of each dialect and are generally peripheral to the core vocabulary.

1. Which one of the following most accurately expresses the main point of the passage?

(A) Linguists who argue that Chinatown Chinese constitutes a distinct new dialect are mistaken because it is intelligible to speakers of the Cantonese dialect.

(B) Because Chinatown Chinese is unfamiliar to many native Chinese people, linguists have concluded that it constitutes a distinct new dialect of Chinese.

(C) The primary claims supporting the view that Chinatown Chinese is a distinct new dialect do not stand up to close examination.

(D) Because visitors from China can fairly easily converse with Chinese Americans living in San Francisco, the variety of language there cannot be designated a distinct new dialect.

(E) Although Chinese dialects are difficult to define with certainty, linguists are now in agreement that Chinatown Chinese does not constitute a distinct new dialect.

GO ON TO THE NEXT PAGE.

2. The passage suggests that a visitor from China who speaks the same traditional dialect as a Chinese-American person in San Francisco would find it most difficult to converse with that person about

(A) news from China
(B) mutual relatives in San Francisco
(C) the Chinese American's daily life in the U.S.
(D) the Chinese visitor's feelings about the U.S.
(E) Chinese cultural traditions

3. The author mentions the words *dang-tang* (second sentence of the second paragraph) and *gong-ngihn ngiht* (third sentence of the second paragraph) in order to

(A) demonstrate the extent to which American English terms dominate Chinatown Chinese
(B) illustrate how Chinese Americans are able to communicate with each other easily despite using different dialects
(C) explain why native Chinese are able to understand Chinese Americans with relative ease
(D) show why Chinatown Chinese should be considered a distinct new dialect
(E) exemplify the ways in which American English terms have become part of or have influenced Chinatown Chinese

4. According to the passage, in San Francisco the traditional Chinese dialects spoken by Chinese immigrants to the U.S.

(A) remain at their core essentially the same over time
(B) eventually merge with other Chinese dialects
(C) undergo subtle changes in sound and grammatical structure
(D) are often abandoned by native speakers for the Cantonese dialect
(E) lose much of their traditional vocabulary as they incorporate transliterated American English terms

5. When the passage refers to "transliterated terms" (second sentence of the second paragraph), the author most likely means words

(A) whose sounds and meanings have been directly incorporated into another language
(B) that name objects, places, and events that are part of local experience
(C) that are written in the same way in another language
(D) that are direct translations from another language
(E) that sound different in different dialects

GO ON TO THE NEXT PAGE.

In a typical Hollywood action movie, the hero skirts death to complete a mission. Bad guys shoot, cars explode, objects fall from the sky, but all just miss. If any one of those things happened just a little differently, the hero would be dead. Yet the hero survives.

In some respects, the story of our universe resembles an action movie. A slight change to any one of the laws of physics would likely have caused some disaster that would have disrupted the normal evolution of the universe and made life impossible. For example, if the strong nuclear force had been slightly stronger or weaker, stars would have forged very little of the carbon that seems necessary to form planets and living things. Indeed, it seems that in order for a universe to support life, the laws of physics must be so finely tuned that the very existence of such a universe becomes improbable.

Some cosmologists have tried to reconcile the existence of our universe with the seeming improbability of its existence by hypothesizing that our universe is but one of many universes within a wider array called the multiverse. In almost all of those universes, the laws of physics might not allow the formation of matter as we know it and therefore of life. But given the sheer number of possibilities, nature would have had a good chance to get the "right" set of laws at least once.

But just how exceptional is the set of physical laws governing our universe? The view that the laws of physics are finely tuned arises largely from the difficulty scientists have had in identifying alternative sets of laws that would be compatible with life.

The conventional way scientists explore whether a particular constant of physics is finely tuned is to tweak it while leaving all other constants unaltered. The scientists then "play the movie" of that universe—they do calculations, what-if scenarios, or computer simulations—to see what disasters occur. But there is no reason to tweak just one parameter at a time. By manipulating multiple constants at once, my colleague and I have identified numerous scenarios—hypothetical universes—where the physical laws would be very different from our own and yet compatible with the formation of complex structures and perhaps even some forms of intelligent life.

Fine tuning has been invoked by some cosmologists as indirect evidence for the multiverse. Do our findings therefore call the concept of the multiverse into question? I do not think this is necessarily the case for two reasons. First, certain models of the birth of the universe would lead us to expect the existence of something like the multiverse. Secondly, the multiverse concept may well prove to be the source of solutions to certain other long-standing puzzles in cosmology.

6. Which one of the following most accurately states the main point of the passage?

(A) Although the universe seems finely tuned for the existence of life, there may be more sets of physical laws that would be compatible with life than commonly thought.

(B) Although the multiverse hypothesis was developed to explain the apparent fine tuning of the physical laws of our universe, it may be useful for explaining other kinds of issues in cosmology.

(C) When scientists have tried modeling hypothetical universes by altering physical laws, they have been unable to find alternate sets of laws that are consistent with life.

(D) The improbability of life occurring in the universe supports the idea that our universe is just one of many universes in a broader multiverse.

(E) The story of our universe resembles an action movie in that, despite all of the circumstances that could have had disastrous consequences for the emergence of life, life exists.

7. It can be inferred from the passage that when the author says that scientists "play the movie" (second sentence of the fifth paragraph), the author means that they

(A) acknowledge the fictional nature of what is being described

(B) follow a theoretical chain of events to its conclusion

(C) highlight how dramatic the situation is that follows

(D) model their work on certain common archetypes

(E) play an active role in shaping the story

GO ON TO THE NEXT PAGE.

8. The passage suggests that the cosmologists mentioned in the third paragraph would be most likely to agree with which one of the following statements?

(A) Our universe is affected by what occurs in other universes.

(B) The existence of multiple universes makes each universe more likely to contain life.

(C) The laws of physics must be the same in every part of the multiverse.

(D) There are enough universes to make it probable that life exists in at least one of them.

(E) There is only one universe in the multiverse that contains life.

9. The author would be most likely to agree with which one of the following statements about the conventional way in which scientists investigate the apparent fine tuning of physical laws?

(A) It focuses on looking for outcomes that are irrelevant to the issue at hand.

(B) It is too unfocused to produce useful results.

(C) It has been conducted without concern for mathematical rigor.

(D) Its methodology results in an overly restricted set of outcomes.

(E) It will eventually produce a workable model of an alternate universe with life.

10. The final paragraph of the passage functions primarily to

(A) demonstrate the inadequacy of the view that the author is arguing against

(B) indicate the kinds of questions to which the author's research can be extended

(C) discuss the implications of the author's research

(D) consider two potential counterarguments to the author's position

(E) suggest a course of future experimentation to test the author's conclusions

11. The author's attitude toward the multiverse hypothesis can best be described as one of

(A) dismissiveness
(B) skepticism
(C) open-mindedness
(D) advocacy
(E) enthusiasm

12. If the multiverse hypothesis as discussed in the third paragraph is correct, then the story of the hero in the first paragraph would be more analogous to the story of our universe if the hero

(A) had a team of supporters working behind the scenes to make sure that the hero succeeded

(B) was actually just one of many people sent on the mission, but almost all of the others failed

(C) had developed the survival skills needed to complete the mission during a series of previous missions

(D) was actually just one of many people sent on the mission, and each person found a unique way to succeed

(E) was equipped with a map that made it possible to know where each danger lurked and how to avoid it

GO ON TO THE NEXT PAGE.

Passage A

Comedians are not amused when their jokes are stolen, and for that reason we might expect joke-stealing disputes to ripen into lawsuits occasionally. Copyright is the most relevant body of law; formally, it applies to jokes and comedic routines. Yet copyright infringement lawsuits between rival comedians are all but unheard of, despite what appears to be a persistent practice of joke stealing among stand-up comedians. The nonexistence of such lawsuits is a product of both practical considerations that render the cost of enforcing the formal law prohibitively expensive, and legal hurdles that make success difficult and uncertain in lawsuits relating to joke stealing. In the end, copyright law simply does not provide comedians with a cost-effective way of protecting their comedic material.

Conventional intellectual property wisdom holds that absent formal legal protection, there would be scant production of creative works, as potential creators would be deterred by the unlikelihood of recouping the cost of their creations. If there is no effective legal protection against joke theft, then why do thousands of comedians keep cranking out new material night after night?

The answer to this question is that, in stand-up comedy, social norms substitute for intellectual property law. Taken as a whole, this norms system governs a wide array of issues that generally parallel those ordered by copyright law. These norms are not merely hortatory. They are enforced with sanctions, including simple badmouthing and refusals to work with an offending comedian. These sanctions, while extralegal, can cause serious reputational harm to an alleged joke thief, and may substantially hamper a comedian's career. Using this informal system, comedians are able to assert ownership of jokes, regulate their use and transfer, impose sanctions on transgressors, and maintain substantial incentives to invest in new material.

Passage B

Accomplished chefs consider their recipes to be a very valuable form of intellectual property. At the same time, recipes are *not* a form of innovation that is effectively covered by current intellectual property laws. Recipes are rarely patentable, and combinations of ingredients cannot be copyrighted. Legal protections are potentially available via trade secrecy laws, but chefs very seldom use them. Instead, three implicit social norms are operative among chefs, and together these norms function in a manner quite similar to law-based intellectual property systems.

First, a chef must not copy another chef's recipe innovation exactly. The function of this norm is analogous to patenting in that the community acknowledges the right of a recipe inventor to exclude others from practicing his or her invention, even if all the information required to do so is publicly available. A second norm mandates that, if a chef reveals recipe-related secret information to a colleague, that colleague

must not pass the information on to others without permission. This norm gives a chef a property right similar to that attainable via a contract under trade secrecy law. A third norm is that colleagues must credit developers of significant recipes as the authors of that information. This norm operates in a manner analogous to copyright protection.

13. Both passages are primarily concerned with investigating which one of the following topics?

   (A) the legal protections available to creators of intellectual property
   (B) the connection between the enforcement of social norms and the incentives these norms provide to creators of intellectual property
   (C) the extent to which the rights of creators of intellectual property must be balanced against the social value of making that property publicly available
   (D) the practical considerations that prompt creators of intellectual property to forgo legal protections of their work
   (E) the ways in which social norms can take the place of laws in protecting intellectual property

14. Passage A, but not passage B, discusses

   (A) the relationship of social norms to intellectual property laws
   (B) the evolution of social norms
   (C) the enforcement of social norms
   (D) the limitations of social norms
   (E) the impact of social norms on creative output

15. Which one of the following questions is addressed by passage A but not by passage B with respect to the group of professionals discussed?

   (A) How can members of the group share their creative work with colleagues without sacrificing their intellectual property rights?
   (B) Why do members of the group usually choose not to make use of the legal protections that are potentially available to them?
   (C) To what extent can patent law protect the creative output of members of the group?
   (D) What is a form of creative output that members of the group regard as intellectual property?
   (E) What social norms prohibit members of the group from violating the intellectual property rights of other members of the group?

GO ON TO THE NEXT PAGE.

16. The author of passage A would be most likely to agree with which one of the following statements?

(A)   Comedians rarely acknowledge the degree to which their own comedic material is influenced by the work of their peers.

(B)   Comedians would be more likely to protect their comedic material through copyright law if they had greater assurance that they could successfully bring infringement lawsuits against perceived perpetrators of joke theft.

(C)   Creative rights to jokes and comedic routines should be protected by trade secrecy law rather than by copyright law.

(D)   The system of social norms operative among comedians is not robust enough to allow comedians to be properly compensated for the expenses they incur when developing new comedic material.

(E)   In the particular context of stand-up comedy, no informal system for protecting intellectual property can be as effective as a formal system.

17. Which one of the following statements is most strongly supported by information given in the passages?

(A)   Intellectual property violations are more frequent among comedians than among chefs.

(B)   A more elaborate system of social norms has developed among chefs than among comedians.

(C)   Chefs enjoy more significant legal protections of their intellectual property than do comedians.

(D)   Most comedians and chefs are satisfied with current intellectual property laws.

(E)   Comedians and chefs both derive some professional benefit from observing the social norms of their profession.

18. The relationship described in passage A as holding between comedians and copyright law is most analogous to the relationship described in passage B as holding between chefs and which one of the following?

(A)   intellectual property
(B)   patent law
(C)   the combinations of ingredients in a recipe
(D)   trade secrecy law
(E)   social norms

19. The author of passage A would be most likely to agree with which one of the following statements?

(A)   The social norms that are operative among comedians make it possible for individual comedians to recoup the costs associated with developing a comedic routine.

(B)   Comedians should increase their reliance on copyright law as a means of protecting their comedic routines.

(C)   Most professional comedians are largely unconcerned with the expense involved in developing new comedic material.

(D)   Law-based intellectual property systems generally work less efficiently than systems based on social norms.

(E)   Existing copyright law should be modified to make it more cost effective for comedians to protect their comedic material through legal means.

20. Which one of the following, if true, would most clearly support the argument made in passage B?

(A)   There is no social norm preventing chefs from using colleagues' recipes as inspiration, as long as those recipes are not copied exactly.

(B)   Chefs are significantly more likely to deny requested information to colleagues whom they believe have violated the operative social norms.

(C)   Recipes published in cookbooks are protected by copyright law from being published in other cookbooks.

(D)   The community of chefs is too small to effectively enforce sanctions against those who violate the operative social norms.

(E)   In practice it is virtually impossible to determine whether a chef has copied a colleague's recipe exactly or has instead independently developed that recipe.

GO ON TO THE NEXT PAGE.

The novelist and social theorist Charlotte Perkins Gilman, whose writings were widely read and discussed in the early twentieth century, played an important role in the debate about the theories of Charles Darwin and their application to society. Darwin's theory of evolution did not directly apply to social ideology, but various intellectuals translated his ideas of natural selection into social language and argued about their interpretation. Some of these Social Darwinist theorists held that the nature of human social interactions is strictly determined by the process of biological evolution, and that it is futile to try to meddle with the competitive struggle for existence and the survival of the fittest. Another, more activist group of Social Darwinists held that although changes in human societies, like those that occur in biological species, do constitute a sort of evolution, this evolution at the level of a human society need not be competitive, but can emerge through collective action within society.

Gilman identified herself with this latter ideological camp and applied evolutionary theory in the movement for social change. The central thesis of this group of Social Darwinists was that although people, like all life, are the products of natural evolutionary forces, the principles of change that determine the development of organisms have brought humans to the point where it is possible for us to contribute consciously to the evolutionary process, to redesign and mold our societies in appropriate ways. This, for Gilman, was not simply a descriptive observation about humanity but was also a source of ethical responsibility. She argued that since a prime source of social evolution is human work, whether in crafts, trades, arts, or sciences, one of the primary ethical responsibilities of a person is to identify and engage in work that is societally relevant and that makes the best use of that person's talents.

Gilman was not merely engaged in an intellectual debate. Motivated by her ethical vision and convinced of the plasticity of human nature, Gilman vehemently sought to break the molds into which people, especially women, had been thrust. In both her fiction and her social theory she urges women to further social evolution by collectively working toward a reorganization of society. A central goal of the reorganization she envisioned would be the abandonment of gender-specific work roles and hierarchical relationships. Gilman believed that at one time such arrangements had been necessary for evolution because what she felt were male traits of assertiveness, combat, and display were essential for the development of a complex society. Future progress, she believed, now required the restoration of a balance that would include what she saw as female qualities of cooperation and nurturance.

21. Which one of the following most accurately expresses the main point of the passage?

(A) Gilman's activist social theory, which called for the abolition of gender-specific work roles, contributed the central doctrine to one type of Social Darwinism that distinguished it from the other, more competitive-minded Social Darwinist camp.

(B) Although Gilman aligned herself with the activist group of Social Darwinists, she rejected some of its doctrines, calling instead for gender equality and the general recognition of traditionally female qualities.

(C) Unlike most Social Darwinists of her time, Gilman saw the issues involved in Social Darwinist debate as transcending abstract theoretical concerns and having important implications for human society, especially for women.

(D) Gilman's version of Social Darwinism held that people can and should contribute actively to the social evolution of humanity, and in her writings she advised women to do so through efforts to eliminate traditional gender roles.

(E) Gilman, whose important contributions to the debate over the application of Darwinism to social ideology were widely recognized in the early twentieth century, should also be recognized for her writings on women's social issues.

22. The passage most strongly suggests that which one of the following statements is true?

(A) Gilman's social theory was unlike other applications of evolutionary theory to the social realm because it was not closely allied with any of the major political movements of her time.

(B) One of Gilman's innovations was the introduction of social discourse into the debate about the theories of Charles Darwin, which prior to her work had focused purely on biological issues.

(C) Gilman worked in direct collaboration with other social activists toward the implementation of a set of social reforms that were based on her evolutionary doctrines.

(D) Charles Darwin's writings on the evolution of biological species influenced Gilman's work only indirectly through the writings of other Social Darwinists.

(E) Other evolutionary theorists contemporary with or prior to Gilman shared her view about whether or not evolutionary theory has implications for social practice.

GO ON TO THE NEXT PAGE.

23. Which one of the following sequences most accurately expresses the organization of the passage?

(A) The author identifies a particular individual as a proponent of one of two versions of a theory, and then describes how that individual drew practical implications from the theory and relates some of those implications.

(B) The author describes the relationship of a particular individual to an intellectual community, characterizes in general terms a theory held by that individual, contrasts that theory with another related theory, and then rejects one of those two competing theories.

(C) The author proposes an interpretation of a particular individual's writings, explains how those writings relate to a more general theoretical context, and then argues for the proposed interpretation of the individual's writings.

(D) The author describes some reasoning used by a group of theorists, evaluates that reasoning, attributes similar reasoning to a particular individual, and then shows how the proposed evaluation applies to specific arguments made by that individual.

(E) The author presents some historical facts about the development of a scientific theory, explains the role played by a particular individual in the formulation of that theory, and then summarizes the responses of critics to that individual's work.

24. The passage indicates that Gilman believed that which one of the following can be a significant factor in the evolution of society?

(A) reclamation of ancient social theories
(B) cross-cultural communication
(C) greater literacy
(D) skilled occupations
(E) future uses of dialectical methods in the social sciences

25. The passage gives evidence that Gilman valued which one of the following as an instrument of social progress in her time?

(A) industrialization
(B) fiction writing
(C) international travel
(D) religious training
(E) combative personality traits

26. The passage can most accurately be described as which one of the following?

(A) a defense of the principles of social theory that were promulgated by a particular group of writers and activists

(B) a description of the role played by a particular writer in an intellectual controversy over the consequences of a scientific theory

(C) an explication of the theoretical points of disagreement between two closely related social theories that have almost identical goals

(D) a defense of one interpretation of a particular writer's views, together with a rejection of a competing interpretation of those views

(E) an introduction to a general type of scientific theory, clarified by a detailed presentation of one writer's version of that theory

27. Which one of the following is implied by Gilman's views as described in the passage?

(A) Some social conditions on which social evolution depends at certain times in human history are detrimental to further social evolution at other times in history.

(B) The types of changes that constitute genuine social evolution can no longer be brought about except through coordinated efforts directed at consciously formulated goals.

(C) Gender-based hierarchical relationships, which predated, and led to the development of, gender-specific work roles, will probably be especially difficult to eradicate.

(D) While Social Darwinist theories are essentially descriptive and thus do not have ethical implications, they can be useful rhetorically in communicating ethical messages.

(E) Continuation of the process of social evolution will lead inevitably to the inclusion of more cooperation and nurturance in social arrangements.

STOP

IF YOU FINISH BEFORE TIME IS CALLED, YOU MAY CHECK YOUR WORK ON THIS SECTION ONLY.
DO NOT WORK ON ANY OTHER SECTION IN THE TEST.

SECTION III
Time—35 minutes
26 Questions

Directions: Each question in this section is based on the reasoning presented in a brief passage. In answering the questions, you should not make assumptions that are by commonsense standards implausible, superfluous, or incompatible with the passage. For some questions, more than one of the choices could conceivably answer the question. However, you are to choose the **best** answer; that is, choose the response that most accurately and completely answers the question and mark that response on your answer sheet.

1. Advertisement: Most nutritionists recommend eating fish twice a week. Eating tilapia fillets is a perfect choice for those who want the benefits of eating fish but do not care for the taste of fish. Tilapia fillets lack the strong fishy taste that many people find objectionable.

   Which one of the following, if true, most seriously weakens the advertisement's argument?

   (A) Eating more than the recommended amount of fish can cause toxins that are present in high concentrations in many varieties of fish to accumulate in a person's body.
   (B) Tilapia are invasive species that crowd out native species of fish in lakes throughout the world.
   (C) Tilapia fillets contain little of the beneficial fish oils that are the main reason nutritionists recommend eating fish frequently.
   (D) Most people who do not care for the taste of fish eat less fish than is recommended by most nutritionists.
   (E) People who rarely or never eat fish usually dislike any food with a strong fishy taste.

2. Domestication of animals is a cooperative activity, and cooperative activities require a sophisticated means of communication. Language provides just such a means. It is likely, therefore, that language developed primarily to facilitate animal domestication.

   A flaw in the argument is that the argument

   (A) conflates being necessary for the development of a phenomenon with guaranteeing the development of that phenomenon
   (B) takes for granted that every phenomenon has a unique cause
   (C) infers that the development of one phenomenon caused the development of another merely because the two phenomena developed around the same time
   (D) draws a conclusion that merely restates a claim presented in support of that conclusion
   (E) assumes that if something serves a purpose it must have developed in order to serve that purpose

3. Many employers treat their employees fairly. Thus, using others as a means to one's own ends is not always morally reprehensible or harmful to others.

   The argument requires the assumption that

   (A) some employers act in a morally reprehensible manner only when they harm those whom they employ
   (B) no employers who act morally use their employees as a means to their own ends
   (C) some or all employers use their employees as a means to their own ends
   (D) making a profit from the labor of others is personally advantageous but never harmful
   (E) it is not possible to harm someone else without treating that person as a means to one's own ends

4. Editorial: It is common to find essays offering arguments that seem to show that our nation is in decline. There is no cause for alarm, however. The anxious tone of these essays shows that the problem is with the psychological state of their writers rather than with the actual condition of our nation.

   Which one of the following most accurately describes a flaw in the editorial's reasoning?

   (A) The editorial dismisses a claim without considering any reasons presented in arguments for that claim.
   (B) The editorial compares two situations without considering the obvious differences between them.
   (C) The editorial confuses claims about a cultural decline with claims about a political decline.
   (D) The editorial overlooks the possibility that the nation is neither thriving nor in decline.
   (E) The editorial dismisses a particular view while offering evidence that actually supports that view.

GO ON TO THE NEXT PAGE.

5. Eating turmeric, a spice commonly found in curries, probably helps prevent Alzheimer's disease. More turmeric is consumed per capita in India than in the rest of the world, and the incidence of Alzheimer's disease is much lower there than it is worldwide. Furthermore, Alzheimer's disease is characterized by the buildup of amyloid protein plaques in the brain, and studies on animals found that curcumin—a compound found in turmeric—reduces the accumulation of amyloid proteins.

Which one of the following, if true, most strengthens the argument?

(A) Rosemary and ginger, which contain compounds that affect amyloid protein accumulation much like curcumin does, are commonly found in the diets of people living in India.

(B) Many scientists believe that the buildup of amyloid protein plaques in the brain is a symptom of Alzheimer's disease rather than a cause.

(C) The proportion of people living in India who fall within the age group that is most prone to developing Alzheimer's disease is smaller than the proportion of people worldwide who fall within that age group.

(D) None of the other compounds found in turmeric have been studied to see whether they affect the accumulation of amyloid proteins.

(E) The parts of India that have the highest per capita rates of curry consumption have the lowest incidence of Alzheimer's disease.

6. Forestry official: Many people think that if forest fires are not extinguished as quickly as possible, the Forestry Department is not doing its job properly. But relatively frequent, small fires clear out small trees and forest debris, which, if allowed to accumulate, would create the conditions for large, devastating fires. Therefore, it's best to let small fires burn.

The statement that relatively frequent, small fires clear out small trees and forest debris plays which one of the following roles in the official's argument?

(A) It is offered as support for the contention that the Forestry Department is not doing its job properly if it does not extinguish forest fires as quickly as possible.

(B) It is used as evidence against the contention that the Forestry Department is not doing its job properly if it does not extinguish forest fires as quickly as possible.

(C) It is used to show what the consequences would be if the Forestry Department based its policies on the ideas most people have about how it should do its job.

(D) It is an example used to illustrate the claim that most people believe the Forestry Department should quickly extinguish all forest fires.

(E) It is a conclusion based on the premise in the argument that it is best to let small forest fires burn.

7. Gerald: Unless a consumer secures his or her home wireless Internet service, anyone strolling by is able to access that person's service with certain laptop computers or smartphones. Such use cannot be considered illegal under current laws: it's no more like trespassing than is enjoying music playing on someone's radio as you walk down the street.

Kendra: But unlike hearing music while walking by, accessing wireless service requires stopping for a considerable length of time. And that could be considered loitering or even harassment.

Gerald's and Kendra's positions indicate that they disagree over whether accessing someone's wireless Internet service while walking down the street

(A) can be considered illegal under current law
(B) is like trespassing
(C) should be prohibited by law
(D) requires a considerable length of time
(E) could be done without intending to do so

GO ON TO THE NEXT PAGE.

8. Over the last thousand years, plant species native to islands have gone extinct at a much faster rate than have those native to mainland regions. Biologists believe that this is because island plants have not adapted the defenses against being eaten by large land mammals that mainland plants have. Ordinarily, populations of large land mammals are not established on islands until after the island is colonized by humans.

Which one of the following, if true, most strongly supports the biologist's explanation cited above?

(A) Most of the plant species in the world that have not yet gone extinct are native to mainland regions.

(B) Many plant species that are not native to islands have become very well established on islands throughout the world.

(C) Commercial development on many islands has resulted in loss of habitat for many native plants.

(D) The rate of extinction of native plant species on an island tends to increase dramatically after human colonization.

(E) Large land mammals tend to prefer plants from species native to mainland regions over plants from species native to islands.

9. As regards memory, the brain responds best to repeated patterns, such as the melodic and rhythmic patterns of music. This is why we can remember long strings of information or text, which would normally be impossible to memorize, when they are put to music. Given that music aids memory, it might seem that funny jokes would be easy to remember, since, like music, they normally elicit an emotional response in us. However, jokes are usually very difficult to remember, since _____.

Which one of the following most logically completes the passage?

(A) jokes, unlike music, always have content that is verbal or at least clearly symbolic

(B) some successful jokes are short and pithy, whereas others are long and involved

(C) jokes work not by conforming to repeated patterns but by breaking them

(D) for most people, certain memories elicit a strong emotional response

(E) people can hold in short-term memory only a few chunks of unpatterned information at a time

10. The prehistoric fish Tiktaalik is the earliest known animal with fingers. Since variations were so great among prehistoric fish species, Tiktaalik would not have stood out as unusual at the time. However, Tiktaalik's fingers were an important development in animal evolution because it is likely that Tiktaalik is an ancestor to the many land animals with fingers.

The statements above, if true, most strongly support which one of the following?

(A) Tiktaalik likely used its fingers to move on land.

(B) Tiktaalik's fingers were its only feature to play a significant role in the development of modern land animals.

(C) Tiktaalik is not the ancestor of any currently surviving fish species.

(D) No fish without fingers would ever be able to move on land.

(E) The evolutionary significance of Tiktaalik could not be determined just through comparison to fish species of its time.

11. Gabriella: By raising interest rates, the government has induced people to borrow less money and therefore to spend less, thereby slowing the country's economy.

Ivan: I disagree with your analysis. The country's economy is tied to the global economy. Whatever happens to the global economy also happens here, and the global economy has slowed. Therefore, the government's action did not cause the economy's slowdown.

Gabriella and Ivan disagree about whether

(A) the economic slowdown in the country has caused people to spend less

(B) the economy of the country is tied to the economies of other countries

(C) raising interest rates caused a significant decrease in borrowing

(D) raising interest rates caused the country's economy to slow

(E) the global economy has slowed

GO ON TO THE NEXT PAGE.

12. In a scene in an ancient Greek play, *Knights*, the character Demosthenes opens a writing tablet on which an oracle had written a prophecy, and while looking at the tablet, he continuously expresses his amazement at its contents. His companion presses him for information, whereupon Demosthenes explains what the oracle had written.

Of the following claims, which one can most justifiably be rejected on the basis of the statements above?

(A) In ancient Greek plays, characters are presumed to know how to read unless their illiteracy is specifically mentioned.

(B) The character of Demosthenes in *Knights* is not based on a historical figure.

(C) In ancient Greek plays, the reading aloud of written texts commonly occurred as part of the on-stage action.

(D) In ancient Greece, people did not read silently to themselves.

(E) Only rarely in ancient Greece were prophecies written down on writing tablets.

13. Science cannot adequately explain emotional phenomena such as feeling frustrated, falling in love, or being moved by a painting. Since they cannot be explained by physics, chemistry, or neurophysiology, human emotions must not be physical phenomena.

The conclusion follows logically if which one of the following is assumed?

(A) Whatever is not a physical phenomenon cannot be explained by science.

(B) Nothing that can be felt by only one subject can be studied scientifically.

(C) Physics, chemistry, and neurophysiology have similar explanatory frameworks.

(D) Whatever is not a physical phenomenon is an emotional one.

(E) Every physical phenomenon can be explained by physics, chemistry, or neurophysiology.

14. Several *Tyrannosaurus rex* skeletons found in North America contain tooth marks that only a large carnivore could have made. At the time *T. rex* lived, it was the only large carnivore in North America. The tooth marks could have resulted only from combat or feeding. But such tooth marks would have been almost impossible to inflict on the skeleton of a live animal.

The information above most strongly supports which one of the following?

(A) *T. rex* regularly engaged in combat with smaller carnivores.

(B) At the time *T. rex* lived, it was common for carnivores to feed on other carnivores.

(C) *T. rex* sometimes engaged in cannibalism.

(D) *T. rex* sometimes engaged in intraspecies combat.

(E) At the time *T. rex* lived, there were large carnivores on continents other than North America.

15. There is a popular view among literary critics that a poem can never be accurately paraphrased because a poem is itself the only accurate expression of its meaning. But these same critics hold that their own paraphrases of particular poems are accurate. Thus, their view that poetry cannot be accurately paraphrased is false.

The reasoning in the argument is most vulnerable to the criticism that the argument

(A) presupposes the falsity of the view that it sets out to refute

(B) takes for granted that the main purpose of poems is to convey information rather than express feelings

(C) takes for granted that a paraphrase of a poem cannot be useful to its readers unless it accurately expresses a poem's meaning

(D) provides no justification for favoring one of the literary critics' beliefs over the other

(E) provides no justification for following one particular definition of "paraphrase"

GO ON TO THE NEXT PAGE.

16. The tax bill passed 2 years ago provides substantial incentives for businesses that move to this area and hire 50 or more employees. Critics say the bill reduces the government's tax revenues. Yet clearly it has already created many jobs in this area. Last year, Plastonica qualified for incentives under the bill by opening a new plastics factory here that hired 75 employees.

The argument's reasoning depends on which one of the following assumptions?

(A) If Plastonica had not opened the plastics factory in the area, it would not have opened a plastics factory at all.

(B) Plastonica would not have opened the plastics factory in the area had it not been for the incentives.

(C) Most critics of the tax bill claim that it will not create any more new jobs.

(D) If Plastonica had not opened the plastics factory in the area, it would have opened it somewhere else.

(E) Critics of the tax bill believe that it has not created any jobs in the area.

17. When a chain of service stations began applying a surcharge of $0.25 per purchase on fuel paid for by credit card, the chain's owners found that this policy made their customers angry. So they decided instead to simply raise the price of fuel a compensatory amount and give a $0.25 discount to customers paying with cash. Customers were much happier with this policy.

Which one of the following generalizations does the situation described above most clearly illustrate?

(A) People usually adopt beliefs without carefully assessing the evidence for and against those beliefs.

(B) People's perceptions of the fairness of a policy sometimes depend on whether that policy benefits them personally.

(C) People usually become emotional when considering financial issues.

(D) People often change their minds about issues that do not make significant differences to their lives.

(E) People's evaluations of a situation sometimes depend less on the situation itself than on how it is presented to them.

18. Herbalist: Many herbal medicines work best when they have a chance to influence the body gently over several months. However, many of these herbal medicines have toxic side effects when taken daily for such long periods. Therefore, at least some people who use herbal medicines daily should occasionally skip their usual dose for a day or two, to give the body a chance to recuperate.

Which one of the following is an assumption required by the herbalist's argument?

(A) At least some people who use herbal medicines daily use them for periods long enough for the medicines to have side effects.

(B) At least some herbal medicines work less well in achieving their desired effects if one occasionally skips one's usual dose than if one does not.

(C) Some herbal medicines have toxic side effects when taken for several months, even if the usual dose is occasionally skipped for a day or two to give the body a chance to recuperate.

(D) Anyone who uses herbal medicines should give those medicines a chance to influence the body gently over several months at least.

(E) One should occasionally skip one's usual dose of an herbal medicine for a day or two only if doing so will reduce or eliminate toxic side effects from several months of use.

GO ON TO THE NEXT PAGE.

19. Business owner: Around noon in one section of the city, food trucks that sell lunch directly to customers on the sidewalk occupy many of the limited metered parking spaces available, thus worsening already bad traffic congestion. This led the city council to consider a bill to prohibit food trucks from parking in metered spaces in any commercially zoned area. This bill should be rejected since there is plenty of available parking and little traffic congestion in most areas of the city.

Which one of the following principles, if valid, most helps to justify the business owner's argument?

(A) Unless a business provides a product or service that is valued by consumers, the business should not be allowed to make use of scarce city resources.

(B) If a serious problem exists in one part of a city, the city government should address the problem before it spreads to another area of the city.

(C) No proposed solution to a city problem should be implemented until the problem has been thoroughly studied.

(D) A law that would disadvantage businesses of a certain type throughout a city should not be used to solve a problem that does not affect most areas of the city.

(E) If a city has a serious problem, then it should not implement any policy that would aggravate that problem even if the policy would address another serious problem.

20. Michele: In my professional experience, it's usually not a good idea for a company to overhaul its databases. The rewards rarely exceed the problems experienced along the way, and I'd suggest that anyone considering a database overhaul think twice before proceeding.

Alvaro: But the problems are always caused by a failure to recode the database properly. The best advice for a company considering a database overhaul is to do the job right.

Michele and Alvaro disagree with each other about which one of the following?

(A) why companies should consider overhauling their databases

(B) whether the problems experienced during a database overhaul ever outweigh the rewards

(C) which kinds of database overhauls have more problems than are justified by the rewards

(D) what a company should do when considering a database overhaul

(E) when professional experience is required to correctly recode a database

GO ON TO THE NEXT PAGE.

21. In an experiment, subjects were shown a series of images on a computer screen, appearing usually at the top but occasionally at the bottom. Subjects were asked to guess each time where the next image would appear on the screen. They guessed correctly less than half of the time. The subjects all reported that they based their guesses on patterns they believed they saw in the sequence. Instead, if they had simply guessed that the next image would always appear at the top, they would have been correct most of the time.

If all of the statements above are true, which one of the following must also be true?

(A) If the subjects had always guessed that the next image would appear at the top, they would not have been basing their guesses on any pattern they believed they saw in the sequence.

(B) Basing one's guesses about what will happen next on the basis of patterns one believes one sees is less likely to lead to correct guesses than always guessing that what has happened before will happen next.

(C) There was no predictable pattern that one could reasonably believe occurred in the series of images on the computer screen.

(D) Some of the subjects sometimes guessed that the next image would appear at the bottom of the computer screen, but were incorrect.

(E) The most rational strategy for guessing correctly where the next image would appear would have been simply to always guess that the image would appear at the top.

22. The temperature in Taychester is always at least 10 degrees lower than the temperature in Charlesville. However, the average resident of Charlesville spends 10 to 20 percent more on winter heating expenses than does the average resident of Taychester.

Each of the following, if true, helps to resolve the apparent paradox described above **except**:

(A) Heat loss due to wind is less in Taychester than in Charlesville.

(B) Although Charlesville is always fairly warm during the daytime, temperatures in Charlesville drop steeply at night.

(C) Utility rates in Taychester are lower than utility rates in Charlesville.

(D) People who are used to warmer temperatures generally keep their homes warmer in the winter than do people who are used to colder temperatures.

(E) Houses in colder climates are usually better insulated than houses in warmer climates.

23. Each new car in the lot at Rollway Motors costs more than $18,000. Any car in their lot that is ten or more years old costs less than $5,000. Thus, if a car in Rollway's lot costs between $5,000 and $18,000, it is a used car that is less than ten years old.

The pattern of reasoning in which one of the following arguments is most similar to that in the argument above?

(A) Each apartment above the fourth floor of the building has more than two bedrooms. But all apartments below the fourth floor have fewer than two bedrooms. Thus, any apartment on the fourth floor of the building has exactly two bedrooms.

(B) Each apartment above the fourth floor of the building has two or three bedrooms. But no apartment below the fourth floor has more than two bedrooms. Thus, all of the building's three-bedroom apartments are on the fourth floor or higher.

(C) No apartment above the fourth floor of the building has fewer than three bedrooms. But all apartments below the fourth floor have fewer than two bedrooms. Thus, if there are apartments in the building with exactly two bedrooms, they are on the fourth floor.

(D) No apartment above the fourth floor of the building has more than two bedrooms. But only three-bedroom apartments have balconies. Thus, if any apartment in the building has a balcony, it is on the fourth floor or lower.

(E) Each apartment above the fourth floor of the building has more than two bedrooms. The building has no vacant apartments on or below the fourth floor. Thus, if there is any vacant apartment in the building, it will have more than two bedrooms.

GO ON TO THE NEXT PAGE.

24. Meteorologist: The number of tornadoes reported annually has more than doubled since the 1950s. But their actual number has probably not increased. Our ability to find tornadoes has improved, so we're probably just finding a higher percentage of them than we used to.

Which one of the following, if true, provides the most support for the meteorologist's argument?

(A) The physical damage caused by the average tornado has remained roughly constant since the 1950s.

(B) The number of tornadoes hitting major population centers annually has more than doubled since the 1950s.

(C) The number of large and medium sized tornadoes reported annually has remained roughly constant since the 1950s.

(D) The annual number of deaths due to tornadoes has increased steadily since the 1950s.

(E) The geographic range in which tornadoes are most prevalent has remained roughly constant since the 1950s.

25. Salesperson: If your vacuuming needs are limited to cleaning small areas of uncarpeted floors, an inexpensive handheld vacuum cleaner is likely to be sufficient. After all, most are easy to use and will likely satisfy all your vacuuming needs on wood and tile floors.

The conclusion of the salesperson's argument is most strongly supported if which one of the following is assumed?

(A) The only types of floor surfaces that most consumers encounter are carpet, wood, and tile.

(B) Inexpensive handheld vacuum cleaners are sufficient for cleaning small areas of carpeted floors.

(C) Any handheld vacuum cleaner that is easy to use but sufficient only for cleaning small areas of uncarpeted floors is likely to be inexpensive.

(D) If your household cleaning needs include cleaning small areas of uncarpeted floors, it is likely that you will need a vacuum cleaner.

(E) The more versatile a vacuum cleaner is, the more likely it is to be expensive.

26. Decreased reliance on fossil fuels is required if global warming is to be halted. The current reliance would decrease if economic incentives to develop alternative energy sources were present. So ending global warming requires offering economic incentives to develop alternative energy sources.

The flawed pattern of reasoning exhibited by the argument above most closely parallels that exhibited by which one of the following?

(A) If we end poverty we will end hunger. Ending unemployment will end poverty. So ending unemployment will end hunger.

(B) Daily exercise guarantees good health. Good health ensures a happy life. So daily exercise is required for good health.

(C) Going to college is required for getting a professional job. Graduating from high school is necessary for going to college. So graduating from high school is necessary for getting a professional job.

(D) Keeping good teachers is necessary for improving education. If teachers' salaries were improved, good teachers would remain in the profession. So an increase in teachers' salaries is necessary to improve education.

(E) Preventing abuse of prescription drugs requires expanding drug education efforts. Increased cooperation between schools and law enforcement agencies is needed if drug education efforts are to be expanded. So, if cooperation between law enforcement and schools increases, the abuse of prescription drugs will be prevented.

S T O P

IF YOU FINISH BEFORE TIME IS CALLED, YOU MAY CHECK YOUR WORK ON THIS SECTION ONLY.
DO NOT WORK ON ANY OTHER SECTION IN THE TEST.

SECTION IV
Time—35 minutes
25 Questions

Directions: Each question in this section is based on the reasoning presented in a brief passage. In answering the questions, you should not make assumptions that are by commonsense standards implausible, superfluous, or incompatible with the passage. For some questions, more than one of the choices could conceivably answer the question. However, you are to choose the **best** answer; that is, choose the response that most accurately and completely answers the question and mark that response on your answer sheet.

1. Dentist: I recommend brushing one's teeth after every meal to remove sugars that facilitate the growth of certain bacteria; these bacteria produce acid that dissolves minerals in tooth enamel, resulting in cavities. And when brushing is not practical, I recommend chewing gum—even gum that contains sugar—to prevent the formation of cavities.

    Which one of the following, if true, would most help to reconcile the dentist's apparently paradoxical recommendations?

    (A) A piece of chewing gum that contains sugar contains far less sugar than does the average meal.
    (B) Tooth decay can be stopped and reversed if it is caught before a cavity develops.
    (C) Chewing gum stimulates the production of saliva, which reduces acidity in the mouth and helps remineralize tooth enamel.
    (D) Sugars can be on teeth for as long as 24 hours before the teeth-damaging bacteria whose growth they facilitate begin to proliferate.
    (E) Chewing gum exercises and relaxes the jaw muscles and so contributes to the overall health of the oral tract.

2. When the ancient fossils of a primitive land mammal were unearthed in New Zealand, they provided the first concrete evidence that the island country had once had indigenous land mammals. Until that discovery, New Zealand had no known native land mammals. The discovery thus falsifies the theory that New Zealand's rich and varied native bird population owes its existence to the lack of competition from mammals.

    Which one of the following, if true, most seriously weakens the argument?

    (A) The unearthed land mammal is only one of several ancient land mammals that were indigenous to New Zealand.
    (B) The recently discovered land mammal became extinct long before the native bird population was established.
    (C) The site at which the primitive land mammal was unearthed also contains the fossils of primitive reptile and insect species.
    (D) Countries with rich and varied native land mammal populations do not have rich and varied native bird populations.
    (E) Some other island countries that are believed to have no native land mammals in fact had indigenous land mammals at one time.

GO ON TO THE NEXT PAGE.

3. Restaurant owner: The newspaper reporter who panned my restaurant acknowledges having no special expertise about food and its preparation. His previous job was as a political reporter. He is a good writer, but he is not a true restaurant critic. A newspaper would never call someone a drama critic who had no special training in theater.

    Which one of the following most accurately expresses the conclusion drawn in the restaurant owner's argument?

    (A) The newspaper reporter who panned the restaurant acknowledges having no special expertise about food and its preparation.
    (B) The previous job of the newspaper reporter who panned the restaurant was as a political reporter.
    (C) The newspaper reporter who panned the restaurant is a good writer.
    (D) The newspaper reporter who panned the restaurant is not a true restaurant critic.
    (E) A newspaper would never call someone a drama critic who had no special training in theater.

4. It has been hypothesized that our solar system was formed from a cloud of gas and dust produced by a supernova—an especially powerful explosion of a star. Supernovas produce the isotope iron-60, so if this hypothesis were correct, then iron-60 would have been present in the early history of the solar system. But researchers have found no iron-60 in meteorites that formed early in the solar system's history, thereby disproving the hypothesis.

    Which one of the following is an assumption required by the argument?

    (A) If a meteorite is formed early in the solar system's history, it contains chemical elements that are unlikely to be found in gas and dust produced by a supernova.
    (B) Other solar systems are not formed from clouds of gas and dust produced by supernovas.
    (C) Supernovas do not produce significant quantities of any form of iron other than iron-60.
    (D) Researchers have found iron-60 in meteorites that were formed relatively late in the solar system's history.
    (E) If there had been iron-60 present in the early history of the solar system, it would be found in meteorites formed early in the solar system's history.

5. Safety expert: Tuna is often treated with carbon monoxide so that it will not turn brown as it ages. Treating tuna with carbon monoxide does not make it harmful in any way. Nonetheless, there is a danger that such treatment will result in more people getting sick from eating tuna.

    Which one of the following, if true, most helps to resolve the apparent discrepancy in the safety expert's statements?

    (A) Workers in fish processing plants can be sickened by exposure to carbon monoxide if the appropriate safety procedures are not followed at those plants.
    (B) Over the last several years, tuna consumption has increased in most parts of the world.
    (C) Tuna that is treated with carbon monoxide provides no visible indication when it has spoiled to the point that it can cause food poisoning.
    (D) Treating tuna with carbon monoxide is the only way to keep it from turning brown as it ages.
    (E) Most consumers strongly prefer tuna that is not brown because they believe that brown tuna is not fresh.

6. Astrophysicist: Gamma ray bursts (GRBs)—explosions of powerful radiation from deep space—have traditionally been classified as either "short" or "long," terms that reflect the explosion's relative duration. However, an unusual GRB has been sighted. Its duration was long, but in every other respect it had the properties of a short GRB. Clearly, the descriptive labels "short" and "long" have now outlived their usefulness.

    The conclusion of the astrophysicist's argument is most strongly supported if which one of the following is assumed?

    (A) No other GRBs with unusual properties have been sighted.
    (B) The classification of GRBs can sometimes be made on the basis of duration alone.
    (C) Properties other than duration are more important than duration in the proper classification of the unusual GRB.
    (D) GRBs cannot be classified according to the different types of cosmic events that create them.
    (E) Descriptive labels are easily replaced with nondescriptive labels such as "type I" and "type II."

GO ON TO THE NEXT PAGE.

7. In one study, hospital patients' immune systems grew stronger when the patients viewed comic videos. This indicates that laughter can aid recovery from illness. But much greater gains in immune system strength occurred in the patients whose tendency to laugh was greater to begin with. So hospital patients with a greater tendency to laugh are helped more in their recovery from illness even when they laugh a little than other patients are helped when they laugh a greater amount.

    The argument is most vulnerable to criticism on the grounds that it

    (A) overlooks the possibility that the patients whose tendency to laugh was greater to begin with laughed more at the comic videos than did the other patients
    (B) fails to address adequately the possibility that the patients whose tendency to laugh was greatest to begin with already had stronger immune systems than the other patients
    (C) presumes, without providing justification, that hospital patients have immune systems representative of those of the entire population
    (D) takes for granted that the gains in immune system strength did not themselves influence the patients' tendency to laugh
    (E) presumes, without providing justification, that the patients whose tendency to laugh was greatest to begin with recovered from their illnesses more rapidly than the other patients

8. A study of guppy fish shows that a male guppy will alter its courting patterns in response to feedback from a female guppy. Males with more orange on one side than the other were free to vary which side they showed to a female. Females were drawn to those males with more orange showing, and males tended to show the females their more orange side when courting.

    Which one of the following, if true, provides the most support for the argument?

    (A) When a model of a female guppy was substituted for the female guppy, male guppies still courted, but were not more likely to show their side with more orange.
    (B) In many other species females show a preference for symmetry of coloring rather than quantity of coloring.
    (C) No studies have been done on whether male guppies with more orange coloring father more offspring than those with less orange coloring.
    (D) Female guppies have little if any orange coloring on their sides.
    (E) The male and female guppies were kept in separate tanks so they could see each other but not otherwise directly interact.

9. Politician: Some proponents of unilateral nuclear arms reduction argue that it would encourage other countries to reduce their own nuclear arsenals, eventually leading to an international agreement on nuclear arms reduction. Our acting on the basis of this argument would be dangerous, because the argument ignores the countries presently on the verge of civil wars. These countries, many of which have nuclear capability, cannot be relied upon to conform to any international military policy.

    Which one of the following most accurately expresses the conclusion of the politician's argument?

    (A) Countries that are on the verge of civil wars are unlikely to agree to reduce either their nuclear arms or their conventional weapons.
    (B) Unilateral nuclear arms reduction by the politician's country would encourage all countries to reduce their nuclear arsenals.
    (C) Many countries cannot be relied upon to disclose the extent of their nuclear capability.
    (D) It is unlikely that an international agreement on nuclear disarmament will ever be achieved.
    (E) It is risky for the politician's country to unilaterally reduce nuclear arms in hopes of achieving an international agreement on arms reduction.

GO ON TO THE NEXT PAGE.

10. Advertisement: Auto accidents are the most common cause of whiplash injury, a kind of injury that is caused by a sudden sharp motion of the neck. However, many other types of accidents can produce a sudden sharp motion of the neck and thereby result in whiplash injury. A sudden sharp motion of the neck can be caused by a fall, a bump on the head, or even by being shoved from behind. That is why you should insist on receiving Lakeside Injury Clinic's complete course of treatment for whiplash after any accident that involves a fall or a bump on the head.

Which one of the following, if true, provides the strongest basis for criticizing the reasoning in the advertisement?

(A) Being shoved from behind rarely causes whiplash.

(B) Auto accidents often involve falling or being bumped on the head.

(C) Nonautomobile accidents other than those involving falls or bumps on the head also occasionally cause whiplash injuries.

(D) It is very uncommon for falling or being bumped on the head to result in a sudden sharp motion of the neck.

(E) The appropriate treatment for whiplash caused by a fall or a bump on the head is no different from that for whiplash caused by an auto accident.

11. A group of citizens opposes developing a nearby abandoned railroad grade into a hiking trail. Its members argue that trail users will likely litter the area with food wrappers and other debris. But this objection is groundless. Most trail users will be dedicated hikers who have great concern for the environment. Consequently, development of the trail should proceed.

The argument above is flawed in that it

(A) bases its conclusion mainly on a claim that an opposing argument is weak

(B) illicitly infers that because each member of a set has a certain property that set itself has the property

(C) illicitly assumes as one of its premises the contention it purports to show

(D) illicitly infers that an attribute of a few users of the proposed trail will characterize a majority of users of the trail

(E) attacks the citizens in the group rather than their objection to developing the trail

12. For years, university administrators, corporations, and government agencies have been predicting an imminent and catastrophic shortage of scientists and engineers. But since there is little noticeable upward pressure on the salaries of scientists and engineers, and unemployment is as high in these fields as any other, these doomsayers are turning out to be wrong.

Which one of the following would, if true, most strengthen the argument above?

(A) The proportion of all research in science and engineering being carried out by corporations is larger than it was five years ago.

(B) Most students choose fields of study that offer some prospect of financial success.

(C) The number of students in university programs in science and engineering has increased significantly in the last five years.

(D) Certain specializations in science and engineering have an oversupply of labor and others have shortages.

(E) The knowledge and skills acquired during university programs in science and engineering need to be kept current through periodic retraining and professional experience.

13. Rhonda: As long as the cost is not too great, you should use your time, energy, or money to help others. People who are active participants in charitable causes have richer lives than miserly hermits, however prosperous the hermits may be.

Brad: You should ignore the problems of complete strangers and focus your generosity on your immediate relatives and close friends, since these are the people who will remember your sacrifices and return the kindness when you yourself need help.

Which one of the following principles, if valid, would most help to justify both Rhonda's and Brad's arguments?

(A) One should always do what will produce the most benefit for the most people.

(B) One should treat others as one expects to be treated by them.

(C) One should act in ways that will benefit oneself.

(D) One should make sacrifices for others only if they will eventually return the favor.

(E) One should always act in a manner that one can reflect on with pride.

GO ON TO THE NEXT PAGE.

14. Columnist: Wildlife activists have proposed that the practice of stringing cable TV lines from the same poles that carry electric power lines should be banned because cable TV lines, while electrically neutral themselves, make it easier for animals to climb near electric power lines, risking electrocution. This particular argument for banning the practice fails, however, since some animals are electrocuted by power lines even where cable TV lines are all underground.

Which one of the following most accurately describes a flaw in the columnist's reasoning?

(A) It takes a sufficient condition for an argument's being inadequate to be a necessary condition for its being inadequate.

(B) It rejects an argument for a proposal merely on the grounds that the proposal would not completely eliminate the problem it is intended to address.

(C) It fails to consider the additional advantageous effects that a proposal to address a problem might have.

(D) It rejects an argument by criticizing the argument's proponents rather than by criticizing its substance.

(E) It rejects a proposal to address a problem merely on the grounds that other proposals to address the problem would also be effective.

15. The ancient reptile *Thrinaxodon*, an ancestor of mammals, had skull features suggesting that it had sensory whiskers. If *Thrinaxodon* had whiskers, it clearly also had hair on other parts of its body, which would have served as insulation that regulated body temperature. Therefore, *Thrinaxodon* was probably warm-blooded, for such insulation would be of little use to a cold-blooded animal.

Which one of the following most accurately describes the role played in the argument by the statement that if *Thrinaxodon* had whiskers, it clearly also had hair on other parts of its body, which would have served as insulation that regulated body temperature?

(A) It is a premise offered in support of the conclusion that insulation regulating body temperature would be of little use to a cold-blooded animal.

(B) It is a premise offered in support of the main conclusion drawn in the argument.

(C) It is a conclusion for which the claim that *Thrinaxodon* had skull features suggesting that it had sensory whiskers is offered as support.

(D) It is a statement of a hypothesis that the argument attempts to show is false.

(E) It is offered as an explanation of the phenomenon described by the argument's main conclusion, but it is not itself used to provide support for that conclusion.

16. Economist: Currently, many countries rely primarily on taxing income to fund government expenditures. But taxing income does nothing to promote savings and investment. Taxing consumption, on the other hand, would encourage savings. The most important challenge facing these countries is improving their economies, and the only way to accomplish this is to increase their savings rates. Hence, _____

Which one of the following most logically completes the economist's argument?

(A) most governments should stop taxing savings and investment

(B) the economies of countries will rapidly improve if their governments adopt tax policies that encourage savings and investment

(C) in most countries taxes on consumption alone could raise adequate revenues to fund government expenditures

(D) the tax laws of many countries should be revised to focus on taxing consumption rather than income

(E) it is detrimental to the economic improvement of any country to continue to tax income

17. Meade: People who are injured as a result of their risky behaviors not only cause harm to themselves but, because we all have important ties to other people, inevitably impose emotional and financial costs on others. To protect the interests of others, therefore, governments are justified in outlawing behavior that puts one's own health at risk.

Which one of the following principles, if valid, most undermines the reasoning in Meade's argument?

(A) Endangering the social ties that one has to other people is itself a harm to oneself.

(B) People who have important ties to others have a personal obligation not to put their own health at risk.

(C) Governments are not justified in limiting an individual's behavior unless that behavior imposes emotional or financial costs on others.

(D) Preventing harm to others is not by itself a sufficient justification for laws that limit personal freedom.

(E) People's obligation to avoid harming others outweighs their obligation to avoid harming themselves.

GO ON TO THE NEXT PAGE.

18. Sanderson intentionally did not tell his cousin about overhearing someone say that the factory would close, knowing that if he withheld this information, his cousin would assume it would remain open. Clearly this was morally wrong. After all, lying is morally wrong. And making a statement with the intention of misleading someone is lying. True, it was Sanderson's failing to state something that misled his cousin. Yet there is no moral difference between stating and failing to state if they are done with the same intention.

Which one of the following is an assumption required by the argument?

(A) Sanderson believed that his cousin would not want to be informed about the factory closing.

(B) No one ever told Sanderson's cousin about the factory closing.

(C) Sanderson believed that the factory would in fact be closing.

(D) Sanderson would have lied to his cousin if his cousin had asked him whether the factory would be closing.

(E) Sanderson had something to gain by his cousin's continuing to believe that the factory would remain open.

19. After a judge has made the first ruling on a particular point of law, judges must follow that precedent if the original ruling is not contrary to the basic moral values of society. In the absence of precedent, when judges' own legal views do not contradict any widespread public opinion—and only then—they may abide by their own legal views in deciding a case.

Of the rulings described below, which one conforms most closely to the principles stated above?

(A) Judge Swoboda is confronted with a legal issue never before decided. Realizing that his own view on the issue contradicts what most people believe, he nonetheless issues a ruling that accords with his own legal views.

(B) Judge Valenzuela decides, in the absence of any precedent, whether children as young as twelve can be legally tried as adults. There is overwhelming public support for trying children twelve and older as adults, a practice that violates Judge Valenzuela's personal moral views. So Judge Valenzuela rules, in keeping with his own legal beliefs, against trying twelve-year-olds as adults.

(C) Judge Levinsky sets a legal precedent when she rules that the "starfish exception" applies to children. In deciding a later case concerning the starfish exception, Judge Wilson adheres to his own legal views rather than Judge Levinsky's ruling, even though he does not believe that Judge Levinsky's ruling opposes the basic moral values of society.

(D) Judge Watanabe must decide a case that depends on an issue for which no legal precedent exists. There is no widespread public opinion on the issue, so Judge Watanabe rules against the defendant because that conforms to her own legal view about the issue.

(E) Judge Balila rules against the defendant because doing so conforms to her own views about the legal issues involved. However, this ruling is contrary to relevant precedents, all of which conform to the basic moral values of society.

GO ON TO THE NEXT PAGE.

20. Neuroscientists subjected volunteers with amusia—difficulty telling different melodies apart and remembering simple tunes—to shifts in pitch comparable to those that occur when someone plays one piano key and then another. The volunteers were unable to discern a difference between the tones. But the volunteers were able to track timed sequences of musical tones and perceive slight changes in timing.

The statements above, if true, most strongly support which one of the following hypotheses?

(A) People who are unable to discern pitch compensate by developing a heightened perception of timing.

(B) Amusia results more from an inability to discern pitch than from an inability to discern timing.

(C) People who are unable to tell pitches apart in isolation are able to do so in the context of a melody by relying upon timing.

(D) The ability to tell melodies apart depends on the discernment of pitch alone and not at all on the perception of timing.

(E) Whereas perception of timing can apparently be learned, discernment of pitch is most likely innate.

21. Literary critic: There is little of social significance in contemporary novels, for readers cannot enter the internal world of the novelist's mind unless they experience that world from the moral perspective of the novel's characters. But in contemporary novels, the transgressions committed by some characters against others are sensationalistic spectacles whose only purpose is to make readers wonder what will happen next, rather than events whose purpose is to be seen as the injustices they are.

Which one of the following principles, if valid, would most help to justify the literary critic's argument?

(A) An artist who wants to engage the moral sensibilities of his or her audience should not assume that forms of artistic expression that previously served this purpose continue to do so.

(B) A novelist who wants to make a reader empathize with a victim of injustice should avoid sensationalistic spectacles whose only purpose is to make readers wonder what will happen next.

(C) A work of art is socially important only if it engages the moral sensibilities of its audience.

(D) If a novel allows a reader to understand injustice from the point of view of its victims, it will be socially significant.

(E) Novels have social significance only to the extent that they allow readers to enter the internal world of the novelist's mind.

22. A recent study revealed that people who follow precisely all the standard recommendations for avoidance of infection by pathogenic microorganisms in meat-based foods are more likely to contract diseases caused by these pathogens than are those who deviate considerably from the standard recommendations. Hence, the standard recommendations for avoidance of infection by these pathogens must be counterproductive.

The argument is most vulnerable to criticism on the grounds that it fails to take into account which one of the following possibilities?

(A) Pathogenic microorganisms can reproduce in foods that are not meat-based.

(B) Many people do follow precisely all the standard recommendations for avoidance of infection by pathogenic microorganisms in meat-based foods.

(C) Not all diseases caused by microorganisms have readily recognizable symptoms.

(D) Preventing infection by pathogenic microorganisms is simply a matter of following the appropriate set of recommendations.

(E) Those most concerned with avoiding pathogenic infections from meat-based foods are those most susceptible to them.

GO ON TO THE NEXT PAGE.

23. No nonfiction book published by Carriage Books has ever earned a profit. Since Carriage Books earned a profit on every book it published last year, it clearly did not publish a nonfiction book last year.

The pattern of reasoning in the argument above is most similar to that in which one of the following arguments?

(A) No actor represented by the talent agent Mira Roberts has ever won an important role in a major movie. Since every actor represented by Ms. Roberts had at least one important acting role last year, it is clear that none of those actors worked in a movie last year.

(B) No hotel owned by the Bidmore Group specializes in serving business travelers. Since the Cray Springs Hotel is owned by the Bidmore Group, it clearly does not specialize in serving business travelers.

(C) Pranwich Corporation has never given a bonus to an employee in its marketing division. Since Pranwich gave bonuses to every one of its systems analysts last year, it is clear that the company employed no systems analysts in its marketing division at that time.

(D) James Benson has never done business with the city of Waldville. Since Waldville only maintains business files on individuals that it does business with, it clearly does not have a business file on James Benson.

(E) Conway Flooring has never installed hardwood flooring for any customer in Woodridge. Since Conway Flooring has had a lot of customers in Woodridge, the company clearly does not install hardwood flooring.

24. All unemployed artists are sympathetic to social justice. And no employed artists are interested in the prospect of great personal fame.

If the claims made above are true, then which one of the following must be true?

(A) If there are artists interested in the prospect of great personal fame, they are sympathetic to social justice.

(B) All artists uninterested in the prospect of great personal fame are sympathetic to social justice.

(C) Every unemployed artist is interested in the prospect of great personal fame.

(D) If an artist is sympathetic to social justice, that artist is unemployed.

(E) All artists are either sympathetic to social justice or are interested in the prospect of great personal fame.

25. The police department has two suspects for the burglary that occurred last night, Schaeffer and Forster. Schaeffer has an ironclad alibi, so Forster must be the burglar.

Which one of the following arguments exhibits a flawed pattern of reasoning that is most similar to that exhibited by the argument above?

(A) It has been known for some time that the Wrightsburg Zoo might build a new primate house and that it might refurbish its polar bear exhibit. There is now good reason to believe the zoo will build a new primate house. Therefore, the zoo will not refurbish its polar bear exhibit.

(B) If Watson, a robbery suspect, had been picked out of a police lineup by the victim, then charging Watson with robbery would have been reasonable. But the victim did not pick Watson out of the lineup. So Watson should not be charged.

(C) If Iano Industries does not borrow money so that it can upgrade its factories, it will be unable to compete. While it is undesirable for Iano to take on more debt, being unable to compete would be even worse. So Iano should borrow the money needed to upgrade its factories.

(D) Baxim Corporation announced last year that it was considering moving its headquarters to Evansville and that it was also considering moving to Rivertown. But Baxim has now decided not to move to Evansville. Thus, we can be sure that Baxim will move to Rivertown.

(E) The only viable candidates in the mayoral race are Slater and Gonzales. Political analysts believe that Slater has little chance of winning. Therefore, it is likely that Gonzales will win the election.

STOP

IF YOU FINISH BEFORE TIME IS CALLED, YOU MAY CHECK YOUR WORK ON THIS SECTION ONLY.
DO NOT WORK ON ANY OTHER SECTION IN THE TEST.

Acknowledgment is made to the following sources from which material has been adapted for use in this test:

Bruce Bower, "Brain Roots of Music Depreciation." ©2004 by Science Service, Inc.

Marjorie K. M. Chan and Douglas W. Lee, "Chinatown Chinese: A Linguistic and Historical Re-evaluation" in *Amerasia Journal*. ©1981 by Marjorie K. M. Chan and Douglas W. Lee.

Emmanuelle Fauchart and Eric von Hippel, "Norms-Based Intellectual Property Systems: The Case of French Chefs" in *Organization Science*. ©2008 by INFORMS.

Alejandro Jenkins and Gilad Perez, "Looking for Life in the Multiverse: Universes with Different Physical Laws Might Still Be Habitable" in *Scientific American*. ©2010 by Scientific American, a division of Nature American, Inc.

Ann J. Lane, Introduction to *Herland*. ©1979 by Ann J. Lane.

Dotan Oliar and Christopher Jon Sprigman, "There's No Free Laugh (Anymore): The Emergence of Intellectual Property Norms and the Transformation of Stand-Up Comedy" in *Virginia Law Review*. ©2008 by Virginia Law Review.

Computing Your Score

Directions:

1. Use the Answer Key on the next page to check your answers.

2. Use the Scoring Worksheet below to compute your raw score.

3. Use the Score Conversion Chart to convert your raw score into the 120–180 scale.*

Scoring Worksheet

1. Enter the number of questions you answered correctly in each section.

	Number Correct
SECTION I	_____
SECTION II	_____
SECTION III	_____
SECTION IV	Unscored

2. Enter the sum here: _____

This is your Raw Score.

Score Conversion Chart

Use the table below to convert your raw score to the corresponding 120–180 scaled score for PrepTest 149.

Raw Score	Scaled Score	Raw Score	Scaled Score
78	180	38	146
77	180	37	145
76	179	36	144
75	177	35	143
74	176	34	142
73	174	33	142
72	173	32	141
71	172	31	140
70	170	30	139
69	169	29	138
68	169	28	138
67	168	27	137
66	167	26	136
65	166	25	135
64	165	24	134
63	164	23	133
62	164	22	132
61	163	21	131
60	162	20	130
59	161	19	129
58	161	18	128
57	160	17	127
56	159	16	126
55	158	15	125
54	158	14	123
53	157	13	122
52	156	12	121
51	156	11	120
50	155	10	120
49	154	9	120
48	153	8	120
47	153	7	120
46	152	6	120
45	151	5	120
44	150	4	120
43	149	3	120
42	149	2	120
41	148	1	120
40	147	0	120
39	146		

*Scores are reported on a 120–180 score scale, with 120 being the lowest possible score and 180 being the highest possible score.

Answer Key

Question	Section I	Section II	Section III	Section IV*
1	C	C	C	C
2	D	C	E	B
3	A	E	C	D
4	C	A	A	E
5	C	A	E	C
6	D	A	B	C
7	A	B	A	A
8	E	D	D	A
9	A	D	C	E
10	C	C	E	D
11	A	C	D	A
12	A	B	D	C
13	C	E	E	C
14	B	C	C	B
15	E	B	D	B
16	C	B	B	D
17	B	E	E	D
18	E	D	A	C
19	A	A	D	D
20	D	B	D	B
21	B	D	D	E
22	A	E	B	E
23	C	A	C	C
24	B	D	C	A
25	C	B	A	D
26		B	D	
27		A		

*Section IV is unscored. The number of items answered correctly in Section IV should not be added to the raw score.

PrepTest 150

SECTION I

Time—35 minutes

27 Questions

Directions: Each set of questions in this section is based on a single passage or a pair of passages. The questions are to be answered on the basis of what is **stated** or **implied** in the passage or pair of passages. For some questions, more than one of the choices could conceivably answer the question. However, you are to choose the **best** answer; that is, choose the response that most accurately and completely answers the question and mark that response on your answer sheet.

The following passage was written in the mid-1990s.

Evidence that the earth's atmosphere has warmed has become quite compelling, in part because it has been reinforced recently by the development of accurate profiles of average annual temperatures throughout the last 1,000 years. These data, inferred from studies of geological patterns and samples of ice deposits, tree rings, and coral growth layers, indicate that the recent increase in average temperature—a rise of about one half of a degree Celsius over the last 100 years—is unprecedented in the previous 1,000 years. At the same time, other recent studies have strengthened the controversial link between this increase and the "greenhouse effect." Proponents of the greenhouse effect claim that the increase was caused by elevated levels in the atmosphere of certain gases that prevent heat from radiating back into space.

Early models charting the greenhouse effect were somewhat inconsistent with observed data; they estimated that the increase in the earth's atmospheric temperature over recent decades should have been higher than the increase observed in actuality, which led opponents to question the validity of the greenhouse theory. But new methods have enabled scientists to gauge the effect of greenhouse gases more accurately by taking into account an important factor that earlier studies overlooked: airborne sulfates. Sulfates from natural sources such as volcanoes as well as from human technological sources tend to counteract the heating effect of greenhouse gases by reflecting solar energy back into space. Taking into account the varying levels of airborne sulfates indicated by the concentration of sulfates in successive ages of glacial ice, these scientists have calculated theoretical temperatures for recent decades that are consistent with observed temperatures.

Another question for proponents of the greenhouse theory comes from scientists who have attempted to tie changes in the earth's atmospheric temperature to variations in solar energy. From observations of cycles in several types of solar phenomena, these scientists have developed models that chart variations in the sun's heating effects, and the models do show a strong decade-by-decade correspondence between solar activity and atmospheric temperature fluctuations. But the models cannot account for the entirety of the recent rise in atmospheric temperature. While researchers have found that the average annual atmospheric temperature fluctuates from one year to the next, its temperature over the long term has been relatively stable—deviations from the long-term average atmospheric temperature have inevitably reverted to this average, or equilibrium, temperature. But the current rise in temperature surpasses the most extreme fluctuations in temperature consistent with the models based on variations in solar energy. In light of all this, it seems reasonable to conclude that changes in the earth's atmosphere have raised its equilibrium temperature, and that greenhouse gases represent the best explanation of that shift.

1. Which one of the following most accurately states the main point of the passage?

(A)   Though many accept the theory that the greenhouse effect is causing the recent global warming, that theory is somewhat questionable in light of recent data concerning sulfates and solar cycles.

(B)   Scientific models of the effects of greenhouse gases, modified to incorporate the effects of airborne sulfates, are important because they predict that the earth's average temperature will continue to rise.

(C)   New scientific evidence shows that the earth's equilibrium temperature has been rising in a way that is consistent with the greenhouse theory, but that the increase has been less than this theory originally estimated.

(D)   Recent scientific data and calculations support the claims that the earth's atmosphere is becoming warmer and that the greenhouse effect is a major cause of this warming trend.

(E)   The greenhouse theory is a reasonable explanation of a recent upward trend in the earth's atmospheric temperatures only if it is combined with the solar-fluctuation theory.

GO ON TO THE NEXT PAGE.

2. Which one of the following most accurately describes the relation between the argumentation in the second paragraph and that in the third paragraph?

    (A)   Two complementary theories that the author compares in the second paragraph are then contrasted in the third paragraph, where the first theory is ultimately rejected in favor of the second.

    (B)   A theory that the author shows to be problematic in the second paragraph is tentatively rejected in the third paragraph in light of compelling evidence that runs counter to the theory.

    (C)   A theory that the author discusses in the second paragraph is tentatively accepted after weighing additional considerations in the third paragraph.

    (D)   A theory that the author proposes and defends in the second paragraph is substantially revised in the third paragraph in response to new findings.

    (E)   A theory whose validity is questioned by the author in the second paragraph is shown in the third paragraph to be consistent with observed data.

3. Which one of the following is mentioned in the passage?

    (A)   the way in which sulfates in the earth's atmosphere produce an effect on temperatures

    (B)   that airborne sulfates are the main greenhouse gases

    (C)   the usual duration of one cycle of varying solar energy output

    (D)   predictions as to the effects of global warming on glacial ice

    (E)   an example of a technological source of airborne sulfates

4. It can be reasonably inferred from the passage that the author considers which one of the following most crucial in judging the success of a model developed to explain the global warming trend of the previous 100 years?

    (A)   a strong correspondence between the model's calculated average global temperatures in the last few years and data from actual temperature observations

    (B)   that the model predicts an increase in the earth's temperature on the basis of a simple explanatory framework

    (C)   the extent to which the model has been revised in light of experimental findings

    (D)   a close fit between the warming mechanisms postulated by the theory and those that are generally acknowledged to be able to raise atmospheric temperatures

    (E)   a long-term match between the model's estimated changes in the earth's temperature and data indicating the actual temperatures that have occurred

5. Which one of the following most accurately states the author's primary purpose in the last two sentences of the second paragraph?

    (A)   to provide an example of a set of observations that has been predicted by a theory

    (B)   to argue that a new theory will need to be formulated in order to accommodate certain recent findings

    (C)   to demonstrate the degree to which a previously accepted theory fails to account for observed phenomena

    (D)   to show that a certain theory that was previously in doubt can be defended in light of additional data

    (E)   to propose a way of resolving a dispute between proponents of two competing theories

GO ON TO THE NEXT PAGE.

When interviewing witnesses to a crime, police interviewers seek to maximize the amount of information that a cooperating eyewitness can give them so that they can generate leads to follow, confirm or disconfirm alibis, and so forth. One method for eliciting information over and above what a cooperative witness might otherwise provide is the cognitive interview.

Developed by psychologists and adopted by police forces around the world, the cognitive interview combines cognitive techniques known to improve recall, such as multiple retrieval attempts, with communication strategies developed by social psychologists, such as conversation-management skills and techniques for building rapport between interviewer and interviewee. The general consensus is that this package has proven successful in increasing the number of details recalled by witnesses, with little impact on the number of incorrect details reported (neither increasing nor decreasing overall accuracy). However, a problem associated with the cognitive interview is that it is a complex procedure, requiring substantial training to learn and a long time to conduct. Because of this complexity, not all officers receive this training, and even trained officers often deviate from the procedures specified in the cognitive interview training.

An alternative to the cognitive interview is hypnosis. Indeed, hypnotic investigative interviewing was a precursor to the cognitive interview. However, even though the techniques involved are much less complex, the evidence suggests that overall accuracy, as determined by the proportion of correct to incorrect responses, is not generally improved with hypnosis; in fact, sometimes it may deteriorate. Hypnosis may also give rise to a "false confidence" effect, whereby witnesses are more confident in their reports generally, including reports of incorrect information. There are other practical difficulties, most notably that not all witnesses are susceptible to hypnosis.

For police interviewers, the ideal method for eliciting additional information from an eyewitness would be one that requires no special training for the interviewer, that can be applied to the entire population of potential witnesses, and that has a positive effect on correct memory reports, with no corresponding increase in false details reported. Research suggests that such a method may in fact be available. Encouraging eyewitnesses to close their eyes during recall attempts is a technique that is common to both hypnosis and the cognitive interview. Recent studies demonstrate that instructed eye-closure can benefit recall for both visual and auditory materials, for events witnessed on video, and for events witnessed through live interactions. These studies indicate an improvement over hypnotic interviewing, with no problems of participant dropout because of lack of hypnotic susceptibility. More significantly, instructed eye-closure by itself appears to improve witness recall to a degree equivalent to that demonstrated by the cognitive interview. And the benefits of eye-closure are achieved with no increase in errors, no specialist training, and no greater complexity of interviewing technique.

6. Which one of the following most accurately expresses the main point of the passage?

(A) For police interviewers, the ideal interview procedure would be one that is simple to apply, universally applicable, and reliably successful at eliciting accurate information.

(B) Interviewing witnesses is a crucial component of law enforcement, but all existing interview procedures require some trade-off between reliability and practicality.

(C) Instructing witnesses to close their eyes during memory-recall tasks is a technique common to both hypnosis and the cognitive interview.

(D) Though difficult to implement on a large scale, the cognitive interview is the most effective procedure police officers can use when questioning an eyewitness.

(E) Instructed eye-closure improves witness recall without sacrificing practicality or reliability, making it an ideal interview technique for police interviewers.

7. According to the passage, each of the following is true of the instructed eye-closure technique **except**:

(A) It requires less training than the cognitive interview.

(B) Studies have shown that it can benefit recall for events witnessed on video.

(C) It does not lead to an increase in erroneous memory reports.

(D) It may give rise to a "false confidence" effect.

(E) It is common to both hypnotic interviewing and the cognitive interview.

8. The author refers to "alibis" (first sentence of the passage) primarily in order to

(A) highlight a positive contribution made by psychological research

(B) exemplify the kind of information police interviewers seek to elicit from suspects

(C) point to a use to which an effective interview procedure might be put

(D) contrast the concerns of police officers with those of psychologists

(E) illustrate the complexity of the cognitive interview

GO ON TO THE NEXT PAGE.

9. The author would be most likely to agree with which one of the following statements?

(A) There is reason to worry that the cognitive interview is less effective if police interviewers deviate from the procedures specified in the training.

(B) An interviewer's success at eliciting valuable information from a witness derives largely from the interviewer's ability to establish a rapport with the witness.

(C) Though it suffers from significant drawbacks, hypnotic interviewing has an advantage over other investigative interviewing procedures in that its effective use requires essentially no training.

(D) When interviewing witnesses, police interviewers may need to use different techniques depending on whether the desired information is visual or auditory in nature.

(E) An increase in the complexity of an interview procedure will usually result in a decrease in the reliability of the information obtained.

10. It can be inferred from the passage that the use of hypnotic interviewing most likely has which one of the following consequences?

(A) Interviews yield more inaccurate information than accurate information.

(B) Interviewers are overly confident that complex interview procedures have been followed correctly.

(C) Interviewers are not able to detect attempts by a witness to intentionally deceive the interviewer.

(D) Interviewers are not able to accurately assess the reliability of a witness's memory reports by asking the witness how sure he or she is concerning those reports.

(E) Interviewees become less susceptible to hypnosis over the course of the interview process, resulting in a steady decrease in the amount of information they are able to provide.

11. Which one of the following describes a relationship that is most analogous to the one that holds between the cognitive interview and instructed eye-closure, as described in the passage?

(A) Studies show that individuals who frequently engage in light exercise enjoy significant health benefits, but equivalent health benefits are enjoyed by those who engage in more strenuous exercise on a less frequent basis.

(B) Reduced consumption of saturated fat combined with an increased consumption of fiber has been shown to produce significant health benefits, but equivalent health benefits have been produced by an increase in fiber consumption alone.

(C) Consumption of moderate amounts of caffeine has been linked to positive health benefits, but excessive caffeine consumption has been shown to elevate blood pressure.

(D) Research has shown that a new vitamin supplement can produce dramatic benefits in women, but data is inconclusive regarding men.

(E) Studies suggest that diet and exercise produce observable health benefits, but less significant benefits can be achieved through exercise alone.

12. The author would be most likely to agree with which one of the following statements?

(A) If all witnesses were susceptible to hypnosis, hypnotic interviewing would be the best procedure for maximizing the amount of accurate information obtained from cooperative witnesses.

(B) Even if police forces had the time and resources to train all of their officers in the cognitive interview, the complexity of the procedure would still pose problems for its use.

(C) Instructed eye-closure should be adopted as an investigative interviewing technique only if police forces lack the resources required to implement the cognitive interview.

(D) Interview procedures that are easy to learn are likely to yield a greater amount of accurate information than interview procedures that are more difficult to learn.

(E) The more information a cooperative witness provides when interviewed, the more likely it is that the witness is experiencing a "false confidence" effect.

GO ON TO THE NEXT PAGE.

Passage A

In a 1978 lecture titled "The Detective Story," Jorge Luis Borges observes that, "The detective novel has created a special type of reader," and adds, "If Poe created the detective story, he subsequently created the reader of detective fiction." For Borges, this "special type of reader" confronts literature with such "incredulity and suspicions" that he or she might read any narrative as a detective story. Borges's interest in this particular genre, of course, inspired a good deal of his own fiction, but his account also draws our attention to an insight into the general nature of literature.

Literature, according to Borges, is "an aesthetic event" that "requires the conjunction of reader and text," and what the detective story highlights, he suggests, is the way in which the reader forms the conditions of possibility for this "aesthetic event." Borges imagines that the participation of the reader is not extrinsic to but instead essential to the literary text. Thus, what unites works belonging to the same genre is the way those works are read, rather than, say, a set of formal elements found within the works.

Passage B

One can, if one wants, define genres of fiction as sets of texts sharing certain thematic similarities, but the taxonomic difficulties of such an approach are notorious. The problem of "borderline cases"— especially in science fiction—arises so often that the definition fails to demarcate genres entirely. A more fruitful way to characterize the distinction between genres is to view it as a distinction between reading protocols: between ways of reading, responding to sentences, and making various sentences and various texts make sense. We are free to read any text by any reading protocol we wish. But the texts most central to a genre are those texts that were clearly written to exploit a particular protocol—texts that yield a particularly rich reading experience when read according to one protocol rather than another.

Our major critical effort must therefore be an exploration of the specific workings of many of the individual rhetorical configurations that contour, exploit, or even create a specific reading protocol. Here—to give an example outside of fiction—is a general description of one aspect of the reading protocols associated with poetry: with poetry, we tend to pay more attention to the sound of the words than we do with prose. Therefore we look for rhetorical figures that exploit, among other things, the phonic aspects of the words making up the text. With science fiction, much of the significance of the story will manifest itself in the alternative workings of the world in which the characters maneuver. Therefore we will pay particular attention to the rhetorical figures by which differences between our world and the world of the story are suggested.

13. Both passages are concerned with answering which one of the following questions?

(A) Can works of fiction that belong to a popular genre have literary value?
(B) Who created the genre of detective fiction?
(C) What determines whether a work of fiction belongs to a particular genre rather than another?
(D) What is an author's role in determining the genre to which a story written by the author belongs?
(E) What does science fiction have in common with detective fiction?

14. The authors of the passages would be most likely to agree with which one of the following statements?

(A) Short works of fiction are easier to categorize by genre than longer works.
(B) The first works of detective fiction and science fiction were written as artistic exercises, rather than as entertainment.
(C) There is no scholarly value in attempting to demarcate the boundaries of a genre of fiction.
(D) Genre stories are typically of literary value in proportion to the degree to which they defy the conventions of the genre to which they belong.
(E) Two works of fiction could have very similar plots, characters, and settings and yet belong to different genres.

15. Which one of the following most accurately describes the stance expressed by the author of passage A toward Borges's view?

(A) complete agreement
(B) reluctant acceptance
(C) cautious neutrality
(D) strong skepticism
(E) outright rejection

GO ON TO THE NEXT PAGE.

16. Which one of the following is true about the argumentative structures of the two passages?

    (A) Passage A moves from the specific to the general, whereas passage B moves from the general to the specific.

    (B) Passage A begins with a discussion of a competing view, whereas passage B builds up to such a discussion.

    (C) Both passages respond to a series of counterexamples to their main thesis.

    (D) Both passages open with a description of an apparent contradiction that they then attempt to resolve.

    (E) Both passages explore the implications of a thought experiment described at the outset.

17. The author of passage B would be most likely to agree with which one of the following?

    (A) Fictional works that were not written to exploit the reading protocol of a particular genre are sometimes borderline cases of that genre.

    (B) Readers' expectations regarding a particular fictional work are not essential to its genre classification.

    (C) Thematic similarities constitute the most useful basis for demarcating genres of fiction.

    (D) The interpretation of a sentence that appears in a fictional work does not depend on the genre to which the work belongs.

    (E) Every work of fiction of a given genre must include the themes and other content elements that are shared by the central works of that genre.

18. Borges and the author of passage B would be most likely to agree with which one of the following statements?

    (A) The genre of fiction to which a story belongs is fully determined by the author's intention.

    (B) Any science fiction story could be read as if it were a detective story.

    (C) Every work of fiction unambiguously belongs to some particular genre or other.

    (D) Some rhetorical figures appear in poetry that never appear in prose fiction.

    (E) A story cannot be truly enjoyed unless the reader knows to which genre it is supposed to belong.

19. Which one of the following is an application of a principle underlying passage B to the view of detective fiction ascribed to Borges in passage A?

    (A) A story in the genre of detective fiction cannot include any supernatural characters or events.

    (B) Stories in the genre of detective fiction portray crimes that inevitably reflect the social anxieties of the time in which they were written.

    (C) Stories in the genre of detective fiction employ rhetorical figures designed to encourage readers' suspicions about characters and events in the story.

    (D) A story in the genre of detective fiction must involve the unraveling of a puzzle, the solution to which is discovered by the reader along with the protagonist of the story.

    (E) The reading protocols associated with detective fiction are too universally applicable to constitute a well defined literary genre.

GO ON TO THE NEXT PAGE.

It might reasonably have been expected that the adoption of cooking by early humans would not have led to any changes in human digestive anatomy. After all, cooking makes food easier to eat, which means that no special adaptations are required to process cooked food. However, current evidence suggests that humans today are capable of living on raw food only under unusual circumstances, such as a relatively sedentary lifestyle in a well supported urban environment. Important theoretical obstacles to living on raw food in the wild today include both the low digestibility of much raw plant food, and the toughness of much raw meat. These points suggest that humans are so evolutionarily constrained to eating foods that are digestible and easily chewed that cooking is normally obligatory. Furthermore, the widespread assumption that cooking could not have had any impact on biological evolution because its practice is too recent appears to be wrong. (Various European and Middle Eastern sites that go back more than 250,000 years contain extensive evidence of hominid use of fire and apparent "earth ovens.") The implication is that the adoption of cooked food created opportunities for humans to use diets of high caloric density more efficiently. Selection for such efficiency, we suggest, led to an inability to survive on raw-food diets in the wild.

Important questions therefore arise concerning what limits the ability of humans to utilize raw food. The principal effect of cooking considered to date has been a reduction in tooth and jaw size over evolutionary time. Human tooth and jaw size show signs of decreasing approximately 100,000 years ago; we suggest that this was a consequence of eating cooked food. Subsequent population variation in the extent and timing of dental reduction is broadly explicable by regional variation in the times when improvements in cooking technology were adopted. It is also possible that the earliest impact of cooking was the reduction of tooth and jaw size that accompanied the evolution of *Homo ergaster* approximately 1.9 million years ago. If so, the decrease in tooth and jaw size that started around 100,000 years ago may prove to result from later modifications in cooking technique, such as the adoption of boiling.

The evolution of soft parts of the digestive system is harder to reconstruct because they leave no fossil record. Human digestive anatomy differs from that of the other great apes in ways that have traditionally been explained as adaptations to a high raw-meat diet. Differences include the smaller gut volume, longer small intestine, and smaller colon. All such features are essentially adaptations to a diet of relatively high caloric density, however, and may therefore be at least as well explained by the adoption of cooking as by eating raw meat. Testing between the cooking and raw-meat models for understanding human digestive anatomy is therefore warranted.

20. Which one of the following most accurately states the main point of the passage?

    (A)   Important questions about why humans are unable to survive on raw food are unresolved by current science.
    (B)   Current evidence suggests that human beings are biologically adapted to the ingestion of cooked rather than raw food.
    (C)   The reduction of human tooth and jaw size over evolutionary time strongly suggests that humans underwent a change in their dietary habits.
    (D)   For at least 250,000 years, humans have been eating a diet that heavily features cooked food.
    (E)   No special biological adaptations were necessary for humans to eat cooked food, since cooking makes food easier to eat.

21. The authors would be most likely to agree with which one of the following statements?

    (A)   Small teeth and jaws limit the ability of humans to routinely utilize raw food.
    (B)   Because of its reliance on plants in its diet, *Homo ergaster* had a smaller intestinal volume than modern humans do.
    (C)   Early humans did not utilize plants for food prior to the adoption of cooking.
    (D)   The properties of the human digestive anatomy are primarily the result of adaptation to a high-meat diet.
    (E)   The human digestive anatomy has changed little over evolutionary time.

22. The primary purpose of the parenthetical sentence near the end of the first paragraph is to

    (A)   identify the amount of time that is required for a behavior to have had an impact on biological evolution
    (B)   provide support for the idea that cooking has been practiced for a relatively long time
    (C)   pinpoint the time and place when humans became unable to survive on raw-food diets
    (D)   undercut the suggestion that the adoption of cooking affected the evolution of the human digestive anatomy
    (E)   indicate the particular technology that early humans used to cook food

GO ON TO THE NEXT PAGE.

23. The authors would be most likely to agree with which one of the following statements?

(A) A raw-food diet is significantly healthier for modern humans than a traditional diet.

(B) Humans would not be able to utilize cooked food in their diet if during their evolution they had not biologically adapted to it.

(C) Early humans controlled fire long before they adopted the practice of cooking their food.

(D) The practice of eating a diet of cooked food did not become standard until humans were able to lead relatively sedentary lives.

(E) Empirical evidence does not yet definitively show that early humans developed biological adaptations to a diet of cooked food.

24. Which one of the following most accurately describes the structure of the passage?

(A) The first paragraph outlines a scientific hypothesis's two predictions, the second paragraph describes the empirical confirmation of the first prediction, and the third paragraph describes the empirical disconfirmation of the second prediction.

(B) The first paragraph describes a scientific theory, the second paragraph considers an alternative to that theory, and the third paragraph describes the empirical test that would show which theory is correct.

(C) The first paragraph argues for a claim, the second paragraph explores a possible objection to that claim, and the third paragraph responds to that objection.

(D) The second and third paragraphs describe the empirical predictions that clarify the difference between the two proposals outlined in the first paragraph.

(E) The second and third paragraphs explore the possible empirical implications of a claim made in the first paragraph.

25. Which one of the following, if true, would provide the most support for the authors' claim in the sentence immediately preceding the parenthetical remark in the first paragraph?

(A) Evidence from cut marks on animal bones suggests that early humans' hominid ancestors used stone flake tools to butcher animals.

(B) Human populations are estimated to have adapted biologically to drinking the milk of domesticated animals in 5,000 years or less.

(C) Archaeological evidence indicates that the adoption of fire use by humans coincided with climatic changes that produced ice ages.

(D) An increase in the quantities of the trace element strontium in bones of early humans indicates an increase in the quantity of plant foods in their diet.

(E) The fossil record indicates that the brain volume of hominid species started growing after tooth and jaw size started decreasing.

26. The authors suggest which one of the following in the second paragraph?

(A) Human teeth and jaws underwent their only major reduction in size about 100,000 years ago.

(B) Adaptation to cooked food limited the ability of humans to survive on a high-meat diet.

(C) The evolution of the human digestive system is not well understood.

(D) Cooking methods changed and improved over evolutionary time.

(E) Cooking was adopted by geographically diverse early human populations at the same time.

27. The authors' primary purpose in the passage is to

(A) describe a scientific puzzle
(B) identify a common scientific misconception
(C) elucidate the meaning of a scientific hypothesis
(D) propose a scientific hypothesis
(E) undermine the support for a scientific principle

S T O P

IF YOU FINISH BEFORE TIME IS CALLED, YOU MAY CHECK YOUR WORK ON THIS SECTION ONLY.
DO NOT WORK ON ANY OTHER SECTION IN THE TEST.

SECTION II
Time—35 minutes
25 Questions

Directions: Each question in this section is based on the reasoning presented in a brief passage. In answering the questions, you should not make assumptions that are by commonsense standards implausible, superfluous, or incompatible with the passage. For some questions, more than one of the choices could conceivably answer the question. However, you are to choose the **best** answer; that is, choose the response that most accurately and completely answers the question and mark that response on your answer sheet.

1. Philosopher: I have been told that most university students today have no interest in philosophical issues, but I know from my own experience that this isn't true. I often go to university campuses to give talks, and the students at my talks have a deep interest in philosophical issues.

    The reasoning in the philosopher's argument is flawed in that the argument

    (A) uses the term "interest" in two different ways when the argument requires that it be used consistently throughout

    (B) treats a group as representative of a larger group when there is reason to believe it is unrepresentative

    (C) appeals to the popularity of an academic field as evidence of the worth of that academic field

    (D) takes for granted that just because there is no evidence that interest in something is decreasing, it must be increasing

    (E) takes for granted that it is good that university students have an interest in a certain subject just because the person making the argument has that interest

2. Ancient humans in eastern North America hunted mammoths until the mammoth disappeared from the area around 13,000 years ago. Recently, a fossil bone with an engraving that depicts a mammoth was found in an ancient settlement in eastern North America. This shows that the settlement was occupied at a time when mammoths lived in this area.

    The argument requires the assumption that

    (A) the engraving was made during the time when the settlement was occupied

    (B) the fossil on which the engraving was made was not a mammoth bone

    (C) when mammoths disappeared from eastern North America, there were no mammoths left anywhere in North America

    (D) the engraving technique employed on the fossil was unique to eastern North America

    (E) there is no scientific way of dating when the engraving of the mammoth was made

3. Durham: The mayor will agree to a tax increase because that is the only way the city council will agree to her road repair proposal, and that proposal is her top priority.

    Espinoza: The mayor will not get her road repair proposal passed because it is more important to her that taxes not increase.

    The dialogue provides the most support for the claim that Durham and Espinoza agree about which one of the following?

    (A) The mayor will agree to a tax increase.

    (B) The only way that the city council will agree to pass the mayor's road repair proposal is if she agrees to a tax increase.

    (C) The mayor's road repair proposal is her top priority.

    (D) The mayor will not get her road repair proposal passed.

    (E) It is more important to the mayor that taxes not increase than it is that her road repair proposal passes.

GO ON TO THE NEXT PAGE.

4. When politicians describe their opponents' positions, they typically make those positions seem implausible and unattractive. In contrast, scholars try to make opposing positions seem as plausible and attractive as possible. Doing so makes their arguments against those positions more persuasive to their professional colleagues. Politicians should take note: they could persuade more voters with their arguments if they simply followed the scholars in charitably formulating their opponents' positions.

The reasoning in the argument is most vulnerable to criticism on the grounds that it

(A) fails to address the possibility that an approach that works with one kind of audience will not work with another

(B) fails to account for the difficulty of coming up with charitable formulations of positions to which one is opposed

(C) focuses on the differences between two styles of argumentation even though those styles might be suited to similar audiences

(D) takes for granted that both scholars and politicians have persuasion as their aim

(E) presumes, without giving justification, that politicians formulate the positions of their opponents uncharitably even when they share those positions

5. Lawyer: In a risky surgical procedure that is performed only with the patient's informed consent, doctors intentionally cause the patient's heart and brain functions to stop by drastically reducing the patient's body temperature. When the procedure is completed, body temperature is quickly restored. Because the doctors deliberately stop the patient's life functions, if these functions do not resume following the procedure, the medical team is technically guilty of manslaughter.

Which one of the following principles, if valid, most helps to justify the lawyer's analysis?

(A) Any time a medical procedure could result in the patient's death, the medical team could be charged with manslaughter.

(B) If a medical procedure is known to carry a very high risk of causing the patient's death, then only if the patient does die can the doctors be guilty of manslaughter.

(C) One is guilty of manslaughter only when one intends to cause irreversible loss of a person's life functions.

(D) Deliberately bringing about the cessation of a person's life functions is manslaughter if and only if the cessation is permanent.

(E) Intentionally stopping a patient's life functions is manslaughter unless the patient agrees to the procedure and might die without treatment.

6. John's literature professor believes that the ability to judge the greatness of literary works accurately can be acquired only after years of specialized training. Such training is, in fact, what is required to become a literature professor. She is also well aware that the vast majority of the reading public does not have access to this specialized training.

Which one of the following statements must be true if what John's literature professor believes is true?

(A) John's literature professor can judge the greatness of works of literature accurately.

(B) Anyone who is not a literature professor cannot judge the greatness of works of literature accurately.

(C) Specialized training like that received by John's literature professor should be more broadly available to members of the reading public.

(D) Literature professors do not belong to the reading public.

(E) The vast majority of the reading public is unable to judge the greatness of works of literature accurately.

7. Geothermal power plants produce power using heat from underground reservoirs of hot water or steam heated by the surrounding rock. In the limited areas of the world where such underground hot water and steam can currently be reached by drilling, geothermal power plants produce power more economically than conventional, fossil fuel power plants. However, advocates contend that in the near future economical power from geothermal power plants will be available in most areas.

Which one of the following, if true, most helps to justify the advocates' contention?

(A) Conventional power plants, unlike geothermal power plants, release large amounts of pollutants into the air.

(B) A typical geothermal power plant produces at least as much energy as a typical conventional power plant.

(C) The high start-up costs of geothermal power plants discourages their construction even in locations where they are more economical than conventional power plants in the long run.

(D) Advanced drilling technology is being developed that will soon make it both feasible and economical to drill wells many times deeper than it is currently possible to drill.

(E) Recent research has led to discoveries that could significantly lower production costs for nearly all types of power plants.

GO ON TO THE NEXT PAGE.

8. One should not confuse a desire for money with a desire for material possessions. Much of what money can buy—education, travel, even prestige—are not material goods at all. Material goods themselves, moreover, are seldom desired for their own sake but rather for the experiences or activities they make possible.

The claim that one should not confuse a desire for money with a desire for material possessions plays which one of the following roles in the argument?

(A) It is a generalization from which the argument draws inferences regarding several particular cases.
(B) It is the overall conclusion of the argument.
(C) It is a subsidiary conclusion used by the argument to support its overall conclusion.
(D) It is a recommendation that the argument evaluates by considering specific counterexamples.
(E) It alludes to a problem for which the conclusion of the argument offers a solution.

9. Yu: The menu at Jason's Restaurant states that no food served there contains products grown with chemical pesticides, but this cannot be true. I recently visited Kelly's Grocery, where Jason goes personally to buy the restaurant's produce, and I noticed workers unloading produce from a truck belonging to MegaFarm, which I know uses chemical pesticides on all of its crops.

Which one of the following, if true, most undermines Yu's claim?

(A) Jason does not know that Kelly's Grocery buys produce from MegaFarm.
(B) Jason buys ingredients from several suppliers besides Kelly's Grocery, and those suppliers sell only products that are grown without chemical pesticides.
(C) At Kelly's Grocery, most of the produce items that are grown without chemical pesticides carry a label to indicate that fact.
(D) None of the farms that supply produce to Kelly's Grocery use any pesticide that has not been approved by the government as safe for use on food crops.
(E) Most people who buy produce at Kelly's Grocery would never knowingly buy produce grown with any chemical pesticides.

10. Various studies have concluded that song overlapping, the phenomenon where one bird begins a song while another of its species is singing, is a signal of aggression. These studies are based solely on receiver-response tests, which seek to derive conclusions about the intent of a signal based on how others respond to it. However, any response—even no response—can be interpreted as a reaction to perceived aggression. Therefore, _____.

Which one of the following most logically completes the argument?

(A) birds do not respond in a predictable manner to signals of aggression
(B) receiver-response tests can provide no insight into bird behavior
(C) song overlapping is likely not a signal of aggression
(D) song overlapping has no communicative function
(E) the conclusion of these studies is unconvincing

11. Psychologists have found that candidates for top political offices who blink excessively during televised debates are judged by viewers to have done less well than competing candidates who exhibit average blink rates. Any impact this phenomenon has on election results is surely deleterious: Many features—knowledgeableness, confidence, and so forth—contribute to a political official's ability to perform well in office, but having an average blink rate is certainly not such a feature.

Which one of the following, if true, most weakens the argument?

(A) Voters' judgments about candidates' debate performances rarely affect the results of national elections.
(B) Blinking too infrequently during televised debates has the same effect on viewers' judgments of candidates as blinking excessively.
(C) Excessive blinking has been shown to be a mostly reliable indicator of a lack of confidence.
(D) Candidates for top political offices who are knowledgeable also tend to be confident.
(E) Viewers' judgments about candidates' debate performances are generally not affected by how knowledgeable the candidates appear to be.

GO ON TO THE NEXT PAGE.

12. Scientist: Some pundits claim that the public is afraid of scientists. This isn't true. I have been a scientist for several decades, and I have never met anyone who is afraid of scientists.

Which one of the following is an assumption required by the scientist's argument?

(A) Alleged scientific claims may be used to manipulate people, and it is understandable that people would be on their guard against such manipulation.

(B) If a person understood what science is really about, then that person would not be afraid of scientists.

(C) People may be apprehensive about technological developments that result from science even if they are not afraid of scientists themselves.

(D) If the public were afraid of scientists, then over several decades a scientist would encounter at least one person who was afraid of scientists.

(E) Anyone who claims to be afraid of scientists is actually afraid of scientists.

13. Scientist: It seems likely that the earliest dinosaurs to fly did so by gliding out of trees rather than, as some scientists think, by lifting off the ground from a running start. Animals gliding from trees are able to fly with very simple wings. Such wings represent evolutionary middle stages toward developing the large wings that we associate with flying dinosaurs.

Each of the following, if true, strengthens the scientist's argument **except**:

(A) Early flying dinosaurs built their nests at the base of trees.

(B) Early flying dinosaurs had sharp claws and long toes suitable for climbing.

(C) Early flying dinosaurs had unusual feathers that provided lift while gliding, but little control when taking flight.

(D) Early flying dinosaurs had feathers on their toes that would have interfered with their ability to run.

(E) Early flying dinosaurs lived at a time when their most dangerous predators could not climb trees.

14. The arousal of anger is sometimes a legitimate artistic aim, and every legitimate artwork that has this aim calls intentionally for concrete intervention in the world. Even granting that most art is concerned with beauty in some way, it follows that those critics who maintain that a concern for beauty is a characteristic of all legitimate art are mistaken.

The conclusion of the argument follows logically if which one of the following is assumed?

(A) There are works that are concerned with beauty but that are not legitimate works of art.

(B) Only those works that are exclusively concerned with beauty are legitimate works of art.

(C) Works of art that call for intervention have a merely secondary concern with beauty.

(D) No works of art that call for intervention are concerned with beauty.

(E) Only works that call for intervention are legitimate works of art.

15. Children clearly have a reasonably sophisticated understanding of what is real and what is pretend. Once they have acquired a command of language, we can ask them which is which, and they generally get it right. Even a much younger child who runs away when she sees her father roaring and prowling like a lion does not act as though she thinks her father is actually a lion. If she believed that, she would be terrified. The pleasure children get from make-believe would be impossible to explain if they could not distinguish the real from the pretend.

Which one of the following most accurately expresses the overall conclusion drawn in the argument?

(A) Children apparently have a reasonably sophisticated understanding of what is real and what is pretend.

(B) Children who have acquired a command of language generally answer correctly when asked about whether a thing is real or pretend.

(C) Even a very young child can tell the difference between a lion and someone pretending to be a lion.

(D) Children would be terrified if they believed they were in the presence of a real lion.

(E) The pleasure children get from make-believe would be impossible to explain if they could not distinguish between what is real and what is pretend.

GO ON TO THE NEXT PAGE.

16. Environment minister: Many countries have signed an international agreement that is intended to reduce pollution in the world's oceans. While conformity to this agreement probably would significantly reduce pollution in the world's oceans, it would also probably reduce economic growth in our country and others. Therefore, our country should not sign the agreement.

Which one of the following principles, if valid, would most help to justify the environment minister's argument?

(A) A country should not sign an agreement that is unlikely to achieve its stated goal.

(B) It is more important to maintain economic growth in one's own country than it is to reduce pollution in the world's oceans.

(C) A country should not sign an agreement designed to achieve a particular goal if it is likely that a better means of achieving that goal is possible.

(D) When deciding whether to sign an agreement, a country should consider the agreement's effects on other countries' economies as well as on its own economy.

(E) If a policy is likely to protect the environment and is unlikely to reduce economic growth, then governments should implement that policy.

17. Advocate: A study of people who had recently recovered from colds found that people who took cold medicine for their colds reported more severe symptoms than those people who did not take cold medicine. Therefore, taking cold medicine is clearly counterproductive.

The reasoning in the advocate's argument is flawed because the argument

(A) treats something as true simply because most people believe it to be true

(B) treats some people as experts in an area in which there is no reason to take them to be reliable sources of information

(C) takes something to be true in one case just because it is true in most cases

(D) rests on a confusion between what is required for a particular outcome and what is sufficient to cause that outcome

(E) confuses what is likely the cause of something for an effect of that thing

18. Some people prefer to avoid facing unpleasant truths and resent those whose unwanted honesty forces them into such a confrontation. Others dislike having any information, however painful, knowingly withheld from them. It is obvious then that if those in the former group are guided by the directive to treat others as they themselves want to be treated, _____.

Which one of the following most reasonably completes the argument above?

(A) they will sometimes withhold comment in situations in which they would otherwise be willing to speak

(B) they will sometimes treat those in the latter group in a manner the members of this latter group do not like

(C) those in the latter group must be guided by an entirely different principle of behavior

(D) those in the latter group will respond by concealing unpleasant truths

(E) the result will meet with the approval of both groups

GO ON TO THE NEXT PAGE.

19. If you study history, then you will appreciate the vast differences among past civilizations, and you will appreciate these differences provided that you reflect on your own civilization. Hence, if you study history you will reflect on your own civilization.

Which one of the following is most closely parallel in its flawed reasoning to the flawed reasoning in the argument above?

(A) By studying ancient art you begin to appreciate how much was accomplished with limited materials. Appreciation of ancient art leads to a deeper understanding of modern art. Therefore, studying ancient art can engender a profound new appreciation for modern art.

(B) If you learn Latin, you can improve your vocabulary, and you can improve your vocabulary if you study great works of literature. So you will study great works of literature if you learn Latin.

(C) Traveling to other countries deepens one's appreciation for their cultures, and this appreciation often encourages one to study the history of those lands. So the study of history increases one's desire to travel.

(D) Studying hard while in school helps you to internalize good habits that will serve you well in the working world, and you will retain those good habits if you maintain a positive mental attitude toward study. So diligent study in school improves the chance of success in the workplace.

(E) One can become informed about the world provided that one reads the newspaper daily. If one is informed about the world, then one has an appreciation of other cultures. So if one reads the newspaper daily, then one can come to appreciate other cultures.

20. A philosophical paradox is a particularly baffling sort of argument. Your intuitions tell you that the conclusion of a philosophical paradox is false, but they also tell you that its conclusion follows logically from true premises. Solving a philosophical paradox requires accepting any one of three things: that its conclusion is true, that at least one of its premises is not true, or that its conclusion does not really follow logically from its premises.

If the statements above are true, which one of the following must also be true?

(A) Solving a philosophical paradox requires accepting something that intuitively seems to be incorrect.

(B) The conclusion of a philosophical paradox cannot be false if all the paradox's premises are true.

(C) Philosophical paradoxes with one or two premises are more baffling than those with several premises.

(D) Any two people who attempt to solve a philosophical paradox will probably use two different approaches.

(E) If it is not possible to accept that the conclusion of a particular philosophical paradox is true, then it is not possible to solve that paradox.

21. A chimp who displays feelings of affection toward the other members of its social group is more likely to be defended by these group members from raiders outside of the group—even at the risk of harm to these defenders—than are those chimps who rarely or never display feelings of affection toward their associates. This shows that, from a sociological perspective, affection plays the same role in chimp communities as in human communities, since humans are more willing to face risks to protect those toward whom they have feelings of affection.

Which one of the following is an assumption on which the argument depends?

(A) Chimps express their emotions behaviorally whenever they feel them.

(B) Feelings of affection in chimp communities are at least sometimes reciprocated.

(C) Feelings of affection are the only reason humans protect each other.

(D) Expression of affection in chimps is limited to members of the social group to which they belong.

(E) Feelings of affection, in both human and chimp communities, are usually displayed through altruistic behavior.

22. The writers of the television show *Ambitions* could make their characters more realistic than they currently are, but they know their viewership would shrink if they did. The writers will choose to maximize their audience, so the characters will not be developed in a more realistic manner.

Which one of the following arguments is most similar in its reasoning to the argument above?

(A)   If a company's failure is due to a broader economic collapse, then it is not fair to blame the company's executives for the failure. There was a broader economic collapse when ViqCo went bankrupt. So it is probably not fair to blame ViqCo's executives for the failure.

(B)   If a company's failure is due to a broader economic collapse, then it is not fair to blame the company's executives for the failure. But there was no broader economic collapse when ViqCo went bankrupt. So ViqCo's executives deserve the blame.

(C)   If ViqCo's executives were responsible for the company's failure, then it must be possible to say what they should have done differently. Therefore, if you cannot say what ViqCo's executives should have done differently, then you should not blame them for the failure.

(D)   If ViqCo's executives were responsible for the company's losses, then ViqCo's losses would have been greater than those of its competitors. But ViqCo's losses were less than those of its competitors. So ViqCo's executives were not responsible for the company's losses.

(E)   Since ViqCo's failure was due to a broader economic collapse, it is not fair to blame the company's executives for the failure. But that means that when ViqCo was succeeding because the broader economy was growing, the executives did not deserve the credit.

23. It has been argued that the immense size of *Tyrannosaurus rex* would have made it so slow that it could only have been a scavenger, not a hunter, since it would not have been able to chase down its prey. This, however, is an overly hasty inference. *T. rex*'s prey, if it was even larger than *T. rex*, would probably have been slower than *T. rex*.

The claim that *T. rex* could only have been a scavenger, not a hunter, plays which one of the following roles in the argument?

(A)   It is a hypothesis that is claimed in the argument to be logically inconsistent with the conclusion advanced by the argument.

(B)   It is a hypothesis that the argument contends is probably false.

(C)   It is a hypothesis that the argument attempts to undermine by calling into question the sufficiency of the evidence.

(D)   It is offered as evidence in support of a hypothesis that the argument concludes to be false.

(E)   It is offered as evidence that is necessary for drawing the conclusion advanced by the argument.

GO ON TO THE NEXT PAGE.

24. Legal theorist: Only two types of theories of criminal sentencing can be acceptable—retributivist theories, which hold that the purpose of sentences is simply to punish, and rehabilitationist theories, which hold that a sentence is a means to reform the offender. A retributivist theory is not acceptable unless it conforms to the principle that the harshness of a punishment should be proportional to the seriousness of the offense. Retributivist theories that hold that criminals should receive longer sentences for repeat offenses than for an initial offense violate this principle, since repeat offenses may be no more serious than the initial offense.

Which one of the following can be properly inferred from the legal theorist's statements?

(A) No rehabilitationist theory holds that punishing an offender is an acceptable means to reform that offender.

(B) Reforming a repeat offender sometimes requires giving that offender longer sentences for the repeat offenses than for the initial offense.

(C) Any rehabilitationist theory that holds that criminals should receive longer sentences for repeat offenses than for an initial offense is an acceptable theory.

(D) All theories of criminal sentencing that conform to the principle that the harshness of a punishment should be proportional to the seriousness of the offense are acceptable.

(E) A theory of criminal sentencing that holds that criminals should receive longer sentences for repeat offenses than for an initial offense is acceptable only if it is a rehabilitationist theory.

25. Sociologists study folktales because they provide a means of understanding the distinctive values of a culture. However, the folktales in almost all cultures are adaptations of the same ancient narratives to the local milieu.

Which one of the following, if true, most helps to resolve the apparent discrepancy in the information above?

(A) Because no single person is the author of a folktale, folktales must reflect the values of a culture rather than those of an individual.

(B) Folktales are often oral traditions that persist from times when few people left written materials.

(C) The manner in which a culture adapts its narratives reveals information about the values of that culture.

(D) The ancient narratives persist largely because they speak to basic themes and features of the human condition.

(E) Folktales are often morality tales, used to teach children the values important to a culture.

S T O P

IF YOU FINISH BEFORE TIME IS CALLED, YOU MAY CHECK YOUR WORK ON THIS SECTION ONLY.
DO NOT WORK ON ANY OTHER SECTION IN THE TEST.

SECTION III
Time—35 minutes
25 Questions

Directions: Each question in this section is based on the reasoning presented in a brief passage. In answering the questions, you should not make assumptions that are by commonsense standards implausible, superfluous, or incompatible with the passage. For some questions, more than one of the choices could conceivably answer the question. However, you are to choose the **best** answer; that is, choose the response that most accurately and completely answers the question and mark that response on your answer sheet.

1. In constructing a self-driving robotic car, engineers face the challenge of designing a car that avoids common traffic problems like crashes and congestion. These problems can also affect fish traveling together in schools. However, the principles fish use to navigate in schools ensure that these problems are much less common within schools of fish than among cars on the road. Hence, _____.

   Which one of the following most logically completes the argument?

   (A) constructing a self-driving robotic car requires expertise in fish biology
   (B) the best drivers use the same navigational principles that fish use in schools
   (C) it is always advisable for engineers facing design challenges to look to the natural world for guidance in addressing those challenges
   (D) studying the principles fish use to navigate in schools could help engineers to design a self-driving robotic car that avoids common traffic problems
   (E) a self-driving robotic car using the navigational principles that fish use in schools would be better than a human-driven car at avoiding crashes and congestion

2. The Common Loon is a migratory bird that winters in warmer regions and returns to its breeding lakes in the spring. Typically, only one pair of loons occupies a single lake. Breeding pairs in search of breeding territory either occupy a vacant lake or take over an already occupied one. Surprisingly, almost half the time, returning loons choose to intrude on a territory already occupied by another pair of loons and attempt to oust its residents. This happens even when there are vacant lakes nearby that are perfectly suitable breeding territories.

   Which one of the following, if true, most helps to explain the surprising behavior described above?

   (A) Most of the nearby vacant lakes have served as successful loon breeding territory in the past.
   (B) Contests for occupied breeding territory may be initiated either by male loons or by female loons.
   (C) Loons that intrude on an occupied breeding territory are successful in ousting its residents about half the time.
   (D) Loons frequently determine that a lake is a suitable breeding territory by observing the presence of a breeding pair there.
   (E) Lakes that are perfectly suitable for loon breeding have fish for food, a site for a nest, and a sheltered area to rear chicks.

GO ON TO THE NEXT PAGE.

3. Taxi driver: My passengers complained when, on a hot day, I turned off my cab's air conditioner while driving up a steep hill. While the engine is powerful enough to both run the air conditioner and climb the hill without slowing, this would have decreased my fuel economy considerably. So turning off the air conditioner was the right decision.

Which one of the following principles, if valid, most supports the taxi driver's reasoning?

(A) A taxi driver should not run a cab's air conditioner if doing so would make it difficult to maintain a consistent speed.

(B) A taxi driver should run a cab's air conditioner only if doing so does not cause fuel economy to drop below normal levels.

(C) A taxi driver should try to balance concern for fuel economy with concern for passenger comfort.

(D) A taxi driver should always act in a way that is most likely to ensure customer satisfaction.

(E) A taxi driver's turning off air-conditioning for a short period of time is acceptable only if passengers do not complain.

4. The reason J. S. Bach is remembered is not that he had a high ratio of outstanding compositions to mediocre compositions. It is rather because he was such a prolific composer. He wrote more than a thousand full-fledged compositions, so it was inevitable that some of them would be outstanding and, being outstanding, survive the ages.

Which one of the following, if true, most seriously weakens the argument?

(A) Several of Bach's contemporaries who produced more works than he did have been largely forgotten.

(B) There are a few highly regarded composers who wrote a comparatively small number of compositions.

(C) Bach wrote many compositions that were considered mediocre in his lifetime, and a large proportion of these compositions have been forgotten.

(D) The exact number of Bach's compositions is not known, since many of them have been lost to posterity.

(E) Some great creative geniuses are remembered because they had a very high ratio of outstanding works to mediocre works.

5. Pundit: Clearly, the two major political parties in this city have become sharply divided on the issues. In the last four elections, for example, the parties were separated by less than 1 percent of the vote.

The reasoning in the argument is most vulnerable to criticism on the grounds that the argument

(A) confuses the cause of the sharp division with an effect of the sharp division

(B) presumes, without argument, that sharp division is a bad thing

(C) has a conclusion that is merely a restatement of one of its premises

(D) fails to indicate how what is happening in one city compares with what is happening in other cities

(E) takes for granted that an almost even division in votes indicates a sharp division on issues

6. The waters surrounding Shooter's Island have long been a dumping ground for ruined ships and boats, and the wreckage there has caused these waters to be exceptionally still. An ornithologist found that the overall abundance of waterbirds around Shooter's Island is similar to that around each of the neighboring islands, but that juvenile waterbirds are much more abundant around Shooter's Island than around those other islands. This suggests that the still waters around Shooter's Island serve as a nursery for the juveniles.

Which one of the following, if true, provides the most support for the argument's conclusion?

(A) The ruined ships and boats around Shooter's Island have been there for decades.

(B) The number of juvenile waterbirds around Shooter's Island, as well as the number around each neighboring island, does not fluctuate dramatically throughout the year.

(C) Waterbirds use still waters as nurseries for juveniles whenever possible.

(D) The waters around the islands neighboring Shooter's Island are much rougher than the waters around Shooter's Island.

(E) Waterbirds are typically much more abundant in areas that serve as nurseries for juvenile waterbirds than in areas that do not.

GO ON TO THE NEXT PAGE.

7. Pollster: When opinion researchers need a population sample that reflects the demographic characteristics of the national population, they choose their sample on the basis of national census data. Not everyone participates in the national census, despite its being mandatory. If, however, census participation became voluntary, as some have proposed, the participation rate would be much lower. So if census participation became voluntary, polls designed to discover the opinions of the national population would have less accurate results.

Which one of the following is an assumption on which the pollster's argument depends?

(A)   Using data from the national census is not the only way for opinion researchers to get a population sample that reflects the demographic characteristics of the national population.

(B)   Among people who do not currently participate in the national census, few, if any, would agree to participate if participation were voluntary.

(C)   The group of people who would participate in a voluntary national census would differ in its demographic characteristics from the group of people who would participate in a mandatory national census.

(D)   The people who refuse to participate in opinion polls comprise a group with approximately the same demographic characteristics as the group of people who do not currently participate in the national census.

(E)   The percentage of the nation's population that does not participate in the mandatory national census does not change significantly from one census to another.

8. Of the many works in a collection from Japan's Tokugawa period that the museum will soon put on display, those that are most sensitive to light, as well as the most valuable pieces, will be on display for two weeks only. Sakai Hoitsu's "Spring and Autumn Maples" will be on display for two weeks only, so it is clearly among the most valuable pieces in the collection.

The flawed pattern of reasoning in the argument above most closely parallels that in which one of the following?

(A)   The city council will soon commission surveyors to update the city map. The new map will reflect existing structures as well as planned housing developments. But the housing development I live in was built several decades ago, so it will not be on the updated map.

(B)   The city map was recently updated. Purple dots now indicate public buildings, whereas on the old map, blue dots indicated public buildings. On the updated map, the bank is designated with a blue dot. So the bank must have been a public building at some time in the past.

(C)   I have just purchased the new city map, whose legend indicates that thoroughfares are marked by solid lines and that dotted lines designate one-way streets. Shearing Street is marked by a dotted line, even though it is a thoroughfare. So the mapmakers must have made a mistake.

(D)   On this city map, a solid line designates the city limits. Solid lines also designate major thoroughfares. So there is no way of determining whether a particular solid line on the map is a thoroughfare or an indicator of the city limits.

(E)   The legend on this city map indicates that historical monuments are designated by purple dots. Hospitals are also designated by purple dots. There is a purple dot on Wilson Street. So there must be a hospital on Wilson Street.

GO ON TO THE NEXT PAGE.

9. Marketing agent: A survey of my business clients reveals that, of those who made a profit last year, 90 percent made at least $100,000 in profit for the year. In prior years, not one of these businesses made an annual profit of more than $10,000. So, 90 percent of my business clients increased their profits at least tenfold last year.

The reasoning in the marketing agent's argument is most vulnerable to criticism on the grounds that the argument

(A) overlooks the possibility that the business clients who made more than $100,000 last year made only slightly more than $100,000

(B) fails to explain why some of the business clients who made a profit did not increase their profits at least tenfold last year

(C) draws a conclusion about all of the business clients from premises about the business clients who made a profit last year

(D) treats conditions that are sufficient for making a profit as though they are necessary for making a profit

(E) overlooks the possibility that not all of the business clients made an annual profit of more than $10,000 last year

10. Changes in Britain's National Health Service have led many British hospitals to end on-site laundry services for their staff. Although the water in a typical residential washing machine, unlike that in the industrial washing machines used by hospitals, does not reach temperatures high enough to kill the dangerous bacterium *Acinetobacter*, hospital officials believe that the discontinuation of these services will not put patients at risk.

Which one of the following, if true, most helps to justify the hospital officials' belief?

(A) Hospital staff typically develop an immunity to *Acinetobacter*.

(B) Hospital patients infected with *Acinetobacter* can be isolated from other patients.

(C) Most hospital staff made use of the on-site laundry services before they were discontinued.

(D) Hospital staff are instructed to use clothes dryers at temperatures high enough to kill *Acinetobacter*.

(E) Water in residential washing machines reaches temperatures high enough to kill all dangerous bacteria other than *Acinetobacter*.

11. Many newspapers have cut back on book reviews, replacing them with other features that, according to focus group research, are of greater interest to potential readers. Such a move is ill-advised. Though meant to increase readership, it actually decreases readership by alienating loyal readers while catering to casual readers who are more likely to watch television than pick up a newspaper.

Which one of the following most accurately expresses the conclusion drawn in the argument?

(A) The newspapers should not have cut back on book reviews.

(B) Many newspapers have cut back on book reviews, replacing them with other features.

(C) Focus group research concluded that features other than book reviews were of greater interest to potential readers.

(D) The move to replace book reviews with other features was meant to increase readership, but it actually decreases it.

(E) The move to replace book reviews with other features alienates loyal readers and caters to casual readers.

12. Doctor: There will be more local cases of flu infection this year than there were last year. In addition to the strains of flu that were present in this area last year, a new strain has infected some people this year.

The conclusion of the doctor's argument can be properly drawn if which one of the following is assumed?

(A) Effective approaches have been developed to deal with the strains of flu that were present last year.

(B) It is rare for new strains of flu to appear.

(C) The new strain of flu cannot be addressed with the approaches used to deal with the strains of flu that were present last year.

(D) The new strain of flu is expected to be more dangerous than the strains of flu that were present last year.

(E) There will be no decline this year in the number of cases of flu infection due to strains that were present last year.

GO ON TO THE NEXT PAGE.

13. Hendry: Most employee strikes should be legally permitted. But strikes by university faculty are an exception. Faculty strikes harm a university's students, and I accept the principle that an employee strike shouldn't be legally permitted if it would harm the employer's customers.

Menkin: If your principle is correct, then, contrary to what you claim, employee strikes should almost never be legally permitted.

On the basis of their statements, Hendry and Menkin are committed to disagreeing over whether

(A) a university's students should be considered customers of the university

(B) most employee strikes would harm the employer's customers

(C) strikes by university faculty should be legally permitted

(D) most employee strikes should be legally permitted

(E) faculty strikes harm a university's students

14. Most popular historical films are not documentaries; they are dramatic presentations of historical events. Such presentations cannot present the evidence for the accuracy of what they portray. Consequently, uninformed viewers of dramatic historical films should not regard them as accurate portrayals of historical events.

Which one of the following principles, if valid, most helps to justify the reasoning in the argument?

(A) Writers of historical dramas should attempt to provide their own distinctive insights into the meaning of the historical events they are portraying.

(B) Historical documentaries should be careful to present all the evidence when attempting to inform their audiences about historical events.

(C) Dramatic presentations of historical events are better suited for educational purposes if evidence supporting the accuracy of the presentation is also presented.

(D) Dramatic presentations of historical events should never sacrifice accuracy in order to tell a more entertaining story.

(E) One should never regard a historical account to be accurate unless one has considered the evidence on which it is based.

15. Carrillo: Using the number of existing primate species, along with measures of the genetic diversity among these primates and among the extinct primate species, our statistical model strongly supports the conclusion that the first primate developed around 81.5 million years ago.

Olson: Given that the oldest primate fossils discovered so far date back only 55 million years, your estimate of how long primate species' development has gone on is sheer speculation.

The dialogue provides the most support for the claim that Carrillo and Olson disagree over whether

(A) primates have been around for more than 55 million years

(B) Carrillo's statistical model is a reliable way of dating the first appearance of primate species

(C) the available sample of primate fossils is representative of the variety of primate species that have existed

(D) the dating of the primate fossils that Olson cites is accurate

(E) fossils of the first primate species that developed have been discovered

16. Automobile executive: Our critics say that the communications devices installed in our automobiles are dangerously distracting to drivers. But these critics are wrong. Drivers who want to use communications devices are going to use them regardless. Our devices are easier for drivers to use, and hence they are safer.

The reasoning in the automobile executive's argument is most vulnerable to criticism on the grounds that it

(A) attempts to apply a general principle to a situation to which that principle is not applicable

(B) fails to address the substantive point of the criticism that it is responding to

(C) treats a condition that is necessary to establish its conclusion as one that is sufficient to establish that conclusion

(D) presumes, without providing justification, that all communications devices are the same with respect to driver distraction

(E) is based on premises that presume the truth of the argument's conclusion

GO ON TO THE NEXT PAGE.

17. Since mosquito larvae are aquatic, outbreaks of mosquito-borne diseases typically increase after extended periods of wet weather. An exception to this generalization, however, occurs in areas where mosquitoes breed primarily in wetland habitats. In these areas, outbreaks of mosquito-borne diseases are worse after periods of drought.

Which one of the following, if true, most helps to resolve the apparent discrepancy described above?

(A) The use of insecticides is typically prohibited in wetland habitats.

(B) Human populations tend to be sparse in areas near wetland habitats.

(C) Wetland habitats contain numerous aquatic insects that prey on mosquito larvae.

(D) Wetland habitats host a wider variety of mosquito species than do other areas where mosquitoes breed.

(E) Periods of drought in wetland habitats create conditions conducive to the emergence of new plant growth.

18. Efforts to get the public to exercise regularly, which have emphasized the positive health effects of exercise rather than the dangers of a sedentary lifestyle, have met with little success. In contrast, efforts to curb cigarette smoking, which have emphasized the dangers of smoking rather than the positive health effects of quitting, have been highly successful. Thus, efforts to get the public to exercise regularly would be more successful if they emphasized the dangers of a sedentary lifestyle rather than the positive health effects of exercise.

Which one of the following is an assumption on which the argument relies?

(A) The health risks associated with a sedentary lifestyle are as great as those associated with smoking.

(B) Efforts to get the public to exercise regularly have been largely ineffective at conveying the message that exercise can have positive health effects.

(C) Although most smokers are aware of the dangers of smoking, few are aware of the positive health effects of quitting.

(D) Efforts to curb cigarette smoking would not be more successful if they emphasized the positive health effects of quitting rather than the dangers of smoking.

(E) The majority of people who successfully quit smoking cite health concerns as the primary motivation for their success.

19. Henry: Engines powered by electricity from batteries cause less pollution than internal combustion engines. Therefore, to reduce urban pollution, we should replace standard automobiles with battery-powered vehicles.

Umit: I disagree. Battery-powered vehicles have very short ranges and must be recharged often. Their widespread use would create a greater demand for electricity generated by power plants, which are themselves a major source of pollution.

Of the following, which one, if true, is the strongest counter Henry could make to Umit's objection?

(A) Pollution caused by power plants is generally confined to a small number of locations a significant distance from major cities.

(B) The increased air pollution resulting from a greater demand for electricity would be offset by the reduction in air pollution emitted by electric vehicles.

(C) Electric motors could be restricted to lighter vehicles such as compact cars, which have smaller batteries and therefore require less power to charge than do the larger batteries needed to power larger vehicles.

(D) Hybrid vehicles using both electric and gasoline power moderate the increased demand for electricity produced by power plants.

(E) Most power plants are currently operating well below capacity and could therefore accommodate the increased demand for electricity.

GO ON TO THE NEXT PAGE.

20. History student: It is unfair for the History Department to prohibit students from citing certain online encyclopedias in their research papers merely because these sources are not peer reviewed. In their research, students should be allowed to read whatever they wish; otherwise, it is censorship.

History professor: Students are allowed to read whatever they like. The rule stipulates only that certain online encyclopedias are not to be cited as references since, given that they are not peer reviewed, they cannot reasonably be treated as reliable support for any claim.

The dialogue provides most support for the claim that the student and the professor disagree over whether

(A) research papers written for a history class require some citations to be from sources that have been peer reviewed

(B) prohibiting a certain sort of online source material from being cited as a research reference amounts to prohibiting students from reading that source material

(C) censorship of the reading of research publications that are peer reviewed can ever be justified

(D) sources that are not peer reviewed often have solid support for the claims that they make

(E) students should be allowed to read whatever they wish to in preparing to write a research paper for a history class

21. Finance minister: The World Bank's "Doing Business" report ranks countries in terms of ease of doing business in them. In producing the rankings, the World Bank assesses how difficult it is for a hypothetical business to comply with regulations and pay taxes. Since the last "Doing Business" report came out, our government has dramatically simplified tax filing for small and even midsized businesses. So our "Doing Business" ranking will probably improve.

The answer to which one of the following questions would most help in evaluating the finance minister's argument?

(A) If the finance minister's country made it easier for small businesses to comply with regulations, would the rate at which new businesses are formed increase?

(B) Has compliance with tax laws by small and midsized businesses increased since tax filing was simplified?

(C) For small and midsized businesses in the finance minister's country, is tax preparation and filing more difficult than complying with other regulations?

(D) Is what the finance minister considers to be a midsized business smaller than the hypothetical business used to produce the "Doing Business" report?

(E) Was the finance minister in office when the last "Doing Business" report was issued?

22. Commentator: Unfortunately, Roehmer's opinion column has a polarizing effect on national politics. She has always taken a partisan stance, and lately she has taken the further step of impugning the motives of her adversaries. That style of argumentation is guaranteed not to change the minds of people with opposing viewpoints; it only alienates them. But that is likely not a problem for Roehmer, since her column is just an attempt to please her loyal readers.

The reasoning in the commentator's argument is most vulnerable to criticism on the grounds that the argument

(A) fails to rule out the possibility that a purported cause of a phenomenon is actually an effect of that phenomenon

(B) criticizes a column merely by invoking the personal characteristics of its author

(C) concludes that one event caused another merely because that event occurred immediately prior to the other

(D) contradicts itself in its portrayal of Roehmer's column

(E) employs a tactic at one point that it elsewhere objects to

GO ON TO THE NEXT PAGE.

23. Fine short story writers are unlikely to become great novelists. Short story writers must master the ability to interweave the many small details that together allow mundane incidents to illuminate important truths. Because the novel drowns in such detail, novelists must focus on larger matters. Only a few writers possess both the ability to weave together many small details and the ability to focus on larger matters.

The reasoning in which one of the following is most similar to the reasoning above?

(A) Engineers can never design an automobile that both meets high standards for comfort and safety and uses fuel efficiently, because high levels of comfort and safety generally require that a car be heavy, while efficient use of fuel usually requires that a car be light.

(B) Historians who write grand histories synthesizing the research of many other scholars are unlikely to make many original archival discoveries, because they are unlikely to think that those with their gifts should spend time sifting through material to find important new documents.

(C) Good painters cannot become good scholars of painting. Painters are inevitably biased toward their own style of painting and, accordingly, cannot be objective scholars.

(D) Because of the vast amount of medical knowledge one needs in order to become a successful specialist and because few people have the motivation required to obtain such knowledge, most people are unlikely to become successful specialists.

(E) Those who excel at one sport are unlikely to excel at another, because it is rare for someone who has the specialized talents necessary for success in one sport to also have the different specialized talents necessary for success in a different sport.

24. Politician: Every regulation currently being proposed by the Committee for Overseas Trade will reduce the trade deficit. Our country's trade deficit is so large that it weakens the economy. Therefore, each of the proposed regulations would help the economy.

The reasoning in the politician's argument is flawed in that the argument

(A) takes for granted that the trade deficit will increase in size if no action is taken to reduce it

(B) takes for granted that the only means of strengthening the economy is reducing the trade deficit

(C) merely appeals to the authority of the committee without evaluating any reasons for the proposed regulations

(D) fails to consider the possibility that one effect of a regulation will be offset by other effects

(E) concludes that every regulation in a set will have the same effects as a set of regulations as a whole

25. Essayist writing in 2012: At its onset, a new medium is limited to carrying content from the old medium it replaces. We are in that phase with e-books— today's e-books take their content from print books. Thus it is too early to understand the e-book as a medium, since it has not yet taken its ultimate form.

Which one of the following principles, if valid, most helps to justify the essayist's reasoning?

(A) A medium cannot be fully understood without first understanding the media that came before it.

(B) No electronic medium can resemble a print medium more than it resembles other electronic media.

(C) The ultimate form that a medium will take depends on available technology.

(D) A medium cannot be understood without observing the evolution of its content.

(E) One medium can replace another only if it can represent richer and more varied content.

S T O P

IF YOU FINISH BEFORE TIME IS CALLED, YOU MAY CHECK YOUR WORK ON THIS SECTION ONLY.
DO NOT WORK ON ANY OTHER SECTION IN THE TEST.

SECTION IV
Time—35 minutes
27 Questions

Directions: Each set of questions in this section is based on a single passage or a pair of passages. The questions are to be answered on the basis of what is **stated** or **implied** in the passage or pair of passages. For some questions, more than one of the choices could conceivably answer the question. However, you are to choose the **best** answer; that is, choose the response that most accurately and completely answers the question and mark that response on your answer sheet.

The following passage is adapted from an article published in 2003.

For two decades, Wynton Marsalis complemented his extraordinary gifts as a jazz trumpeter with persuasive advocacy of the importance of jazz history and jazz masters. At his peak, Marsalis ruled the jazz universe, enjoying virtually unqualified admiration as a musician and unsurpassed influence as the music's leading promoter and definer. But after drawing increasing fire from critics and fellow musicians alike for his neotraditionalism, the biggest name in jazz faces an uncertain future, as does jazz itself.

In 1999, to mark the end of the century, Marsalis issued a total of fifteen new CDs. In the following two years he did not release a single collection of new music. In fact, after two decades with Columbia Records—the prestigious label historically associated with Duke Ellington, Thelonious Monk, and Miles Davis—Marsalis has no record contract with any company. Over the past few years Columbia has drastically reduced its roster of active jazz musicians, shifting its emphasis to reissues of old recordings. Atlantic Records folded its jazz catalog into the operations of its parent company, Warner Music, and essentially gave up on developing new artists.

For this grim state of affairs in jazz, Marsalis, the public face of the music and the evident master of its destiny, has been accused of being at least partly culpable. Critics charge that, by leading jazz into the realm of unbending classicism and by sanctifying a canon of their own choosing, Marsalis and his adherents have codified the music into a stifling orthodoxy and inhibited the innovative impulses that have always advanced jazz. As a former executive with Columbia noted, "For many people, Marsalis has come to embody some retro ideology that is not really of the moment—it's more museumlike in nature, a look back."

Indeed, in seeking to elevate the public perception of jazz and to encourage young practitioners to pay attention to the music's traditions, Marsalis put great emphasis on its past masters. Still, he never advocated mere revivalism, and he has demonstrated in his compositions how traditional elements can be alluded to, recombined, and reinvented in the name of individualistic expression, taking the nature of that tradition and trying to push it forward. However, record executives came away with a different message: if the artists of the past are so great and enduring, why continue investing so much in young talent? So they shifted their attention to repackaging their catalogs of vintage recordings.

Where the young talent saw role models and their critics saw idolatry, the record companies saw brand names—the ultimate prize of marketing. For long-established record companies with vast archives of historic recordings, the economics were irresistible: it is far more profitable to wrap new covers around albums paid for generations ago than it is to find, record, and promote new artists.

1. Which one of the following most accurately expresses the main point of the passage?

    (A)   Although he was once heralded as the leading promoter and definer of jazz, Wynton Marsalis's recent turn toward traditional elements in his music has made record companies reluctant to contract with him.

    (B)   Contrary to critics who accuse him of narrow neotraditionalism that stifles the evolution of jazz, Wynton Marsalis plays jazz that is new and innovative and his emphasis on past masters has widened the audience for jazz.

    (C)   Though Wynton Marsalis enjoyed great success for two decades, the shift in focus by record companies to re-releasing traditional recordings has caused him to move away from the traditionalism that initially fueled his success.

    (D)   By emphasizing appreciation of traditional jazz, Wynton Marsalis has unintentionally led major record companies to shun developing new talent in favor of re-releasing vintage jazz recordings.

    (E)   Despite widespread acknowledgement of his musical gifts, Wynton Marsalis has come under increasing criticism for what many regard as excessive traditionalism.

GO ON TO THE NEXT PAGE.

2. By stating that many people consider Marsalis to embody a "retro ideology," the former executive quoted at the end of the third paragraph most likely means that they believe that Marsalis

(A) revived a discredited set of ideas
(B) merely recombined other people's ideas
(C) overemphasized strict adherence to tradition
(D) reinvented and reinterpreted traditional forms
(E) seized on a set of inauthentic musical ideas

3. The author would most likely be less negative about the state of affairs in jazz if

(A) critics were to soften their outspoken indictment of what they view as Marsalis's neotraditionalism
(B) Marsalis were to continue focusing on releasing new music that was informed by traditional jazz
(C) Marsalis were to speak out against those who describe his adherence to tradition as unbending
(D) record companies were to emphasize developing new artists while reissuing old recordings
(E) young jazz musicians were to favor a respect for tradition over impulsive innovation

4. Which one of the following describes a situation most analogous to the situation facing Marsalis, as described in the passage?

(A) A town council's successful plan to slow the pace of housing development on its remaining rural lands has the unintended consequence of forcing housing prices to rise significantly faster than in neighboring towns.
(B) A well-known seed research firm aggressively markets new hybrid tomatoes designed to taste like older traditional varieties, but as a result, sales of traditional varieties skyrocket while hybrid sales decline.
(C) A producer of wool fabrics finds that business has increased substantially since synthetic-fabric producers have begun marketing fabrics that most consumers find less attractive than wool fabric.
(D) A firm that has been selling and promoting herbal medicines for several decades finds that sales are slumping because of increasing competition from upstart herbal products companies.
(E) A campaign to save an endangered fish species in a chain of lakes backfires when a ban on fishing in those lakes allows a predatory fish species to thrive and diminish stocks of the endangered species.

5. According to the passage, Marsalis encouraged young jazz musicians to

(A) restrain their revolutionary, innovative impulses
(B) learn to compose as well as perform jazz
(C) play sessions with older musicians
(D) ignore the prevailing public perceptions of jazz
(E) stay in touch with the traditions of jazz

6. The author would be most likely to agree with which one of the following?

(A) Ironically, record companies have embraced a kind of classicism that is more rigid than that attributed to Marsalis by critics.
(B) Contrary to what critics charged, Marsalis energetically promoted new artists.
(C) Understandably, Marsalis's fellow musicians have been more vocal in their displeasure with his views than have music critics.
(D) Surprisingly, most of today's young artists take issue with critics' increasingly negative views of Marsalis's neotraditionalism.
(E) In saturating the market with fifteen new collections of music in 1999, Marsalis made himself especially vulnerable to criticism.

7. The passage provides information sufficient to answer which one of the following questions?

(A) In the two years after 1999, did Marsalis compose any new music?
(B) Are Marsalis's fans drawn mainly from younger or from older jazz lovers?
(C) Has Marsalis ever released a CD consisting of only jazz standards?
(D) Why did Marsalis have no recording contract at the time the passage was written?
(E) What is a factor that contributed to the shift by record companies toward reissuing vintage jazz recordings?

GO ON TO THE NEXT PAGE.

Common sense suggests that we know our own thoughts directly, but that we infer the thoughts of other people. The former process is noninferential and infallible, while the latter is based on others' behavior and can always be wrong. But this assumption is challenged by experiments in psychology demonstrating that in certain circumstances young children tend to misdescribe their own thoughts regarding simple phenomena while nonetheless correctly describing those phenomena. It seems that these children have the same thoughts that adults have regarding the phenomena but are much less capable of identifying these thoughts. Some psychologists argue that this indicates that one's awareness of one's own thoughts is every bit as inferential as one's awareness of another person's thoughts. According to their interpretation of the experiments, thoughts are unobservable entities that, among other things, help to explain why we act as we do. It follows from this that we are wrong to think of ourselves as having noninferential and infallible access to our own thoughts.

Recognizing an obligation to explain why we cling so tenaciously to an illusory belief in noninferential and infallible knowledge of our own thoughts, these psychologists suggest that this illusion is analogous to what happens to us when we become experts in a particular area. Greater expertise appears to change not only our knowledge of the area as a whole, but our very perception of entities in that area. It appears to us that we become able to see and to grasp these entities and their relations directly, whereas before we could only make inferences about them. For instance, chess experts claim the ability to see without calculation whether a position is weak or strong. From a psychological perspective, we become so expert in making incredibly fast introspective inferences about our thinking that we fail to notice that we are making them. This failure leads naturally to the supposition that there is no way for us to be wrong in our identification of what we ourselves think because we believe we are perceiving it directly.

In claiming that we have only inferential access to our thoughts, the psychologists come perilously close to claiming that we base our inferences about what we ourselves are thinking solely on observations of our own external behavior. But, in fact, their arguments do not commit them to this claim; the psychologists suggest that we are somehow able to base our inferences about what we are thinking on internal cognitive activity that is not itself thought—e.g., fleeting and instantaneous sensations and emotions. The frequent occurrence of such internal activities explains why we develop the capacity to make quick and reliable inferences. Their internality makes it impossible for anyone else to make an inference based on them that contradicts our own. Thus, they are crucial in creating the illusion of noninferentiality and infallibility.

8. Which one of the following most accurately expresses the main point of the passage?

(A) Only experts within a given domain have noninferential and infallible access to their own thoughts; other people must infer their own thoughts as they do others' thoughts.

(B) In opposition to the common belief that thoughts are directly perceived, some psychologists argue that people infer what their own thoughts are.

(C) In response to the common belief that thoughts are directly perceived, some psychologists claim that this belief is an illusion resulting from our inability to make quick and reliable inferences.

(D) Some psychologists have recently attributed children's failure to give an accurate description of their own thoughts to their lack of expertise.

(E) Some psychologists hold that people are able to make inferences about what they are thinking that are based solely on observing their own external behavior.

9. Which one of the following, if true, would most call into question the psychologists' interpretation of the experiments with children (fourth and fifth sentences of the passage)?

(A) Some children who took part in the experiments were no less capable than some adults at identifying their own thoughts.

(B) Experiments with older children found that they were as accurate as adults in identifying their thoughts.

(C) The limited language skills possessed by young children make it difficult for them to accurately communicate their thoughts.

(D) Most young children cannot be expected to know the difference between direct and indirect access to one's thoughts.

(E) The psychologists who conducted the experiments with children were concerned with psychological issues other than the nature of people's access to their own thoughts.

GO ON TO THE NEXT PAGE.

10. Based on the passage, the author is most likely to believe which one of the following about the view that "we base our inferences about what we ourselves are thinking solely on observations of our own external behavior" (first sentence of the last paragraph)?

(A) It constitutes a denial of the possibility of scientifically studying thinking processes.
(B) It has often been misunderstood by psychologists.
(C) It was the prevailing view until undermined by recent psychology experiments.
(D) It seems to contradict common sense but is basically sound.
(E) It is not considered to be an intellectually defensible position.

11. Which one of the following is most closely analogous to the explanation in the passage of how persons fail to notice that they are making inferences about their thoughts?

(A) An anthropologist cannot describe his own culture accurately because he has become too familiar with its workings and therefore takes them for granted.
(B) Science is limited with regard to studying the human mind because science necessarily depends on human reasoning.
(C) As they develop, children become increasingly comfortable with formal abstraction and therefore become vulnerable to failures to learn from concrete experiences.
(D) Judges are barred from trying cases involving their family members because of a potential conflict of interest.
(E) A ship's commander must delegate certain duties and decisions to other officers on her ship because she is too busy to attend to those duties and decisions.

12. According to the passage, one's gaining greater expertise in a field appears to result in

(A) an altered way of expressing one's judgments about issues in that field
(B) a more detail-oriented approach to questions in that field
(C) an increased tendency to ignore one's own errors in judgment within that field
(D) a substantively different way of understanding relations within that field
(E) a reduced reliance on sensations and emotions when inferring one's thoughts regarding that field

13. According to the psychologists cited in the passage, the illusion of direct knowledge of our own thoughts arises from the fact that

(A) we ignore the feedback that we receive regarding the inaccuracy of the inferences we make about our thought processes
(B) knowledge of our own thoughts is usually unmediated due to our expertise, and we simply overlook instances where this is not the case
(C) we are unaware of the inferential processes that allow us to become aware of our thoughts
(D) our inferences regarding our own thoughts are generally extremely accurate, as are our perceptions of the world
(E) our inferences regarding our own thoughts are sometimes clouded and uncertain, as are our perceptions of the world

14. It can most reasonably be inferred that the choice of children as the subjects of the psychology experiments discussed in the passage was advantageous to the experimenters for which one of the following reasons?

(A) Experiments involving children are more likely to give interesting results because children are more creative than adults.
(B) Adults are more likely than children to give inaccurate reports of their thought processes.
(C) Since adults are infallible in their access to their own thoughts, only the thought processes of children shed light on the nature of inference.
(D) Mental processes are sometimes easier to study in children because children are more likely than adults to make certain cognitive errors.
(E) Children are less experienced than adults in inferring the thoughts of others from observations of their behavior.

GO ON TO THE NEXT PAGE.

The following passage is based on an article written in 1995.

Dowsing is the practice of detecting resources or objects beneath the ground by passing handheld, inert tools such as forked sticks, pendulums, or metal rods over a terrain. For example, dowsers typically determine prospective water-well drilling locations by walking with a horizontally held forked tree branch until it becomes vertical, claiming the branch is pulled to this position. The distance to the water from the surface and the potential well's flow rate are then determined by holding the branch horizontally again and either walking in place or backwards while the branch is pulled vertical again. The number of paces indicates the distance to the water, and the strength of the pull felt by the dowser correlates with the potential well's flow rate.

Those skeptical of dowsing's efficacy point to the crudeness of its methods as a self-evident reason to question it. They assert that dowsers' use of inert tools indicates that the dowsers themselves actually make subconscious determinations concerning the likely location of groundwater using clues derived from surface conditions; the tools' movements merely reflect the dowsers' subconscious thoughts. Further, skeptics say, numerous studies show that while a few dowsers have demonstrated considerable and consistent success, the success rate for dowsers generally is notably inconsistent. Finally, skeptics note, dowsing to locate groundwater is largely confined to areas where groundwater is expected to be ubiquitous, making it statistically unlikely that a dowsed well will be completely dry.

Proponents of dowsing point out that it involves a number of distinct techniques and contend that each of these techniques should be evaluated separately. They also note that numerous dowsing studies have been influenced by a lack of care in selecting the study population; dowsers are largely self-proclaimed and self-certified, and verifiably successful dowsers are not well represented in the typical study. Proponents claim that successful dowsers may be sensitive to minute changes in Earth's electromagnetic field associated with variations in subsurface conditions. They also claim that these dowsers have higher success rates than geologists and hydrologists who use scientific tools such as electromagnetic sensors or seismic readings to locate groundwater.

The last two claims were corroborated during a recent and extensive study that utilized teams of the most successful dowsers, geologists, and hydrologists to locate reliable water supplies in various arid countries. Efforts were concentrated on finding groundwater in narrow, tilted fracture zones in bedrock underlying surface sediments. The teams were unfamiliar with the areas targeted, and they agreed that no surface clues existed that could assist in pinpointing the locations of fracture zones. The dowsers consistently made significantly more accurate predictions regarding

drill sites, and on request even located a dry fracture zone, suggesting that dowsers can detect variations in subsurface conditions.

15. Which one of the following most accurately describes the primary purpose of the second paragraph?

(A) to add detail to the description presented in the first paragraph

(B) to offer two perspectives that are synthesized into a new perspective presented in the final paragraph

(C) to present arguments against which the third paragraph presents counterarguments

(D) to explore in detail the ramifications of one claim made in the first paragraph

(E) to clarify the issues on both sides in a dispute that the third paragraph attempts to resolve

16. According to the passage, dowsing's skeptics acknowledge which one of the following?

(A) A few dowsers have shown considerable and consistent success.

(B) Dowsing techniques are generally rejected by scientists.

(C) Successful dowsers are not well represented in the typical study of dowsing's efficacy.

(D) Successful dowsers may be sensitive to minute changes in Earth's electromagnetic field.

(E) Each dowsing technique should be evaluated separately.

GO ON TO THE NEXT PAGE.

17. The reasoning in which one of the following is most analogous to an argument explicitly attributed to dowsing's skeptics in the passage?

(A) Some weather analysts claim that no one can forecast the weather a week ahead with better than 40 percent accuracy, but some computer models have been known to perform with more accuracy than that.

(B) Some people claim to have seen ghosts, but very few of these people can adduce even the smallest piece of credible evidence to support their claims.

(C) Some musicians perform so well that their performances have been said to express a pure, innate talent, but such performances are in fact due to years of very intense practice.

(D) Some people claim to be able to sense where the area's good fishing spots are, but the lakes in the area are so loaded with fish it would be difficult not to pick a good spot.

(E) Some people have memories of participating in historical events in which they did not actually participate, but this does not prove that they have been reincarnated.

18. The author of the passage would be most likely to agree with which one of the following statements about the results of the groundwater-locating study discussed in the final paragraph?

(A) The results suggest that geologists and hydrologists would likely be of little service to any groundwater-locating effort.

(B) The results leave open the possibility that dowsers can sense minute changes in Earth's electromagnetic field.

(C) The results prove conclusively that dowsing is the most dependable technique for finding water in arid countries.

(D) The results demonstrate that dowsers are most successful in their efforts to locate groundwater when they use tools that are typically employed by geologists and hydrologists.

(E) The results do not help to refute skeptics' arguments, because the results provide evidence for dowsing's efficacy in only one type of terrain.

19. The passage provides information most helpful in answering which one of the following questions?

(A) When was dowsing first employed as a means of locating groundwater?

(B) Is the success of dowsers affected by rainstorms that may have saturated the ground in the area being dowsed?

(C) What proportion of successful dowsers use forked sticks in locating groundwater?

(D) Is dowsing ever utilized to try to locate anything other than water?

(E) What are some of the specific surface clues that can indicate the presence of groundwater?

20. The passage provides the most support for inferring which one of the following statements?

(A) Narrow, tilted fracture zones in underlying bedrock are more likely to be found in arid regions than in other regions.

(B) There are no reliable studies indicating that dowsers are consistently able to locate subsurface resources other than groundwater.

(C) A dowser attempting to locate a dry fracture zone would not use the same tools as a dowser attempting to locate groundwater.

(D) Geologists and hydrologists participating in the groundwater-locating study described in the final paragraph could not locate a dry fracture zone upon request.

(E) The groundwater-locating study described in the final paragraph was not a typical dowsing study.

GO ON TO THE NEXT PAGE.

Passage A

Why do some trial court judges oppose conducting independent research to help them make decisions? One of their objections is that it distorts the adversarial system by requiring an active judicial role and undermining the importance of evidence presented by the opposing parties. Another fear is that judges lack the wherewithal to conduct first-rate research and may wind up using outlier or discredited scientific materials.

While these concerns have some merit, they do not justify an absolute prohibition of the practice. First, there are reasons to sacrifice adversarial values in the scientific evidence context. The adversarial system is particularly ill-suited to handling specialized knowledge. The two parties prescreen and compensate expert witnesses, which virtually ensures conflicting and partisan testimony. At the same time, scientific facts are general truths not confined to the immediate cases. Because scientific admissibility decisions can exert considerable influence over future cases, erroneous decisions detract from the legitimacy of the system. Independent research could help judges avoid such errors.

Second, a trial provides a structure that guides any potential independent research, reducing the possibility of a judge's reaching outlandish results. Independent research supplements, rather than replaces, the parties' presentation of the evidence, so the parties always frame the debate.

Passage B

Regardless of what trial courts may do, appellate courts should resist the temptation to conduct their own independent research of scientific literature.

As a general rule, appellate courts do not hear live testimony. Thus these courts lack some of the critical tools available at the trial level for arriving at a determination of the facts: live testimony and cross-examination. Experts practicing in the field may have knowledge and experience beyond what is reflected in the available scientific literature. And adverse parties can test the credibility and reliability of proffered literature by subjecting the expert witness to the greatest legal engine ever invented for the discovery of truth—cross-examination. The trial judge may even participate in the process by questioning live witnesses. However, these events can only occur at the trial level.

Literature considered for the first time at the appellate level is not subject to live comment by practicing experts and cannot be tested in the crucible of the adversarial system. Thus one of the core criticisms against the use of such sources by appellate courts is that doing so usurps the trial court's fact-finding function. Internet sources, in particular, have come under criticism for their potential unreliability.

When an appellate court goes outside the record to determine case facts, it ignores its function as a court of review, and it substitutes its own questionable research results for evidence that should have been tested in the trial court. This criticism applies with full force to the use of outside-the-record texts and treatises, regardless of the medium in which they are found.

21. Which one of the following principles underlies the arguments in both passages?

(A) It is more appropriate for trial judges to conduct independent research than for appellate judges to do so.

(B) Judges should conduct independent research in order to determine what evidence parties to a trial should be allowed to present.

(C) Independent research by judges should not supersede evidence presented by the opposing parties in a trial.

(D) Judges' questioning of witnesses should be informed by the judges' own independent research.

(E) Both trial and appellate judges should conduct research based on standard, reliable sources.

22. It can be inferred that each author would agree that if judges conduct independent research, that research

(A) should be constrained by the structure of a trial

(B) is typically confined to standard, reliable sources

(C) replaces, rather than supplements, party-presented evidence

(D) should be conducted at the trial level but not at the appellate level

(E) usurps the trial court's fact-finding function

23. Which one of the following phrases is used by the author of passage B to express a concern that is most closely related to the concern expressed by the author of passage A using the phrase "lack the wherewithal" (last sentence of the first paragraph of passage A)?

(A) experience beyond what is reflected (third sentence of the second paragraph of passage B)

(B) may even participate in the process (second to last sentence of the second paragraph of passage B)

(C) subject to live comment (first sentence of the third paragraph of passage B)

(D) questionable research results (first sentence of the last paragraph of passage B)

(E) outside-the-record texts (last sentence of passage B)

GO ON TO THE NEXT PAGE.

24. Given the statements about cross-examination in the fourth sentence of the second paragraph of passage B, the author of passage B would be most likely to take issue with which one of the following claims by the author of passage A?

    (A)   An absolute prohibition of independent research by trial judges is not justified.

    (B)   The adversarial system is particularly ill-suited to handling specialized knowledge.

    (C)   Scientific admissibility decisions exert considerable influence over future cases.

    (D)   Erroneous decisions can be readily exposed by third parties.

    (E)   A trial provides a structure that guides any potential independent research.

25. Which one of the following words as used in passage B comes closest to having the same reference as the word "crucible" in the first sentence of the third paragraph of passage B?

    (A)   temptation (first sentence of passage B)

    (B)   credibility (fourth sentence of the second paragraph of passage B)

    (C)   engine (fourth sentence of the second paragraph of passage B)

    (D)   function (second sentence of the third paragraph of passage B)

    (E)   medium (last sentence of passage B)

26. It can be inferred, based on their titles, that the relationship between which one of the following pairs of documents is most analogous to the relationship between passage A and passage B, respectively?

    (A)   "Negative Effects of Salt Consumption" "Unhealthy Amounts of Salt in the Diet"

    (B)   "Salt Can Be Beneficial for Some People" "People with High Blood Pressure Should Avoid Salt"

    (C)   "Debunking the Alleged Danger Posed by Salt" "Inconclusive Research Results on the Health Effects of Salt Consumption"

    (D)   "Substitutes for Dietary Salt" "Salt Substitutes Come Under Fire"

    (E)   "The Health Effects of Salt Consumption" "Salt Deficiency in a Sample Population"

27. The stances of the authors of passage A and passage B, respectively, toward independent research on the part of trial judges are most accurately described as

    (A)   resigned acceptance and implicit disapproval

    (B)   cautious ambivalence and strict neutrality

    (C)   reasoned skepticism and veiled antipathy

    (D)   qualified approval and explicit noncommitment

    (E)   forceful advocacy and tentative opposition

S T O P

IF YOU FINISH BEFORE TIME IS CALLED, YOU MAY CHECK YOUR WORK ON THIS SECTION ONLY.
DO NOT WORK ON ANY OTHER SECTION IN THE TEST.

Acknowledgment is made to the following sources from which material has been adapted for use in this test:

Hans-Dieter Betz, "Unconventional Water Detection: Field Test of the Dowsing Technique in Dry Zones: Part 1" in *Journal of Scientific Exploration*. ©1998 by Society for Scientific Exploration.

Paul Bloom, "The Pleasures of Imagination" in *The Chronicle of Higher Education*. ©2010 by The Chronicle of Higher Education.

Edward K. Cheng, "Should Judges Do Independent Research on Scientific Issues?" in *Judicature*. ©2006 by American Judicature Society.

Samuel R. Delany, "Some Reflections on SF Criticism" in *Science Fiction Studies*. ©1981 by SF-TH Inc.

Alison Gopnik, "How We Know Our Minds: The Illusion of First-Person Knowledge of Intentionality." ©1993 by Cambridge University Press.

David Hajdu, "Wynton's Blues." ©March 2003 by the Atlantic Monthly.

Sharon Keller and Donald Cimics, "Appellate Courts Should Resist the Temptation to Conduct Their Own Independent Research on Scientific Issues" in *Judicature*. ©2006 by American Judicature Society.

Timothy J. Perfect, et al., "How Can We Help Witnesses to Remember More? It's an (Eyes) Open and Shut Case" in *Law and Human Behavior*. ©2007 by American Psychology-Law Society/Division 41 of the American Psychological Association.

Emilio Sauri, "'A la Pinche Modernidad': Literary Form and the End of History in Roberto Bolano's *Los Detectives Salvajes*" in *Modern Language Notes*. ©2010 by The Johns Hopkins University Press.

Eva Wisten, "What Do You Think Marshall McLuhan Would Have Said About Ebooks? How Do They Change the Message of Books?" in *Edge*. ©2012 by Edge Foundation, Inc.

Richard Wrangham and NancyLou Conklin-Brittain, "Cooking as a Biological Trait" in *Comparative Biochemistry and Physiology*. ©2003 by Elsevier Science Inc.

Computing Your Score

Directions:

1. Use the Answer Key on the next page to check your answers.

2. Use the Scoring Worksheet below to compute your raw score.

3. Use the Score Conversion Chart to convert your raw score into the 120–180 scale.*

Scoring Worksheet

1. Enter the number of questions you answered correctly in each section.

	Number Correct
SECTION I	_____
SECTION II	_____
SECTION III	_____
SECTION IV	Unscored

2. Enter the sum here: _____

This is your Raw Score.

*Scores are reported on a 120–180 score scale, with 120 being the lowest possible score and 180 being the highest possible score.

Score Conversion Chart

Use the table below to convert your raw score to the corresponding 120–180 scaled score for PrepTest 150.

Raw Score	Scaled Score	Raw Score	Scaled Score
77	180	38	147
76	180	37	146
75	179	36	146
74	178	35	145
73	176	34	144
72	174	33	143
71	173	32	143
70	172	31	142
69	171	30	141
68	169	29	140
67	168	28	139
66	168	27	138
65	167	26	138
64	166	25	137
63	165	24	136
62	164	23	135
61	163	22	133
60	162	21	132
59	162	20	131
58	161	19	130
57	160	18	128
56	160	17	127
55	159	16	125
54	158	15	124
53	157	14	122
52	157	13	120
51	156	12	120
50	155	11	120
49	155	10	120
48	154	9	120
47	153	8	120
46	153	7	120
45	152	6	120
44	151	5	120
43	151	4	120
42	150	3	120
41	149	2	120
40	149	1	120
39	148	0	120

Answer Key

Question	Section I	Section II	Section III	Section IV*
1	D	B	D	D
2	C	A	D	C
3	A	B	B	D
4	E	A	A	B
5	D	D	E	E
6	E	E	C	A
7	D	D	C	E
8	C	B	E	B
9	A	C	C	C
10	D	E	D	E
11	B	C	A	A
12	B	D	E	D
13	C	A	B	C
14	E	D	E	D
15	A	A	B	C
16	A	B	B	A
17	A	E	C	D
18	B	B	D	B
19	C	B	A	D
20	B	A	B	E
21	A	B	D	C
22	B	D	E	A
23	E	C	E	D
24	E	E	D	B
25	B	C	D	C
26	D			B
27	D			D

---

*Section IV is unscored. The number of items answered correctly in Section IV should not be added to the raw score.

PrepTest 151

SECTION I
Time—35 minutes
27 Questions

Directions: Each set of questions in this section is based on a single passage or a pair of passages. The questions are to be answered on the basis of what is **stated** or **implied** in the passage or pair of passages. For some questions, more than one of the choices could conceivably answer the question. However, you are to choose the **best** answer; that is, choose the response that most accurately and completely answers the question and mark that response on your answer sheet.

The United States Supreme Court's 1948 ruling in *Shelley v. Kraemer* famously disallowed state courts from enforcing racially restrictive covenants. Such covenants are, in essence, private legal obligations included in the deed to a property requiring that only members of a certain race be allowed to occupy the property. Because it prohibited the enforcement of these covenants, the Court's decision in *Shelley v. Kraemer* is justly celebrated for overturning a key instrument of housing discrimination. However, while few would deny that racially restrictive covenants are unjust, the stated legal rationale for the *Shelley* decision has nevertheless proven to be problematic.

The *Shelley* Court relied on the Fourteenth Amendment to the U.S. Constitution, which grants equal protection under the law to all U.S. citizens. This amendment had long been held to apply to state actors but not individuals. *Shelley* did not purport to alter this. But where, then, was the state action that is necessary for invoking the Fourteenth Amendment, given that the restrictive covenants were private contracts? The Court's answer was that although the restrictive covenants themselves were perfectly legal, judicial enforcement of the covenants violated the Fourteenth Amendment because responsibility for a contract's substantive provisions should be attributed to the state when a court enforces it. According to this "attribution" rationale, courts could enforce only those contractual provisions that could have been enacted into general law. Because the Fourteenth Amendment would not have allowed a law that banned members of a certain race from purchasing property, it followed from *Shelley*'s analysis that judicial enforcement of racially restrictive covenants also was unconstitutional.

Shelley's attribution logic threatened to dissolve the distinction between state action, to which Fourteenth Amendment limitations apply, and private action, which falls outside of the Fourteenth Amendment's purview. After all, *Shelley*'s approach, consistently applied, would require individuals to conform their private agreements to constitutional standards whenever, as is almost always the case, the individuals want the option of later seeking judicial enforcement. Primarily for this reason, neither the Supreme Court nor lower courts later applied *Shelley*'s approach. Courts routinely enforce contracts whose substantive provisions could not have been constitutionally enacted by government. For instance, courts regularly enforce settlement agreements that limit the settling party's ability to speak publicly

in various respects, despite the fact that statutory limitations on the identical speech would represent an unconstitutional violation of free speech.

Additionally, there is a particularly noxious aspect of the *Shelley* Court's analytics—namely, the Court's conclusion that racially restrictive covenants themselves were perfectly legal. The legal rationale behind the *Shelley* decision thus failed to target the genuine problem with racially restrictive covenants: what was troubling was not the covenants' enforcement but their substantive content.

1. The primary purpose of the passage is to

    (A) question the reasoning behind a particular judicial decision
    (B) draw a distinction between private action and state action
    (C) defend the way in which scholars and courts have traditionally explained a particular judicial decision
    (D) highlight the shortcomings of the U.S. Constitution
    (E) extend the rationale offered in a particular judicial decision to additional cases

2. An answer to which one of the following questions would be most relevant to determining whether an action can be classified a "state action" (fourth sentence of the second paragraph), as the author uses that phrase in the second paragraph?

    (A) What range of people can the action be expected to affect?
    (B) To what agent can performance of the action be ascribed?
    (C) What principle or principles can be said to govern the action?
    (D) In what ways can the action be expected to affect others?
    (E) What motivations can be attributed to those performing the action?

GO ON TO THE NEXT PAGE.

3. The author's attitude towards the reasoning offered in the U.S. Supreme Court's decision in *Shelley v. Kraemer* is most accurately reflected in the author's use of which one of the following phrases?

(A) "famously disallowed" (first sentence of the passage)
(B) "justly celebrated" (third sentence of the passage)
(C) "perfectly legal" (fifth sentence of the second paragraph)
(D) "consistently applied" (second sentence of the third paragraph)
(E) "noxious aspect" (first sentence of the last paragraph)

4. Which one of the following describes an attribution of responsibility that is most analogous to the attribution central to what the author refers to as *Shelley*'s "attribution" rationale (sixth sentence of the second paragraph)?

(A) If a trucking company fails to properly inspect its vehicles, the company can be held responsible for any accidents in which those vehicles are involved.
(B) If an individual signs a private contract, that person can be held responsible for the provisions of that contract even if the person did not read or comprehend those provisions.
(C) If a newspaper publishes a columnist's op-ed piece, the newspaper, and not just the columnist, can be held responsible for the content of the piece.
(D) If a person is in a position to rescue someone in peril, but chooses not to do so, that person can be held responsible for any injuries suffered by the person in peril.
(E) If a company discovers that it has manufactured and distributed a faulty product, the company is responsible for issuing a recall of that product.

5. In the second paragraph, the author asks the question, "...where, then, was the state action that is necessary for invoking the Fourteenth Amendment, given that the restrictive covenants were private contracts?" (fourth sentence) primarily in order to

(A) demonstrate the conceptual incoherence of a distinction employed by the *Shelley* Court
(B) highlight a potentially confusing issue central to understanding the *Shelley* Court's decision
(C) suggest that the *Shelley* Court did not properly attend to the facts of the case in its decision
(D) cast suspicion on the motivations of the individual judges who served on the *Shelley* Court
(E) challenge the presuppositions upon which the Fourteenth Amendment to the U.S. Constitution is based

6. Which one of the following principles is most clearly operative in the author's argument?

(A) If a judicial decision is deemed by legal scholars to be problematic, subsequent courts should refrain from appealing to that decision.
(B) If a private agreement is deemed judicially unenforceable, the substantive content of that agreement should be considered for inclusion in a statute.
(C) If a judicial decision fails to address the most troubling aspect of a practice, then measures should be taken to prevent this practice from continuing in an altered form.
(D) If courts are hesitant to apply the rationale given in a past decision, this should be taken as evidence that the rationale is questionable.
(E) If the rationale given in a judicial decision is found to be controversial, the decision should be supported by offering a new rationale.

GO ON TO THE NEXT PAGE.

Through years of excavations and careful analysis of her finds around Krasnyi Yar in Kazakhstan, archaeologist Sandra Olsen has assembled what may be evidence of the earliest known people to have domesticated and ridden horses, a momentous development in human history. In remains of pit houses of the Botai people, who inhabited this area some 6,000 years ago, are large numbers of bones, 90 percent of them from horses. It is not immediately evident whether the horses were wild or domesticated, because unlike other animals such as dogs and sheep, domestic horses' bones are not morphologically different from those of their wild counterparts. So Olsen relies heavily on statistical tabulations of the Botai horses by sex and age at death, looking for mortality patterns that might correlate with expectations regarding domesticated herds or wild victims of hunting.

Herders of domesticated animals used for meat or milk typically kill off all but a few males before they are fully mature, but not the females, and archaeologists have evidence of a similar pattern for prehistoric goat herding. At the Botai sites, however, Olsen has found that most of the male horses were fully grown and slightly outnumber the females. One might suppose, then, that they were wild rather than domesticated animals; with many large animal species, hunters would preferentially target adult males so as to maximize size and meat yield. However, it is different with horses. Wild horses live in two types of groups: families consisting of one stallion, six or so adult females, and their young; and bachelor pods consisting of a few males. The families stick together when attacked, but the male groups tend to scatter, so to maximize success in hunting horses, one would target the families. Thus, if the Botai had merely hunted horses, Olsen argues, the proportion of adult male bones should be lower. But if they were in domesticated herds, why were the young males not culled, as would typically occur with, say, herds of goats? Olsen reasons that if the Botai had indeed begun riding, they would likely have kept males alive to ride.

Another clue that at least some of the horses may have been domesticated and that some may have even been ridden is in the fact that their remains include full skeletons, entire vertebral columns, and pelvises. It is unreasonable to suppose that hunters dragged whole 1,000-pound carcasses back to their dwellings. Olsen reasons that these were probably domesticated horses, together with, perhaps, some wild ones hunted and transported using the power of domesticated horses. A number of these nearly whole horse skeletons were discovered buried in a carefully arranged pattern with some of the only human remains yet found in the area, which further suggests a relationship to horses beyond that of merely hunting them as a source of meat.

7.   Which one of the following most accurately expresses the main point of the passage?

(A)   Olsen's careful analysis of her finds in Kazakhstan illustrates the kinds of conclusions that archaeologists can draw based on a correlation between statistical information and expectations.

(B)   Olsen's excavations and analysis of her finds in Kazakhstan indicate that horses played a critical role in Botai culture.

(C)   Olsen's findings regarding bones excavated from ancient Botai dwellings provide evidence that the Botai people domesticated horses and may have ridden them.

(D)   Olsen's findings regarding excavations from ancient Botai dwellings provide evidence confirming that the domestication of horses was a momentous development in human history.

(E)   Olsen's findings regarding the excavation of horse skeletons and human remains from Botai dwellings suggest that horses were revered by the Botai people.

8.   Which one of the following most accurately describes the author's attitude toward the conclusions that Olsen reaches?

(A)   forthright advocacy
(B)   implicit endorsement
(C)   critical ambivalence
(D)   reasoned skepticism
(E)   general disagreement

9.   Which one of the following could replace the word "beyond" in the last sentence of the passage while least altering the meaning of the sentence in which it appears?

(A)   basically parallel to
(B)   more elusive than
(C)   hard to grasp in relation to
(D)   less clearly defined than
(E)   more complex than

GO ON TO THE NEXT PAGE.

10. If the horse remains found at the Botai sites had consisted primarily of the bones of fully grown females and young males, the findings would have provided evidence for which one of the following hypotheses?

   (A) The Botai targeted male pods when hunting horses.
   (B) The Botai caught, trained, and rode only wild horses.
   (C) The Botai had domesticated horses but did not ride them.
   (D) The Botai had developed sources of food other than horses.
   (E) The Botai incorporated the remains of horses into their cultural rituals.

11. Based on the discussion in the passage, the author would be most likely to agree with which one of the following statements?

   (A) Developing mortality patterns based on an examination of excavated animal remains is always required in order to establish whether a prehistoric culture domesticated animals.
   (B) An analysis of evidence at a particular archaeological site is not necessarily conclusive unless it is corroborated by evidence at similar archaeological sites from the same era.
   (C) Any prehistoric culture that consciously arranges the bones of animals in complex patterns should be considered to have reached a high level of social organization.
   (D) The interpretation of archaeological finds at prehistoric sites often requires a consideration of facts beyond those that can be determined from the excavated remains alone.
   (E) The morphological differences between wild and domesticated prehistoric animals help to explain why some modern animals are more easily domesticated than others.

12. The reference by the author of the passage to the practices of herders of domesticated animals (first sentence of the second paragraph) serves primarily as

   (A) a point of comparison for reaching conclusions about the use of horses by the Botai
   (B) an example of an earlier case that, like the Botai case, is inconsistent with accepted hypotheses concerning the domestication of horses
   (C) a refutation of traditional beliefs and assumptions about Botai goat herding
   (D) a simplification of a hypothesis about the relationship between humans and animals in cultures 6,000 years ago
   (E) an analogy meant to clarify the facts known about the domestication of animals by the Botai 6,000 years ago

13. Which one of the following most accurately describes the organization of the passage?

   (A) A set of findings is described and then various explanations of the findings are evaluated.
   (B) A set of specific observations is enumerated and then a general conclusion is drawn from those observations.
   (C) A general principle is presented and then examples of the application of the principle are given.
   (D) A hypothesis is outlined and then a line of reasoning in support of that hypothesis is developed.
   (E) A proposition is stated and then arguments both for and against the proposition are summarized.

14. Data from which one of the following sources would be most relevant to evaluating Olsen's hypothesis?

   (A) tabulation of the number of butchered horse bones versus untouched horse bones in a Botai archaeological site
   (B) tabulation of the number of sheep and goat bones versus the number of horse bones in a Botai archaeological site
   (C) determination of the number of hunting tribes contemporary with the Botai as opposed to the number of modern hunting tribes in the same area
   (D) analysis of mortality patterns in the remains of any other species of animal found at Botai sites
   (E) analysis of the ratio of human remains to horse remains found in Botai ceremonial sites

GO ON TO THE NEXT PAGE.

Passage A

Music does not always gain by association with words. Like images, words can excite the deepest emotions but are inadequate to express the emotions they excite. Music is more adequate, and hence will often seize an emotion that may have been excited by images or words, deepen its expression, and, by so doing, excite still deeper emotion. That is how words can gain by being set to music.

But to set words to music—as in opera or song—is in fact to mix two arts together. A striking effect may be produced, but at the expense of the purity of each art. Poetry is a great art; so is music. But as a medium for emotion, each is greater alone than in company, although various good ends arise from linking the two, providing that the words are subordinated to the more expressive medium of music. What good could any words do for Beethoven's *Fifth Symphony*? So too an opera is largely independent of words, and depends for its aesthetic value not upon the poetry of the libretto (the words of the opera), or even the plot or scenery, but upon its emotional range—a region dominated by the musical element.

Passage B

Throughout the history of opera, two fundamental types may be distinguished: that in which the music is primary, and that in which there is, essentially, parity between music and other factors. The former, sometimes called "singer's opera"—a term which has earned undeserved contempt—is exemplified by most Italian operas, while the latter, exemplified by the operas of German composer Richard Wagner, depend for their effect on a balance among many factors of which music is only one, albeit the most important. Theoretically, it would seem that there should be a third kind of opera, in which the music is subordinated to the other features. While the earliest operas were of this kind, their appeal was limited, and a fuller participation of music was required to establish opera on a secure basis.

In any event, in any aesthetic judgment of opera, regardless of the opera's type, neither the music nor the poetry of the libretto should be judged in isolation. The music is good not if it would make a good concert piece but if it serves the particular situation in the opera in which it occurs, contributing something not supplied by other elements. Similarly, the poetry is good not because it reads well by itself but primarily if, while embodying a sound dramatic idea, it furnishes opportunity for effective musical and scenic treatment. True, the elements of music and poetry may be considered separately, but only for purposes of analyzing their formal features. In actuality these elements are as united as hydrogen and oxygen are united in water. It is this union—further enriched and clarified by the visual action—that results in opera's inimitable character.

15. The authors of both passages attempt to answer which one of the following questions?

   (A) Is music inherently a more expressive medium than poetry?
   (B) Is the emotive power of poetry enhanced when it is set to music?
   (C) Should opera be accorded the same respect as other forms of classical music?
   (D) How important are words to the artistic effectiveness of opera?
   (E) How is opera different from all other musical art forms?

16. Which one of the following issues is addressed by the author of passage A but not by the author of passage B?

   (A) the importance of music to any aesthetic judgment of an operatic work
   (B) how music is affected when it is combined with words
   (C) the ability of music to evoke an emotional response in the listener
   (D) whether music should ever be subordinated to words with which it is combined
   (E) whether music should be judged in isolation from the libretto in opera

17. Passage B, but not passage A, includes which one of the following topics in its discussion of opera?

   (A) the importance of plot and scenery to an opera's aesthetic value
   (B) the ability of images and words to excite deep emotion
   (C) the consequences of combining poetry and music into a single art form
   (D) the relative roles of music and libretto in opera
   (E) the differences among different types of opera

18. It can be inferred that the author of passage B has which one of the following opinions of opera in which the words are subordinated to the music?

   (A) It is primarily a popular art form.
   (B) It has been justly criticized for betraying opera's main objectives.
   (C) It is emotionally more expressive than other types of opera.
   (D) It is as legitimate as other types of opera.
   (E) It should be judged as though it were a concert piece.

GO ON TO THE NEXT PAGE.

19. Which one of the following is a principle that is implicit in the argument made by the author of passage B but that would most likely be rejected by the author of passage A?

(A) An opera's nonmusical elements are essential to the opera's aesthetic value.

(B) Even in operas where there is relative parity among the various elements, the music is the most important element.

(C) An opera cannot be artistically successful unless it skillfully balances many factors.

(D) In order for an opera to be artistically successful, the music should not be subordinated to other features of the opera.

(E) An opera's libretto has formal features that can be analyzed independently of the opera's music.

20. The author of passage B defines a "singer's opera" as an opera

(A) in which there is relative parity between the music and other elements

(B) in which the drama is of paramount importance

(C) that is generally of lower artistic merit

(D) from the art form's earliest historical period

(E) in which nonmusical elements are subordinate

21. The author of passage A would be most likely to regard the discussion in passage B regarding "a third kind of opera" (last two sentences of the first paragraph of passage B) as evidence of which one of the following propositions?

(A) Both poetry and music are diminished by being joined in one art form.

(B) The aesthetic value of an opera depends largely on the quality of its music.

(C) The musical and nonmusical elements of opera are indivisible from one another.

(D) Music invariably gains by being combined with poetry.

(E) Opera requires the careful balancing of many competing but equal elements.

GO ON TO THE NEXT PAGE.

According to the generally accepted theory of plate tectonics, the earth's crust consists of a dozen or so plates of solid rock moving across the mantle—the slightly fluid layer of rock between crust and core. Most earthquakes can then be explained as a result of the grinding of these plates against one another as they collide. When two plates collide, one plate is forced under the other until it eventually merges with the underlying mantle. According to this explanation, this process, called subduction, causes an enormous build-up of energy that is abruptly released in the form of an earthquake. Most earthquakes take place in the earth's seismic "hot zones"—regions with very high levels of subduction. Contrary to expectations, however, global seismic data indicate that there are also regions with high levels of subduction that are nonetheless nearly free of earthquakes. Thus, until recently, there remained a crucial question for which the plate tectonics theory had no answer—how can often intense subduction take place at certain locations with little or no seismic effect?

One group of scientists now proposes that the relative quiet of these zones is tied to the nature of the collision between the plates. In many seismic hot zones, the plates exhibit motion in opposite directions—that is, they collide because they are moving toward each other. And because the two plates are moving in opposite directions, the subduction zone is relatively motionless relative to the underlying mantle. In contrast, the plate collisions in the quiet subduction zones occur between two plates that are moving in the same general direction—the second plate's motion is simply faster than that of the first, and its leading edge therefore becomes subducted. But in this type of subduction, the collision zone moves with a comparatively high velocity relative to the mantle below. Thus, rather like an oar dipped into the water from a moving boat, the overtaking plate encounters great resistance from the mantle and is forced to descend steeply as it is absorbed into the mantle. The steep descent of the overtaking plate in this type of collision reduces the amount of contact between the two plates, and the earthquake-producing friction is thereby reduced as well. On the other hand, in collisions in which the plates move toward each other the subducted plate receives relatively little resistance from the mantle, and so its angle of descent is correspondingly shallow, allowing for a much larger plane of contact between the two plates. Like two sheets of sandpaper pressed together, these plates offer each other a great deal of resistance.

This proposal also provides a warning. It suggests that regions that were previously thought to be seismically innocuous—regions with low levels of subduction—may in fact be at a significant risk of earthquakes, depending on the nature of the subduction taking place.

22. Which one of the following most accurately expresses the main point of the passage?

(A) As a result of differences in resistance when colliding plates are moving in the same or in opposite directions, the amount of subduction in a region is strongly correlated with the number of earthquakes.

(B) The differences between how colliding plates interact when moving in the same or in opposite directions offer scientists a plausible explanation of the rarity of earthquakes in some regions of intense subduction.

(C) Some scientists theorize that seismic "quiet zones" with almost no earthquakes occur where plates are traveling in the same direction and, consequently, do not collide with each other.

(D) A new version of the theory of plate tectonics that abandons the generally accepted explanation of earthquakes as resulting from the process of subduction has been posited by some scientists.

(E) The generally accepted theory of plate tectonics is threatened by new evidence that there are regions of the earth with high levels of subduction but which, nevertheless, have relatively low levels of seismic activity.

23. According to the passage, what results when two plates moving in the same direction collide?

(A) The trailing edge of the slower-moving plate is subducted under the faster-moving plate.

(B) The leading edge of the slower-moving plate is subducted under the faster-moving plate.

(C) The trailing edge of the faster-moving plate is subducted under the slower-moving plate.

(D) The leading edge of the faster-moving plate is subducted under the slower-moving plate.

(E) The leading edge of the smaller plate is subducted under the larger plate.

GO ON TO THE NEXT PAGE.

24. Which one of the following, if true, would present the greatest challenge to the new proposal relating the amount of seismic activity to the type of collision between tectonic plates?

(A) Some regions where seismic activity is infrequent but subduction regularly occurs are regions in which the colliding plates move across the mantle in the same direction.

(B) There are areas in which plates collide but in which there is little or no seismic activity.

(C) There are areas where a plate has descended at a shallow angle during subduction but where there have been few, if any, earthquakes.

(D) The size of the plane of contact between colliding plates is related only to the angle at which subduction occurs.

(E) There is an area where a plate descended at a steep angle during subduction but there has been little or no seismic activity.

25. Based on the information in the passage, which one of the following sentences would most logically complete the last paragraph?

(A) Depending on the relationship between plate velocity and mantle, there is always the possibility that plate velocity could increase.

(B) The lower the level of subduction in an area, the greater the probability that any subduction there is occurring at a shallow angle.

(C) Any region where subduction occurs could suffer an increase in the level of subduction and a consequent increase in seismic activity.

(D) Even at low levels, the process known as subduction inevitably results in a significant amount of seismic activity.

(E) Even in such a region, a plate descending at a shallow angle is likely to cause a great deal of earthquake-producing friction.

26. According to the information in the passage, which one of the following kinds of regions experiences the most earthquakes?

(A) regions where the nature of the collision between plates is such that one plate descends sharply into the mantle

(B) regions where resistance from the mantle during subduction is greatest

(C) regions where subduction occurs at shallow angles

(D) regions where there is the greatest amount of subduction

(E) regions where plates are traveling in the same general direction

27. Which one of the following statements regarding seismic activity can be inferred from the passage?

(A) Earthquakes are frequent in any zones where there is considerable motion of colliding plates in relation to the underlying mantle.

(B) Earthquakes are equally likely to occur at any point along the plane of contact between two colliding plates.

(C) Seismic quiet zones are at particular risk due to the very gradual accumulation of energy, which gets released relatively infrequently.

(D) No region can be identified as a subduction zone unless earthquakes occur there.

(E) Earthquakes are more likely to result where there is a large plane of contact between plates during subduction.

S T O P

IF YOU FINISH BEFORE TIME IS CALLED, YOU MAY CHECK YOUR WORK ON THIS SECTION ONLY.
DO NOT WORK ON ANY OTHER SECTION IN THE TEST.

SECTION II
Time—35 minutes
26 Questions

Directions: Each question in this section is based on the reasoning presented in a brief passage. In answering the questions, you should not make assumptions that are by commonsense standards implausible, superfluous, or incompatible with the passage. For some questions, more than one of the choices could conceivably answer the question. However, you are to choose the **best** answer; that is, choose the response that most accurately and completely answers the question and mark that response on your answer sheet.

1. Ullman: Plato argued that because of the harmful ways in which music can manipulate the emotions, societies need to put restrictions on the music their citizens hear. However, because musicians seek not to manipulate the emotions but to create beauty, this argument is misguided.

    Ullman's argument is most vulnerable to criticism on the grounds that it fails to consider the possibility that

    (A) what musicians intend their music to do and what it actually does are different
    (B) those with the power to censor music would not censor other forms of expression
    (C) there are other, more convincing arguments for allowing the censorship of music
    (D) other forms of art have more potential to be harmful to society than music has
    (E) artists who are trying to manipulate people's emotions to control them are not likely to admit it

2. Physician: A tax on saturated fat, which was intended to reduce consumption of unhealthy foods, has been repealed after having been in effect for only seven months. The tax was apparently having some undesirable and unintended consequences, encouraging people to travel to neighboring countries to purchase certain foods, for example. Nonetheless, the tax should not have been repealed so soon.

    Which one of the following principles, if valid, most helps to justify the physician's conclusion regarding the tax?

    (A) A tax on unhealthy foods should be implemented only if it can be known with a high degree of certainty that it will actually improve people's health.
    (B) It is not possible to adequately gauge the impact of a tax intended to affect people's health until the tax has been in effect for at least one year.
    (C) Before any law intended to improve people's health is implemented, all foreseeable negative consequences should be carefully considered.
    (D) A law intended to improve people's health should be repealed if it is clear that most people are evading the law.
    (E) A tax on unhealthy foods should be applied only to those foods that are widely believed to be the most unhealthy.

3. Legislator: A foreign company is attempting to buy FerroMetal, a domestic iron-mining company. We should prohibit this sale. Since manufacturing is central to our economy, we need a dependable supply of iron ore. If we allow a foreign company to buy FerroMetal, we will have no grounds to stop foreign companies from buying other iron-mining companies. Soon foreigners will control most of the iron mining here, leaving our manufacturers at their mercy. The end result will be that our manufacturers will no longer be able to rely on a domestic supply of iron ore.

    Which one of the following most accurately describes a flaw in the reasoning of the legislator's argument?

    (A) The argument draws a conclusion that simply restates a premise presented in support of that conclusion.
    (B) The argument takes for granted that what is true of one particular industry is true of industry in general.
    (C) The argument defends a practice solely on the grounds that the practice is widely accepted.
    (D) The argument presents a chain of possible consequences of a given event as if it were the only possible chain of consequences of that event.
    (E) The argument concludes that one event would cause a second event even though the second event would have to precede the first.

GO ON TO THE NEXT PAGE.

4. Food company engineer: I stand by my decision to order the dumping of small amounts of chemicals into the local river even though there is some evidence that this material may pose health problems. I fish in the river myself and will continue to do so. Furthermore, I will have no problem if other food manufacturers do what our company does.

The engineer's reasoning most closely conforms to which one of the following principles?

(A) One is justified in performing an act if other people are also planning to perform that kind of act.

(B) One should always choose to act in a way that will benefit the greatest number of people.

(C) One is justified in performing an act if one is willing to submit oneself to the consequences of that action performed by oneself or others.

(D) One should never perform an act until one has fully analyzed all the ways in which that act could impact others.

(E) One has the right to perform an act as long as that act does not harm anyone else.

5. Political strategist: Clearly, attacking an opposing candidate on philosophical grounds is generally more effective than attacking the details of the opponent's policy proposals. A philosophical attack links an opponent's policy proposals to an overarching ideological scheme, thereby telling a story and providing context. This makes the attack emotionally compelling.

Which one of the following is an assumption required by the political strategist's argument?

(A) The stories that people are most likely to remember are those that are emotionally compelling.

(B) Political attacks that are emotionally compelling are generally more effective than those that are not.

(C) Political attacks that tell a story are able to provide more context than those that do not.

(D) Voters are typically uninterested in the details of candidates' policy proposals.

(E) Most candidates' policy proposals are grounded in an overarching ideological scheme.

6. Michaela: I think doctors who complain about patients doing medical research on the Internet are being a little unfair. It seems only natural that a patient would want to know as much as possible about his or her condition.

Sam: It is not unfair. Doctors have undergone years of training. How can you maintain that a doctor's opinion is not worth more than something an untrained person comes up with after searching the Internet?

Sam's response indicates that he interpreted Michaela's remarks to mean that

(A) health information found on the Internet is trustworthy

(B) the opinion of a patient who has done Internet research on his or her condition should have at least as much weight as the opinion of a doctor

(C) the opinion of a patient's own doctor should not be given more weight than the opinions of doctors published on websites

(D) a doctor's explanation of a patient's symptoms should be taken more seriously than the patient's own view of his or her symptoms

(E) patients who do not research their conditions on the Internet give their doctors' opinions more consideration

7. Principle: People should not feed wild animals because it makes them dependent on humans and less likely to survive on their own.

Situation: Bird lovers commonly feed wild birds to attract them to their yards and gardens.

Which one of the following, if assumed, would most help to justify treating the human feeding of wild birds as an exception to the principle above?

(A) Congregating around human bird feeders makes wild birds more vulnerable to predators and diseases.

(B) Some species of wild birds benefit humans by consuming large numbers of mosquitoes and other insect pests.

(C) Wild birds are much more likely to congregate in yards where they are fed than in yards where they are not fed.

(D) Most bird lovers are very active in efforts to preserve the habitats of threatened species of wild birds and other animals.

(E) Human settlement is so pervasive in the habitat of most wild birds that they must depend in part on human sources of food for survival.

8. Normally, political candidates send out campaign material in order to influence popular opinion. But the recent ads for Ebsen's campaign were sent to too few households to serve this purpose effectively. The ads were evidently sent out to test their potential to influence popular opinion. They covered a wide variety of topics, and Ebsen's campaign has been spending heavily on follow-up to gauge their effect on recipients.

Which one of the following most accurately expresses the conclusion drawn in the argument above?

(A) Normally, political candidates send out campaign material to influence popular opinion.

(B) The recent ads for Ebsen's campaign were sent to too few households to influence popular opinion effectively.

(C) The recent ads for Ebsen's campaign were sent out to test their potential to influence popular opinion.

(D) The recent ads for Ebsen's campaign covered a wide variety of topics.

(E) Ebsen's campaign has been spending heavily on follow-up surveys to gauge the ads' effect on recipients.

9. Last year, pharmaceutical manufacturers significantly increased the amount of money they spent promoting new drugs, which they do mainly by sending sales representatives to visit physicians in their offices. However, two years ago there was an average of 640 such visits per representative, whereas last year that figure fell to 501. So the additional promotion must have been counterproductive, making physicians less willing to receive visits by pharmaceutical sales representatives.

Which one of the following, if true, most weakens the argument?

(A) Most pharmaceutical manufacturers increased the size of their sales forces so that their sales representatives could devote more time to each physician.

(B) Physicians who receive visits from pharmaceutical sales representatives usually accept free samples of medication from the representatives' companies.

(C) Most pharmaceutical companies did not increase the amount of money they spend promoting drugs through advertising targeted directly at consumers.

(D) Most physicians who agree to receive a visit from a pharmaceutical sales representative will see that representative more than once during a given year.

(E) The more visits a physician receives from a pharmaceutical sales representative, the more likely he or she is to prescribe drugs made by that representative's company.

10. Archaeologist: The extensive network of ancient tracks on the island of Malta was most likely created through erosion caused by the passage of wheeled vehicles. Some researchers have suggested that the tracks were in fact manually cut to facilitate the passage of carts, citing the uniformity in track depth. However, this uniformity is more likely indicative of wheel diameter: Routes were utilized until tracks eroded to a depth that made vehicle passage impossible.

Which one of the following is the overall conclusion of the archaeologist's argument?

(A) The extensive network of ancient tracks on the island of Malta was most likely created through erosion caused by the passage of wheeled vehicles.

(B) Some researchers have suggested that the ancient tracks on the island of Malta were in fact manually cut to facilitate the passage of carts.

(C) Some researchers cite the uniformity of the depth of the ancient tracks on the island of Malta to support the suggestion that they were manually cut.

(D) The uniformity of depth of the ancient tracks on the island of Malta is probably indicative of the wheel diameter of the carts that passed over them.

(E) The ancient tracks on the island of Malta were utilized until they eroded to a depth that made vehicle passage impossible.

11. The goal of reforesting degraded land is to create an area with a multitude of thriving tree species. But some experienced land managers use a reforesting strategy that involves planting a single fast-growing tree species.

Which one of the following, if true, most helps to resolve the apparent discrepancy in the information above?

(A) Tree species that require abundant sunlight tend to grow quickly on degraded land.

(B) An area with a multitude of thriving tree species tends to be more aesthetically pleasing than an area with only a single tree species.

(C) The reforestation of degraded land is generally unsuccessful unless the land is planted with tree species that are native to the area designated for reforestation.

(D) The growth of trees attracts wildlife whose activities contribute to the dispersal of a large variety of tree seeds from surrounding areas.

(E) The process of reforesting degraded sites is time consuming and labor intensive.

GO ON TO THE NEXT PAGE.

12. An independent computer service company tallied the service requests it receives for individual brands of personal computers. It found that, after factoring in each brand's market share, KRV brand computers had the largest proportion of service requests, whereas ProBit brand computers had the smallest proportion of service requests. Obviously, ProBit is the more reliable personal computer brand.

Which one of the following, if true, most seriously weakens the argument?

(A) The proportions of service requests for the other computer brands in the tally were clustered much closer to the ProBit level of service requests than to the KRV level.

(B) For some computer brands, but not for others, most service requests are made to the manufacturer's service department rather than to an independent service company.

(C) The company that did the tally receives more service requests for ProBit brand computers than does any other independent computer service company.

(D) The computer brands covered in the computer service company's tally differ greatly with respect to their market share.

(E) ProBit has been selling personal computers for many more years than has KRV.

13. When scientific journals began to offer full online access to their articles in addition to the traditional printed volumes, scientists gained access to more journals and easier access to back issues. Surprisingly, this did not lead to a broader variety of articles being cited in new scientific articles. Instead, it led to a greater tendency among scientists to cite the same articles that their fellow scientists cited.

Which one of the following, if true, most helps to explain the surprising outcome described above?

(A) A few of the most authoritative scientific journals were among the first to offer full online access to their articles.

(B) Scientists who wrote a lot of articles were the most enthusiastic about accessing journal articles online.

(C) Scientists are more likely to cite articles by scientists that they know than they are to cite articles by scientists they have never met, even if the latter are more prominent.

(D) Several new scientific journals appeared at roughly the same time that full online access to scientific articles became commonplace.

(E) Online searching made it easier for scientists to identify the articles that present the most highly regarded views on an issue, which they prefer to cite.

14. Researcher: People are able to tell whether a person is extroverted just by looking at pictures in which the person has a neutral expression. Since people are also able to tell whether a chimpanzee behaves dominantly just by looking at a picture of the chimpanzee's expressionless face, and since both humans and chimpanzees are primates, we conclude that this ability is probably not acquired solely through culture but rather as a result of primate biology.

Which one of the following, if true, most strengthens the researcher's argument?

(A) People are generally unable to judge the dominance of bonobos, which are also primates, by looking at pictures of them.

(B) People are able to identify a wider range of personality traits from pictures of other people than from pictures of chimpanzees.

(C) Extroversion in people and dominant behavior in chimpanzees are both indicators of a genetic predisposition to assertiveness.

(D) Any common ancestor of humans and chimpanzees would have to have lived over 7 million years ago.

(E) Some of the pictures of people used in the experiments were composites of several different people.

15. All the apartments on 20th Avenue are in old houses. However, there are twice as many apartments on 20th Avenue as there are old houses. Therefore, most old houses on 20th Avenue contain more than one apartment.

The reasoning in the argument above is most vulnerable to criticism on the grounds that the argument

(A) overlooks the possibility that some of the buildings on 20th Avenue are not old houses

(B) draws a conclusion that simply restates one of the premises offered in support of the conclusion

(C) fails to consider the possibility that some buildings on 20th Avenue may offer types of rental accommodation other than apartments

(D) confuses a condition whose presence would be sufficient to ensure the truth of the argument's conclusion with a condition whose presence is required in order for the conclusion to be true

(E) fails to address the possibility that a significant number of old houses on 20th Avenue contain three or more apartments

GO ON TO THE NEXT PAGE.

16. Scientist: An orbiting spacecraft detected a short-term spike in sulfur dioxide in Venus's atmosphere. Volcanoes are known to cause sulfur dioxide spikes in Earth's atmosphere, and Venus has hundreds of mountains that show signs of past volcanic activity. But we should not conclude that volcanic activity caused the spike on Venus. No active volcanoes have been identified on Venus, and planetary atmospheres are known to undergo some cyclical variations in chemical composition.

Which one of the following, if true, most weakens the scientist's argument?

(A) Conditions on Venus make it unlikely that any instrument targeting Venus would detect a volcanic eruption directly.

(B) Evidence suggests that there was a short-term spike in sulfur dioxide in Venus's atmosphere 30 years earlier.

(C) Levels of sulfur dioxide have been higher in Venus's atmosphere than in Earth's atmosphere over the long term.

(D) Traces of the sulfur dioxide from volcanic eruptions on Earth are detectable in the atmosphere years after the eruptions take place.

(E) Most instances of sulfur dioxide spikes in the Earth's atmosphere are caused by the burning of fossil fuels.

17. Increasing the electrical load carried on a transmission line increases the line's temperature, and too great a load will cause the line to exceed its maximum operating temperature. The line's temperature is also affected by wind speed and direction: Strong winds cool the line more than light winds, and wind blowing across a line cools it more than does wind blowing parallel to it.

Which one of the following is most strongly supported by the information above?

(A) Electrical utility companies typically increase the electrical load on their transmission lines on days on which the wind has a strong cooling effect.

(B) Transmission lines that run parallel to the prevailing winds can generally carry greater electrical loads than otherwise identical lines at a right angle to the prevailing winds.

(C) The electrical load that a transmission line can carry without reaching its maximum operating temperature increases when the wind speed increases.

(D) Air temperature has less effect on the temperature of a transmission line than wind speed does.

(E) The maximum operating temperature of a transmission line is greater on windy days than on calm days.

18. In grasslands near the Namib Desert there are "fairy circles"—large, circular patches that are entirely devoid of vegetation. Since sand termite colonies were found in every fairy circle they investigated, scientists hypothesize that it is the burrowing activities of these termites that cause the circles to form.

Which one of the following, if true, most supports the scientists' hypothesis?

(A) Dying grass plants within newly forming fairy circles are damaged only at the roots.

(B) The grasses that grow around fairy circles are able to survive even the harshest and most prolonged droughts in the region.

(C) The soil in fairy circles typically has higher water content than the soil in areas immediately outside the circles.

(D) Fairy circles tend to form in areas that already have numerous other fairy circles.

(E) Species of animals that feed on sand termites are often found living near fairy circles.

GO ON TO THE NEXT PAGE.

19. Munroe was elected in a landslide. It is impossible for Munroe to have been elected without both a fundamental shift in the sentiments of the electorate and a well-run campaign. Thus, one cannot avoid the conclusion that there has been a fundamental shift in the sentiments of the electorate.

Which one of the following arguments is most closely parallel in its reasoning to the argument above?

(A) The Park Street Cafe closed this year even though its customer base was satisfied. So, because its customer base was satisfied, the only conclusion one can draw is that the Park Street Cafe closed because it was facing strong competition.

(B) The Park Street Cafe closed this year. So we must conclude that the Park Street Cafe was facing strong competition, since it would not have closed unless it was true both that it was facing strong competition and that its customer base was unsatisfied.

(C) No one can argue that the Park Street Cafe closed this year because its customer base was not satisfied. Even if its customer base was not satisfied, the Park Street Cafe would have closed only if it was facing strong competition.

(D) The Park Street Cafe closed this year. There was no reason for it to remain open if it was facing strong competition and had an unsatisfied customer base. So one cannot rule out the possibility that it was both facing strong competition and had an unsatisfied customer base.

(E) The Park Street Cafe closed this year. In order to stay open, it needed a lack of competition and it needed a satisfied customer base. Because it had neither, the unavoidable conclusion is that the Park Street Cafe could not have stayed open this year.

20. For pollinating certain crops such as cranberries, bumblebees are far more efficient than honeybees. This is because a bumblebee tends to visit only a few plant species in a limited area, whereas a honeybee generally flies over a much broader area and visits a wider variety of species.

Which one of the following is most strongly supported by the information above?

(A) If a honeybee visits a wider variety of plant species than a bumblebee visits, the honeybee will be less efficient than the bumblebee at pollinating any one of those species.

(B) The number of plant species other than cranberries that a bee visits affects the efficiency with which the bee pollinates cranberries.

(C) The broader an area a bee flies over, the smaller the number of plant species that bee will be able to visit.

(D) Cranberries are typically found concentrated in limited areas that bumblebees are more likely than honeybees ever to visit.

(E) The greater the likelihood of a given bee species visiting one or more plants in a given cranberry crop, the more efficient that bee species will be at pollinating that crop.

21. Economist: Currently the interest rates that banks pay to borrow are higher than the interest rates that they can receive for loans to large, financially strong companies. Banks will not currently lend to companies that are not financially strong, and total lending by banks to small and medium-sized companies is less than it was five years ago. So total bank lending to companies is less than it was five years ago.

The economist's conclusion follows logically if which one of the following is assumed?

(A) Banks will not lend money at interest rates that are lower than the interest rates they pay to borrow.

(B) Most small and medium-sized companies were financially stronger five years ago than they are now.

(C) Five years ago, some banks would lend to companies that were not financially strong.

(D) The interest rates that banks currently pay to borrow are higher than the rates they paid five years ago.

(E) The interest rates that small and medium-sized companies pay to borrow are higher than those paid by large, financially strong companies.

GO ON TO THE NEXT PAGE.

22. Counselor: To be kind to someone, one must want that person to prosper. Yet, even two people who dislike each other may nevertheless treat each other with respect. And while no two people who dislike each other can be fully content in each other's presence, any two people who do not dislike each other will be kind to each other.

If the counselor's statements are true, then which one of the following must be false?

(A) Some people who like each other are not fully content in each other's presence.

(B) Some people who are fully content in each other's presence do not want each other to prosper.

(C) Some people who treat each other with respect are not fully content in each other's presence.

(D) Some people who want each other to prosper dislike each other.

(E) Some people who are kind to each other do not treat each other with respect.

23. A gram of the artificial sweetener aspartame is much sweeter than a gram of sugar. Soft drinks that are sweetened with sugar are, of course, sweet, so those sweetened with aspartame must be even sweeter. Thus people who regularly drink soft drinks sweetened with aspartame will develop a preference for extremely sweet products.

Which one of the following arguments exhibits flawed reasoning that is most similar to flawed reasoning in the argument above?

(A) People sometimes develop a preference for foods that they initially disliked. So if you dislike a new food, then you will eventually develop a preference for it.

(B) Most people own more books than televisions. Moreover, it takes longer to read a book than to watch an episode of a television show. So most people must spend more time reading than they do watching television.

(C) Joe's piggy bank has only pennies in it, and Maria's has only nickels. Nickels are worth much more than pennies. It therefore follows that there is more money in Maria's piggy bank than in Joe's.

(D) Stephanie likes hot summer weather much more than Katherine does. So the place where Stephanie grew up must have had more days of hot summer weather than the place where Katherine grew up.

(E) Guillermo has a much shorter drive to work than Abdul does. So Guillermo's estimate of the average commute for workers in the country as a whole is likely to be lower than Abdul's estimate.

24. Economist: If minimum wage levels are low, employers have a greater incentive to hire more workers than to buy productivity-enhancing new technology. As a result, productivity growth, which is necessary for higher average living standards, falls off. Conversely, high minimum wage levels result in higher productivity. Thus, raising our currently low minimum wage levels would improve the country's overall economic health more than any hiring cutbacks triggered by the raise would harm it.

Which one of the following, if true, most strengthens the economist's argument?

(A) Productivity growth in a country usually leads to an eventual increase in job creation.

(B) The economist's country has seen a slow but steady increase in its unemployment rate over the last decade.

(C) A country's unemployment rate is a key factor in determining its average living standards.

(D) The economist's country currently lags behind other countries in the development of new technology.

(E) Productivity-enhancing new technology tends to quickly become outdated.

GO ON TO THE NEXT PAGE.

25. Mayor: Periodically an ice cream company will hold a free ice cream day as a promotion. Showing up may not cost you any money, but it sure does cost you time. We learn from this that when something valuable costs no money you get overconsumption and long lines. Currently, those who drive to work complain about the congestion they face in their rush-hour commutes. What is needed is a system for charging people for the use of roads during rush hour. Then rush hour congestion will abate.

The claim that when something valuable costs no money you get overconsumption and long lines plays which one of the following roles in the mayor's argument?

(A)   It is a hypothesis that is rejected in favor of the hypothesis stated in the argument's overall conclusion.

(B)   It is a concession made to those who dispute an analogy drawn in the argument.

(C)   It helps establish the importance of the argument's overall conclusion, but is not offered as evidence for that conclusion.

(D)   It is a general claim used in support of the argument's overall conclusion.

(E)   It is the overall conclusion of the argument.

26. The advertising campaign for Roadwise auto insurance is notable for the variety of its commercials, which range from straightforward and informative to funny and offbeat. This is unusual in the advertising world, where companies typically strive for uniformity in advertising in order to establish a brand identity with their target demographic. But in this case variety is a smart approach, since purchasers of auto insurance are so demographically diverse.

Which one of the following, if true, adds the most support for the conclusion of the argument?

(A)   Advertising campaigns designed to target one demographic sometimes appeal to a wider group of people than expected.

(B)   Consistent efforts to establish a brand identity are critical for encouraging product interest and improving company recognition.

(C)   Fewer people are influenced by auto insurance commercials than by commercials for other types of products.

(D)   Advertising campaigns that target one demographic often alienate people who are not part of the target demographic.

(E)   Efforts to influence a target demographic do not pay off when the content of the advertising campaign falls short.

S T O P

IF YOU FINISH BEFORE TIME IS CALLED, YOU MAY CHECK YOUR WORK ON THIS SECTION ONLY.
DO NOT WORK ON ANY OTHER SECTION IN THE TEST.

SECTION III
Time—35 minutes
25 Questions

Directions: Each question in this section is based on the reasoning presented in a brief passage. In answering the questions, you should not make assumptions that are by commonsense standards implausible, superfluous, or incompatible with the passage. For some questions, more than one of the choices could conceivably answer the question. However, you are to choose the **best** answer; that is, choose the response that most accurately and completely answers the question and mark that response on your answer sheet.

1. Researchers put two electrodes in a pool that a dolphin swam in. When the dolphin swam near the electrodes, the researchers would sometimes create a weak electric field by activating the electrodes. The dolphin would swim away if the electrodes were activated; otherwise it acted normally. The researchers then placed a plastic shield over small organs called vibrissal crypts located on the dolphin's snout. With the crypts covered, the dolphin no longer swam away when the electrodes were activated.

    The statements above, if true, most strongly support which one of the following?

    (A)   In the wild, dolphins sometimes encounter strong electric fields.
    (B)   Vibrissal crypts enable dolphins to sense electric fields.
    (C)   Dolphins do not instinctually avoid electric fields, but they can be trained to do so.
    (D)   Electric fields interfere with the normal functioning of dolphins' vibrissal crypts.
    (E)   Under normal circumstances, dolphins are unable to sense electric fields.

2. In a study of honesty conducted in various retail stores, customers who paid in cash and received change were given an extra dollar with their change. Few people who received an extra dollar returned it. So, among those who received an extra dollar, most behaved dishonestly.

    The answer to which one of the following questions would most help in evaluating the argument?

    (A)   Did those who received an extra dollar count their change?
    (B)   What percentage of the retail transactions studied were cash transactions?
    (C)   Would the people who returned the extra dollar describe themselves as honest?
    (D)   Did the people who returned the extra dollar suspect that it was given to them intentionally?
    (E)   Does increasing the extra change to five dollars have an effect on people's behavior?

3. Dario: The government should continue to grant patents for all new drug compounds. Patents promote innovation by rewarding pharmaceutical companies for undertaking the costly research needed to develop new drugs.

    Cynthia: Promoting innovation is certainly important. For this reason, patents should be granted only for truly innovative drugs, not for minor variants of previously existing drugs. Since it is much less expensive to tweak an existing drug than to develop a wholly new one, pharmaceutical companies tend to focus primarily on the cheaper alternative.

    Dario and Cynthia disagree over whether

    (A)   pharmaceutical companies should be rewarded for pursuing innovation
    (B)   patents should be granted for all drug compounds
    (C)   developing truly innovative drugs is costly
    (D)   pharmaceutical companies have an incentive to create minor variants of existing drugs
    (E)   drug patents can promote innovation

4. There are only two possible reasons that it would be wrong to engage in an activity that causes pollution: because pollution harms ecosystems, which are valuable in themselves; or, ecosystems aside, because pollution harms human populations. Either way, it would not be wrong to perform mining operations on Mars. Although doing so would pollute Mars, the small human presence needed to run the mining operation would be completely protected from the Martian environment and would suffer no harm.

    The conclusion drawn above follows logically if which one of the following is assumed?

    (A)   Mining creates less pollution than many other human activities.
    (B)   There are no ecosystems on Mars.
    (C)   The economic benefits of mining on Mars would outweigh its costs.
    (D)   It is technologically feasible to perform mining operations on Mars.
    (E)   The more complex an ecosystem is, the more valuable it is.

GO ON TO THE NEXT PAGE.

5. A person with low self-esteem will be treated disrespectfully more often than will a person with high self-esteem. Moreover, a recent experiment found that, when people with low self-esteem and those with high self-esteem are both confronted with the same treatment by others, people with low self-esteem are much more likely to feel that they have been treated disrespectfully. Thus, _____.

Which one of the following most logically completes the argument?

(A) people with low self-esteem are usually right when they think they have been treated disrespectfully

(B) being treated disrespectfully tends to cause a person to develop lower self-esteem

(C) if an individual has been treated disrespectfully, it is probably because the individual was perceived to have low self-esteem

(D) people with low self-esteem more frequently think that they are being treated disrespectfully than do people with high self-esteem

(E) a person with low self-esteem will be more inclined to treat others disrespectfully than will a person with high self-esteem

6. Watanabe: To protect the native kokanee salmon in the lake, we must allow fishing of native trout. Each mature trout eats about 250 mature kokanee annually.

Lopez: The real problem is mysis shrimp, which were originally introduced into the lake as food for mature kokanee; but mysis eat plankton—young kokanees' food. The young kokanee are starving to death. So eradicating the shrimp is preferable to allowing trout fishing.

Which one of the following principles, if valid, most strongly supports Lopez's conclusion?

(A) Eliminating a non-native species from a habitat in which it threatens a native species is preferable to any other method of protecting the threatened native species.

(B) When trying to protect the food supply of a particular species, it is best to encourage the method that will have the quickest results, all else being equal.

(C) The number of species in a given habitat should not be reduced if at all possible.

(D) No non-native species should be introduced into a habitat unless all the potential effects of that introduction have been considered.

(E) When seeking to increase the population of a given species, it is most important that one preserve the members of the species who are in the prime reproductive stage of their lives.

7. If rational-choice theory is correct, then people act only in ways that they expect will benefit themselves. But this means that rational-choice theory cannot be correct, because plenty of examples exist of people acting in ways that result in no personal benefit whatsoever.

The argument above is most vulnerable to criticism on the grounds that it

(A) assumes as a premise the contention the argument purports to establish

(B) concludes that a theory is false merely on the grounds that the evidence for it is hypothetical

(C) takes for granted that people who are acting in ways that are personally beneficial expected that their actions would be personally beneficial

(D) presumes, without justification, that examples of people acting in ways that are not personally beneficial greatly outnumber examples of people acting in ways that are personally beneficial

(E) fails to consider that people acting in ways that result in no personal benefit may nonetheless have expected that acting in those ways would produce personal benefit

8. Winds, the movement of gases in the atmosphere of a planet, are ultimately due to differences in atmospheric temperature. Winds on Earth are the result of heat from the Sun, but the Sun is much too far away from Jupiter to have any significant impact on the temperature of Jupiter's atmosphere. Nevertheless, on Jupiter winds reach speeds many times those of winds found on Earth.

Which one of the following, if true, most helps to explain the facts cited above about Jupiter and its winds?

(A) Unlike Earth, Jupiter's atmosphere is warmed by the planet's internal heat source.

(B) Jupiter's atmosphere is composed of several gases that are found in Earth's atmosphere only in trace amounts.

(C) Gaseous planets such as Jupiter sometimes have stronger winds than do rocky planets such as Earth.

(D) There are more planets that have winds stronger than Earth's than there are planets that have winds weaker than Earth's.

(E) Planets even farther from the Sun than Jupiter are known to have atmospheric winds.

GO ON TO THE NEXT PAGE.

9. Until recently it was widely believed that only a limited number of species could reproduce through parthenogenesis, reproduction by a female alone. But lately, as interest in the topic has increased, parthenogenesis has been found in a variety of unexpected cases, including sharks and Komodo dragons. So the number of species that can reproduce through parthenogenesis must be increasing.

    The reasoning in the argument is most vulnerable to criticism on the grounds that the argument

    (A) equates mere interest in a subject with real understanding of that subject
    (B) takes for granted that because one thing follows another, the one must have been caused by the other
    (C) takes ignorance of the occurrence of something as conclusive evidence that it did not occur
    (D) overlooks a crucial difference between two situations that the argument presents as being similar
    (E) presumes that because research is new it is, on that basis alone, better than older research

10. Physician: Clinical psychologists who are not also doctors with medical degrees should not be allowed to prescribe psychiatric medications. Training in clinical psychology includes at most a few hundred hours of education in neuroscience, physiology, and pharmacology. In contrast, doctors with medical degrees must receive years of training in these fields before they are allowed to prescribe psychiatric medications.

    Which one of the following principles, if valid, would most help to justify the reasoning in the physician's argument?

    (A) Clinical psychologists who are also doctors with medical degrees should be allowed to prescribe psychiatric medications.
    (B) Doctors without training in clinical psychology should not be allowed to prescribe psychiatric medications.
    (C) No one without years of training in neuroscience, physiology, and pharmacology should be allowed to prescribe psychiatric medications.
    (D) The training in neuroscience, physiology, and pharmacology required for a medical degree is sufficient for a doctor to be allowed to prescribe psychiatric medications.
    (E) Clinical psychologists should receive years of training in neuroscience, physiology, and pharmacology.

11. Lobbyist: Those who claim that automobile exhaust emissions are a risk to public health are mistaken. During the last century, as automobile exhaust emissions increased, every relevant indicator of public health improved dramatically rather than deteriorated.

    The flaw in the lobbyist's reasoning can most effectively be demonstrated by noting that, by parallel reasoning, we could conclude that

    (A) inspecting commercial airplanes for safety is unnecessary because the number of commercial airplane crashes has decreased over the last decade
    (B) smoking cigarettes is not bad for one's health because not all cigarette smokers get smoking-related illnesses
    (C) using a cell phone while driving is not dangerous because the number of traffic accidents has decreased since the invention of the cell phone
    (D) skydiving is not dangerous because the number of injuries to skydivers has decreased in recent years
    (E) people with insurance do not need to lock their doors because if anything is stolen the insurance company will pay to replace it

12. A recently discovered fossil, which is believed by some to come from *Archaeoraptor liaoningensis*, a species of dinosaur, can serve as evidence that birds evolved from dinosaurs only if the entire fossil is from a single animal. However, the fossil is a composite of bones collected from various parts of the discovery site, so it does not provide evidence that birds evolved from dinosaurs.

    The conclusion drawn in the argument follows logically if which one of the following is assumed?

    (A) The only paleontologists who believe that the entire fossil is from a single animal are those who were already convinced that birds evolved from dinosaurs.
    (B) If the fossil is a composite, then it has pieces of more than one animal.
    (C) There are other fossils that provide evidence that birds evolved from dinosaurs.
    (D) If the entire fossil is from a single animal, then it is a well-preserved specimen.
    (E) The fossil was stolen from the discovery site and sold by someone who cared much more about personal profit than about the accuracy of the fossil record.

GO ON TO THE NEXT PAGE.

13. A new screening test has been developed for syndrome Q. Research has shown that the test yields a positive for syndrome Q whenever the person tested has that syndrome. So, since Justine shows positive on the test, she must have syndrome Q.

Which one of the following most accurately describes a flaw in the reasoning in the argument?

(A) It confuses the claim that a subject will test positive when the syndrome is present with the claim that any subject who tests positive has the syndrome.

(B) It makes a general claim regarding the accuracy of the test for syndrome Q without providing adequate scientific justification for that claim.

(C) It fails to adequately distinguish between a person's not having syndrome Q and that person's not testing positive for syndrome Q.

(D) It confuses a claim about the accuracy of a test for syndrome Q in an arbitrary group of individuals with a similar claim about the accuracy of the test for a single individual.

(E) It confuses the test's having no reliable results for the presence of syndrome Q with its having no reliable results for the absence of syndrome Q.

14. Music historian: In the past, radio stations would not play rock songs that were more than three minutes in length. Rock musicians claimed that such commercial barriers limited their creativity, and some critics argue that only since those barriers have been lifted has rock music become artistic. In fact, however, when these barriers were lifted, the standards for song structures broke down and the music became aimless, because the styles from which rock derived were not well suited to songs of extended length.

Which one of the following is most strongly supported by the music historian's claims?

(A) Rock music is not a good outlet for creative musicians who have a great many ideas.

(B) Rock music must borrow from styles more conducive to songs of extended length if it is to become artistic.

(C) Rock music requires more discipline than some other forms of music.

(D) Rock music can sometimes benefit from the existence of commercial barriers rather than being harmed by them.

(E) Rock music is best when it is made by musicians who do not think of themselves as being self-conscious artists.

15. Some food historians conclude that recipes compiled by an ancient Roman named Apicius are a reliable indicator of how wealthy Romans prepared and spiced their food. Since few other recipes from ancient Rome have survived, this conclusion is far too hasty. After all, the recipes of Apicius may have been highly atypical, just like the recipes of many notable modern chefs.

The argument does which one of the following?

(A) It rejects a view held by some food historians solely on the grounds that there is insufficient evidence to support it.

(B) It offers support for a view held by some food historians by providing a modern analogue to that view.

(C) It takes issue with the view of some food historians by providing a modern analogue that purportedly undercuts their view.

(D) It uses a conclusion drawn by some food historians as the basis for a conclusion about a modern analogue.

(E) It tries to bolster a conclusion about the similarity of historical times to modern times by comparing a conclusion drawn by some food historians to a modern analogue.

GO ON TO THE NEXT PAGE.

16. Wood that is waterlogged or desiccated can be preserved for a significant period, but, under normal conditions, wood usually disintegrates within a century or two. For this reason, archaeologists have been unable to find many remains of early wheeled vehicles to examine. However, archaeologists have found small ceramic models of wheeled vehicles made at approximately the same time as those early vehicles. Since these models have been much less susceptible to disintegration than the vehicles themselves, the main evidence regarding early wheeled vehicles has come from these models.

Which one of the following is most strongly supported by the information above?

(A) Most of the small ceramic models of early wheeled vehicles were made by the very individuals who made the vehicles upon which the ceramic vehicles were modeled.

(B) Few, if any, small models of early wheeled vehicles were made of wood or other materials equally susceptible to disintegration under normal conditions.

(C) The individuals who made the early wheeled vehicles were not always aware that wood can be preserved through waterlogging or desiccation.

(D) An artifact will be more difficult for archaeologists to find if it has been preserved through waterlogging or desiccation than if it has been preserved under more normal conditions.

(E) Of the early wheeled vehicles not preserved, more were made of wood than were made of materials no more susceptible to disintegration than are ceramic items.

17. Traditional hatcheries raise fish in featureless environments and subject them to dull routines, whereas new, experimental hatcheries raise fish in visually stimulating environments with varied routines. When released into the wild, fish from the experimental hatcheries are bolder than those from traditional hatcheries in exploring new environments and trying new types of food. Fish raised in the experimental hatcheries, therefore, are more likely to survive after their release.

Which one of the following is an assumption required by the argument?

(A) It is economically feasible for hatchery operators to expose fish to greater visual stimulation and to more varied routines.

(B) The quality of the environments into which hatchery-raised fish are released has little effect on the fish's survival rate.

(C) Some fish raised in traditional hatcheries die because they are too timid in their foraging for food.

(D) Hatchery-raised fish that are released into the wild need to eat many different types of food to survive.

(E) Fish in the wild always live in visually stimulating environments.

18. An analysis of the language in social media messages posted via the Internet determined that, on average, the use of words associated with positive moods is common in the morning, decreases gradually to a low point midafternoon, and then increases sharply throughout the evening. This shows that a person's mood typically starts out happy in the morning, declines during the day, and improves in the evening.

The reasoning in the argument is most vulnerable to criticism on the grounds that the argument overlooks the possibility that

(A) people's overall moods are lowest at the beginning of the workweek and rise later, peaking on the weekend

(B) many people who post social media messages use neither words associated with positive moods nor words associated with negative moods

(C) the frequency in the use of words in social media is not necessarily indicative of the frequency of the use of those words in other forms of communication

(D) the number of social media messages posted in the morning is not significantly different from the number posted in the evening

(E) most of the social media messages posted in the evening are posted by people who rarely post such messages in the morning

GO ON TO THE NEXT PAGE.

19. Economist: The wages of many of the lowest-paid corporate employees in this country would be protected from cuts by enacting a maximum wage law that prohibits executives at any corporation from earning more than, say, 50 times what the corporation's lowest-paid employees in this country earn. Currently, some executives try to increase corporate profits—and their own salaries—by cutting the pay and benefits of their corporations' employees. A maximum wage law would remove this incentive for these executives to cut the wages of their lowest-paid employees.

Which one of the following is an assumption the economist's argument requires?

(A) All of the lowest-paid corporate employees in the economist's country are employed at corporations at which the executives earn more than 50 times what the corporations' lowest-paid employees in the economist's country earn.

(B) Some corporate executives who cut the pay of their corporations' lowest-paid employees in the economist's country in order to increase their own salaries already earn less than 50 times what their corporations' lowest-paid employees in the economist's country earn.

(C) No corporate executives in the economist's country would raise the wages of their corporations' lowest-paid employees in the economist's country unless such a maximum wage law linked executive wages to those of their corporations' lowest-paid employees in the economist's country.

(D) If corporate executives could not increase their own salaries by cutting the pay and benefits of their corporations' lowest-paid employees in the economist's country, they would never change the wages of those employees.

(E) If such a maximum wage law were enacted in the economist's country, one or more corporate executives would not cut the pay and benefits of their corporations' lowest-paid employees in the economist's country.

20. The level of triglycerides in the blood rises when triglycerides are inadequately metabolized. Research shows that patients with blood triglyceride levels above 1 milligram per milliliter are twice as prone to heart attacks as others. Thus, it is likely that consuming large amounts of fat, processed sugar, or alcohol, each known to increase triglyceride levels in the blood, is a factor causing heart disease.

Which one of the following, if true, most weakens the argument?

(A) People with a high-fat diet who engage in regular, vigorous physical activity are much less likely to develop heart disease than are sedentary people with a low-fat diet.

(B) Triglyceride levels above 2 milligrams per milliliter increase the risk of some serious illnesses not related to heart disease.

(C) Shortly after a person ceases to regularly consume alcohol and processed sugar, that person's triglyceride levels drop dramatically.

(D) Heart disease interferes with the body's ability to metabolize triglycerides.

(E) People who maintain strict regimens for their health tend to adopt low-fat diets and to avoid alcohol and processed sugar.

GO ON TO THE NEXT PAGE.

21. In an experiment, some volunteers were assigned to take aerobics classes and others to take weight-training classes. After three months, each performed an arduous mathematical calculation. Just after that challenge, the measurable stress symptoms of the volunteers in the aerobics classes were less than those of the volunteers in the weight-training classes. This provides good evidence that aerobic exercise helps the body handle psychological stress.

Which one of the following is an assumption the argument requires?

(A) Three months is enough time for the body to fully benefit from aerobic exercise.

(B) The volunteers who were assigned to the aerobics classes did not also lift weights outside the classes.

(C) On average, the volunteers who were assigned to the aerobics classes got more exercise in the months in which they took those classes than they had been getting before beginning the experiment.

(D) On average, the volunteers assigned to the aerobics classes found it less difficult to perform the mathematical calculation than did the volunteers assigned to the weight-training classes.

(E) On average, the volunteers assigned to the aerobics classes got a greater amount of aerobic exercise overall during the experiment, including any exercise outside the classes, than did the volunteers assigned to the weight-training classes.

22. Insurers and doctors are well aware that the incidence of lower-back injuries among office workers who spend long hours sitting is higher than that among people who regularly do physical work of a type known to place heavy stresses on the lower back. This shows that office equipment and furniture are not properly designed to promote workers' health.

Which one of the following, if true, most undermines the reasoning above?

(A) When they are at home, laborers and office workers tend to spend similar amounts of time sitting.

(B) Insurance companies tend to dislike selling policies to companies whose workers often claim to have back pain.

(C) People who regularly do physical work of a type known to place heavy stress on the lower back are encouraged to use techniques that reduce the degree of stress involved.

(D) Most of the lower-back injuries that office workers suffer occur while they are on the job.

(E) Consistent physical exercise is one of the most effective ways to prevent or recover from lower-back injuries.

23. Researchers have found that some unprotected areas outside of a national park that was designed to protect birds have substantially higher numbers of certain bird species than comparable areas inside the park.

Which one of the following, if true, most helps to explain the researchers' finding?

(A) Moose are much more prevalent inside the park, where hunting is prohibited, than outside the park, and moose eat much of the food that the birds need to survive.

(B) The researchers also found that some unprotected areas outside of the park have substantially higher numbers of certain reptile species than comparable areas inside the park.

(C) Researchers tagged a large number of birds inside the park; three months later some of these birds were recaptured outside the park.

(D) Both inside the park and just outside of it, there are riverside areas containing willows and other waterside growth that the bird species thrive on.

(E) The park was designed to protect endangered bird species, but some of the bird species that are present in higher numbers in the unprotected areas are also endangered.

GO ON TO THE NEXT PAGE.

24. A recent poll of a large number of households found that 47 percent of those with a cat had at least one person with a university degree, while 38 percent of households with a dog had at least one person with a university degree. Clearly, people who hold university degrees are more likely to live in a household with a cat than one with a dog.

The reasoning in the argument is flawed in that the argument

(A) ignores the possibility that a significant number of households might have both a cat and a dog

(B) takes for granted that there are not significantly more households with a dog than ones with a cat

(C) fails to consider how many of the households have at least one person without a university degree

(D) fails to consider to what extent people with university degrees participate in decisions about whether their households have a cat or dog

(E) ignores the possibility that two things can be correlated without being causally connected

25. Keeler wanted the institute to receive bad publicity. He and Greene were the only ones in a position to tell the press about the institute's potentially embarrassing affiliations, but Greene had no reason to do so. Therefore, it must have been Keeler who notified the press.

Which one of the following arguments is most closely parallel in its reasoning to the argument above?

(A) The only people who had any reason to write the anonymous letter were Johnson and Ringwold. Johnson and Ringwold both deny doing so. Ringwold, however, admits that she has written anonymous letters in the past. Thus, it must have been Ringwold who wrote the letter.

(B) Carter and Whitequill were the only ones who had any motive to bribe the public official. But Whitequill would have been too fearful that the bribery might somehow be made public. Carter, therefore, must be the person who bribed the public official.

(C) Other than Helms and Lapinski, no one had access to the equipment on Thursday, the day it was tampered with. Thus, since Helms had reason to tamper with the equipment and Lapinski did not, it must have been Helms who did it.

(D) When the bridge was designed, Fleming and Solano were the only ones capable of creating such a design. Fleming, however, had a strong reason to take credit for the design if it were his. Thus, since no one took credit for the design, it must have been the work of Solano.

(E) Cutter and Rengo are the only serious candidates for designing the new monument. Rengo has designed several beautiful monuments and has connections to the selection committee. Therefore, it will probably be Rengo who is awarded the job of designing the monument.

S T O P

IF YOU FINISH BEFORE TIME IS CALLED, YOU MAY CHECK YOUR WORK ON THIS SECTION ONLY.
DO NOT WORK ON ANY OTHER SECTION IN THE TEST.

SECTION IV
Time—35 minutes
25 Questions

Directions: Each question in this section is based on the reasoning presented in a brief passage. In answering the questions, you should not make assumptions that are by commonsense standards implausible, superfluous, or incompatible with the passage. For some questions, more than one of the choices could conceivably answer the question. However, you are to choose the **best** answer; that is, choose the response that most accurately and completely answers the question and mark that response on your answer sheet.

1. Joe: All vampire stories are based on an absurd set of premises. Since, according to such stories, every victim of a vampire becomes a vampire, and vampires have existed since ancient times and are immortal, vampires would by now have almost completely eliminated their prey.

    Maria: In most of the vampire stories I am familiar with, vampires turn only a few of their victims into vampires. The rest are permanently dead.

    Joe and Maria disagree over the truth of which one of the following?

    (A) Vampires are always depicted in vampire stories as immortal.
    (B) Vampires are always depicted in vampire stories as having existed since ancient times.
    (C) No vampire stories are incoherent.
    (D) No vampire stories depict the vampire population as being very large.
    (E) In all vampire stories, every victim of a vampire becomes a vampire.

2. A company decided to scan all of its salespersons' important work that existed only in paper form into a central computer database that could be easily accessed using portable computers, thereby saving salespersons the effort of lugging their paper files all over the country. The project was a dismal failure, however; salespersons rarely accessed the database and continued to rely on many paper files, which they had refused to turn over to the staff responsible for creating the database.

    Which one of the following, if true, most helps to account for the failure described above?

    (A) Some of the salespersons gave huge paper files to the staff responsible for creating the database while other salespersons gave them much smaller files.
    (B) Most of the salespersons already had portable computers before the new database was created.
    (C) The papers that the salespersons found most important all contained personal information about employees of client companies, which the salespersons did not want in a central database.
    (D) All of the salespersons were required to attend a series of training sessions for the new database software even though many of them found the software easy to use even without training.
    (E) The number of staff required to create the database turned out to be larger than anticipated, and the company had to pay overtime wages to some of them.

GO ON TO THE NEXT PAGE.

3. Politician: The legal right to free speech does not
    protect all speech. For example, it is illegal
    to shout "Fire!" in a crowded mall if the
    only intent is to play a practical joke; the
    government may ban publication of information
    about military operations and the identity of
    undercover agents; and extortion threats and
    conspiratorial agreements are also criminal acts.
    The criminalization of these forms of speech is
    justified, since, although they are very different
    from each other, they are all likely to lead directly
    to serious harm.

    In the statements above, the politician argues that

    (A)   it is legitimate to prohibit some forms of speech
           on the grounds that they are likely to lead
           directly to serious harm
    (B)   a form of speech can be restricted only if it
           is certain that it would lead directly to
           serious harm
    (C)   in all but a few cases, restricting speech
           eventually leads directly to serious harm
    (D)   any form of speech may, one way or another, lead
           directly to serious harm
    (E)   all but one of several possible reasons for
           restricting freedom of speech are unjustified

4. Art critic: Nowadays, museum visitors seldom pause to
    look at a work of art for even a full minute. They
    look, perhaps take a snapshot, and move on. This
    tells us something about how our relationship to
    art has changed over time. People have become
    less willing to engage with works of art than they
    once were.

    The art critic's argument depends on the assumption that

    (A)   museum visitors today generally look at more
           pieces of art during each museum visit than
           museum visitors looked at in the past
    (B)   the ease with which museum visitors can take
           snapshots of art contributes to the speed with
           which they move through art museums
    (C)   visitors would enjoy their museum experiences
           more if they took more time with individual
           works of art
    (D)   museum visitors who take snapshots of works of
           art rarely look at the pictures afterward
    (E)   the amount of time spent looking at a work of
           art is a reliable measure of engagement with
           that work

5. Heavy tapestry fabrics are appropriate only for use in
    applications that will not need to be laundered frequently.
    These applications do not include any types of clothing—
    such as skirts or even jackets—but instead include
    swags and balloon valances, which are types of window
    treatments.

    Which one of the following statements is most supported
    by the information above?

    (A)   If a fabric is not a heavy tapestry fabric, then it is
           not appropriate for use in swags.
    (B)   Heavy tapestry fabrics should not be used unless
           swags or balloon valances are being made.
    (C)   If heavy tapestry fabrics are appropriate for a
           particular application, then that application must
           be a window treatment.
    (D)   If a fabric is appropriate for use in a skirt or
           jacket, then that fabric is not a heavy tapestry
           fabric.
    (E)   Heavy tapestry fabrics are sometimes appropriate
           for use in types of clothing other than skirts and
           jackets.

6. The construction of new apartments in Brewsterville
    increased the supply of available housing there.
    Ordinarily, increasing the supply of available housing
    leads to lower rents for existing apartments. But in
    Brewsterville, rents for existing apartments rose.

    Which one of the following, if true, most helps to
    explain the discrepancy described above?

    (A)   Fewer new apartments were constructed than
           originally planned.
    (B)   The new apartments were much more desirable
           than the existing apartments.
    (C)   Rents in some areas close to Brewsterville
           dropped as a result of the construction of the
           new apartments.
    (D)   A sizeable number of people moved out of the
           existing apartments while the new apartments
           were being constructed.
    (E)   The new apartments were constructed at the
           outset of a trend of increasing numbers of
           people seeking residence in Brewsterville.

GO ON TO THE NEXT PAGE.

7. Politicians often advocate increased overall economic productivity while ignoring its drawbacks. For example, attempting to increase the productivity of a corporation means attempting to increase its profitability, which typically leads to a reduction in the number of workers employed by that corporation. Thus, attempting to increase productivity in the economy as a whole may benefit business owners, but will increase the number of unemployed workers.

The reasoning in the argument is most vulnerable to criticism on the grounds that the argument

(A)   presumes, without providing justification, that increased unemployment is sufficient reason to abandon increased productivity as an economic goal

(B)   fails to justify its presumption that attempting to increase productivity in the economy as a whole would produce results similar to those produced by attempting to increase productivity in a single corporation

(C)   unfairly criticizes politicians in general on the basis of the actions of a few who are unwilling to consider the drawbacks of attempting to increase productivity

(D)   fails to justify its presumption that attempting to increase productivity in the economy as a whole is always more important than the interests of workers or business owners

(E)   fails to address all potential drawbacks and benefits of attempting to increase productivity at a single corporation

8. A good movie reviewer should be able to give favorable reviews of movies that are not to his or her taste. Because movie reviewers have seen so many movies, their tastes are very different from and usually better informed than those of most moviegoers. Yet the function of movie reviewers, as opposed to film critics, is to help people determine which movies they might enjoy seeing, not to help them better appreciate movies.

Which one of the following most accurately expresses the overall conclusion drawn in the argument?

(A)   Movie reviewers' tastes in movies are very different from and usually better informed than those of most moviegoers.

(B)   If a movie reviewer is good, he or she should be able to give favorable reviews of movies that are not to his or her taste.

(C)   The function of a movie reviewer is different from that of a film critic.

(D)   Movie reviewers see many more movies than most moviegoers see.

(E)   The role of movie reviewers is to help people determine which movies they might enjoy seeing, not to help people better appreciate movies.

9. The brain area that enables one to distinguish the different sounds made by a piano tends to be larger in a highly skilled musician than in someone who has rarely, if ever, played a musical instrument. This shows that practicing on, and playing, a musical instrument actually alters brain structure.

Which one of the following most accurately describes a flaw in the argument?

(A)   The argument presumes, without providing justification, that what is true about the brain structures of highly skilled pianists is also true of the brain structures of other highly skilled musicians.

(B)   The argument fails to address the possibility that people who become highly skilled musicians do so, in part, because of the size of a certain area of their brains.

(C)   The argument draws a conclusion about a broad range of phenomena from evidence concerning a much narrower range of phenomena.

(D)   The argument fails to address the possibility that a certain area of the brain is smaller in people who have listened to a lot of music but who have never learned to play a musical instrument than it is in people who have learned to play a musical instrument.

(E)   The argument presumes, without providing justification, that highly skilled musicians practice more than other musicians.

10. Researcher: Overhearing only one side of a cell-phone conversation diverts listeners' attention from whatever they are doing. Hearing only part of a conversation leaves listeners constantly trying to guess what the unheard talker has just said. Listeners' attention is also diverted because cell-phone talkers speak abnormally loudly.

The researcher's statements, if true, most strongly support which one of the following?

(A)   The risk that a driver will cause an accident is increased when the driver is talking on a cell phone.

(B)   When a driver hears a passenger in the driver's vehicle talking on a cell phone, that detracts from the driver's performance.

(C)   Overhearing one side of a conversation on a traditional telephone does not divert listeners' attention from tasks at hand.

(D)   People who overhear one side of a cell-phone conversation inevitably lose track of their thoughts.

(E)   Conversing on a cell phone requires making more guesses about what one's conversational partner means than other forms of conversation do.

GO ON TO THE NEXT PAGE.

11. A new treatment for muscle pain that looked very promising was tested in three separate studies. Although the results were positive, it turned out that all three studies had critical methodological flaws. So the treatment is probably not actually effective.

The flawed nature of the argument above can most effectively be demonstrated by noting that, by parallel reasoning, we could conclude that

(A) since the judges in a baking contest did not have uniform criteria for selecting a winner, the cake that won is probably a bad one

(B) since some people who fish seldom catch any fish, they probably have some reason for fishing other than catching fish

(C) since some foods have very little nutritional value, people who include those foods in their diets are probably malnourished

(D) since all scarves are at least somewhat decorative, it is likely that when scarves were first adopted, they were purely decorative

(E) since all members of the city council have a financial stake in the city's development, any development proposal they make is likely to be motivated purely by self-interest

12. If future improvements to computer simulations of automobile crashes enable computers to provide as much reliable information about the effectiveness of automobile safety features as is provided by actual test crashes, then manufacturers will use far fewer actual test crashes. For the costs of designing and running computer simulations are much lower than those of actual test crashes.

Which one of the following, if true, most strongly supports the argument?

(A) Apart from information about safety features, actual test crashes provide very little information of importance to automobile manufacturers.

(B) It is highly likely that within the next 20 years computer simulations of automobile crashes will be able to provide a greater amount of reliable information about the effectiveness of automobile safety features than can be provided by actual test crashes.

(C) If computer simulations will soon be able to provide more information about the effectiveness of automobile safety features, automobile manufacturers will soon be able to produce safer cars.

(D) The cost per automobile of testing and designing safety features is decreasing and will continue to decrease for the foreseeable future.

(E) For years, the aviation industry has been successfully using computer simulations of airplane crashes to test the effectiveness of safety features of airplane designs.

13. Legislator: My colleague says we should reject this act because it would deter investment. But because in the past she voted for legislation that inhibited investment, this surely is not the real reason she opposes the act. Since she has not revealed her real reason, it must not be very persuasive. So we should vote to approve the act.

The reasoning in the legislator's argument is most vulnerable to the criticism that the argument

(A) treats a personal character trait as if it were evidence of the professional viewpoint of the person having that trait

(B) fails to address the grounds on which the colleague claims the act should be rejected

(C) presumes, without providing justification, that the colleague's opposition to the act is the minority position in the legislature

(D) presumes, without providing justification, that voters will oppose legislation that deters investment

(E) fails to consider that the colleague's opposition to the act may be a response to constituents' wishes

14. A new computer system will not significantly increase an organization's efficiency unless the computer system requires the organization's employees to adopt new, more productive ways of working. The Ministry of Transportation is having a new computer system custom built to fit the ministry's existing ways of working, so

_____.

Which one of the following most logically completes the argument?

(A) the new computer system will not increase the efficiency of the Ministry of Transportation to any appreciable degree

(B) it is likely that the new computer system will not function correctly when it is first installed

(C) the leaders of the Ministry of Transportation must not be concerned with the productivity of the ministry's employees

(D) the new computer system will be worthwhile if it automates many processes that are currently performed manually

(E) it will be easy for employees of the Ministry of Transportation to learn to use the new computer system

GO ON TO THE NEXT PAGE.

15. Columnist: Many car manufacturers trumpet their cars' fuel economy under normal driving conditions. For all three of the cars I have owned, I have been unable to get even close to the fuel economy that manufacturers advertise for cars of those makes. So manufacturers probably inflate those numbers.

The reasoning in the columnist's argument is most vulnerable to criticism on the grounds that the argument

(A) draws a conclusion on the basis of a sample that is too small

(B) presumes, without providing justification, that driving conditions are the same in every geographical region

(C) overlooks the possibility that the source of a cited claim may be biased and hence unreliable

(D) presumes, without providing justification, that car manufacturers knowingly market cars that fail to meet minimum fuel efficiency standards

(E) uses the term "fuel economy" in two different senses

16. Tenants who do not have to pay their own electricity bills do not have a financial incentive to conserve electricity. Thus, if more landlords install individual electricity meters on tenant dwellings so that tenants can be billed for their own use, energy will be conserved as a result.

Which one of the following, if true, most weakens the argument?

(A) Tenants who do not have to pay their own electricity bills generally must compensate by paying more rent.

(B) Many initiatives have been implemented to educate people about how much money they can save through energy conservation.

(C) Landlords who pay for their tenants' electricity have a strong incentive to make sure that the appliances they provide for their tenants are energy efficient.

(D) Some tenant dwellings can only support individual electricity meters if the dwellings are rewired, which would be prohibitively expensive.

(E) Some people conserve energy for reasons that are not related to cost savings.

17. The position that punishment should be proportional to how serious the offense is but that repeat offenders should receive harsher punishments than first-time offenders is unsustainable. It implies that considerations as remote as what an offender did years ago are relevant to the seriousness of an offense. If such remote considerations were relevant, almost every other consideration would be too. But this would make determining the seriousness of an offense so difficult that it would be impossible to apply the proportionality principle.

The statement that considerations as remote as what an offender did years ago are relevant to the seriousness of an offense plays which one of the following roles in the argument?

(A) It is a statement the argument provides grounds to accept and from which the overall conclusion is inferred.

(B) It is a statement inferred from a position the argument seeks to defend.

(C) It is the overall conclusion in favor of which the argument offers evidence.

(D) It is an allegedly untenable consequence of a view rejected in the argument's overall conclusion.

(E) It is a premise offered in support of an intermediate conclusion of the argument.

18. Blogger: Traditionally, newspapers have taken objectivity to be an essential of good journalism. However, today's newer media are more inclined to try to create a stir with openly partisan reporting. This contrast in journalistic standards is best understood in terms of differing business strategies. The newer media outlets need to differentiate themselves in a crowded marketplace. The standard of objectivity developed primarily among newspapers with no serious rivals, so the most important objective was to avoid offending potential readers.

Which one of the following is an assumption required by the blogger's argument?

(A) Journalists at traditional newspapers are just as partisan as journalists who work for newer media outlets.

(B) People prefer objective reporting to partisan reporting that merely reinforces their own partisan leanings.

(C) The newer media outlets are increasing in popularity at the expense of traditional newspapers.

(D) Newspapers have regarded objective reporting as less likely to offend people than openly partisan reporting.

(E) There can be no basis for taking objectivity to be an essential journalistic standard.

GO ON TO THE NEXT PAGE.

19. Any government practice that might facilitate the abuse of power should not be undertaken except in cases in which there is a compelling reason to do so. The keeping of government secrets is one such practice. Though government officials are sometimes justified in keeping secrets, too often they keep secrets for insubstantial reasons, and in so doing they wind up enabling abuses of power. When government officials conceal from the public the very fact that they are keeping a secret, this practice opens up even greater opportunity for abuse.

Which one of the following can be properly inferred from the statements above?

(A) In most cases in which government officials conceal information from the public, they are not justified in doing so.

(B) In those cases in which government officials have a compelling reason to keep a secret, doing so does not facilitate an abuse of power.

(C) A government official who justifiably keeps a secret should not conceal its existence without having a compelling reason to do so.

(D) Government officials who conceal information without a compelling reason are thereby guilty of an abuse of power.

(E) Government officials should keep information secret only if doing so does not make it easier for those officials to abuse their power.

20. According to a theory embraced by some contemporary musicians, music is simply a series of sounds, bereft of meaning. But these musicians, because they understand that their theory is radically nonconformist, encourage audience acceptance by prefacing their performances with explanations of their intentions. Thus, even their own music fails to conform to their theory.

Which one of the following, if assumed, enables the argument's conclusion to be properly drawn?

(A) The human ability to think symbolically and to invest anything with meaning makes it very difficult to create music that has no meaning.

(B) It will be possible for musicians to create music that means nothing only when listeners are able to accept such a theory of music.

(C) The fact that music is distinguishable from a random series of sounds only when it has meaning makes music with meaning more appealing to audiences than music without meaning.

(D) Music that opposes current popular conceptions of music is less likely to be enjoyed by audiences than is music that accords with such conceptions.

(E) Musicians whose music has no meaning do not preface their performances with explanations of their intentions.

21. Evolution does not always optimize survival of an organism. Male moose evolved giant antlers as a way of fighting other males for mates, giving those with the largest antlers an evolutionary advantage. But those antlers also make it harder to escape predators, since they can easily get tangled in trees. All male moose would be better off with antlers half the current size: they would all be less vulnerable to predators, and those with the largest antlers would maintain their relative advantage.

Which one of the following is a technique of reasoning used in the argument?

(A) citing an example to cast doubt on a competing argument

(B) employing an analogy in order to dispute a generalization

(C) challenging a general claim by presenting a counterexample

(D) disputing the relevance of an example thought to support an opposing view

(E) undermining a claim by showing that it is self-contradictory

GO ON TO THE NEXT PAGE.

22. Biologist: When bacteria of a particular species are placed in a test tube that has different areas lit with different colors of light, the bacteria move only into the areas lit with a particular shade of red. The bacteria contain chlorophyll, a chemical that allows them to produce energy more effectively from this color of light than from any other. This suggests that the bacteria detect this color of light by monitoring how much energy their chlorophyll is producing.

Which one of the following, if true, most weakens the biologist's argument?

(A) If the chlorophyll is removed from the bacteria, but the bacteria are otherwise unharmed, they no longer show any tendency to move into the areas lit with the particular shade of red.

(B) The bacteria show little tendency to move into areas containing light in colors other than the particular shade of red, even if their chlorophyll can produce some energy from light in those colors.

(C) The areas of the test tube lit with the particular shade of red favored by the bacteria are no warmer, on average, than areas lit with other colors.

(D) The bacteria show no tendency to move into areas lit with blue even when those areas are lit so brightly that the bacteria's chlorophyll produces as much energy in those areas as it does in the red areas.

(E) There are species of bacteria that do not contain chlorophyll but do move into areas lit with particular colors when placed in a test tube lit with different colors in different places.

23. If a piece of legislation is the result of negotiation and compromise between competing interest groups, it will not satisfy any of those groups. So, we can see that the recently enacted trade agreement represents a series of compromises among the various interest groups that are concerned with it, because all of those groups are clearly unhappy with it.

Which one of the following most accurately describes a logical flaw in the argument?

(A) It draws a conclusion that is merely a disguised restatement of one of its premises.

(B) It concludes that a condition is necessary for a certain result merely from the claim that the condition leads to that result.

(C) It relies on understanding a key term in a quite different way in the conclusion from the way that term is understood in the premises.

(D) It takes for granted that no piece of legislation can ever satisfy all competing interest groups.

(E) It bases a conclusion about a particular case on a general principle that concerns a different kind of case.

GO ON TO THE NEXT PAGE.

24. After a nuclear power plant accident, researchers found radioactive isotopes of iodine, tellurium, and cesium—but no heavy isotopes—in the atmosphere downwind. This material came either from spent fuel rods or from the plant's core. Spent fuel rods never contain significant quantities of tellurium isotopes. Radioactive material ejected into the atmosphere directly from the core would include heavy isotopes. After the accident, steam, which may have been in contact with the core, was released from the plant. The core contains iodine, tellurium, and cesium isotopes, which are easily dissolved by steam.

Of the following statements, which one is most strongly supported by the information above?

(A) Radioactive material ejected into the environment directly from a nuclear power plant's core would not include tellurium isotopes.

(B) The radioactive material detected by the researchers was carried into the atmosphere by the steam that was released from the plant.

(C) The nuclear power plant's spent fuel rods were not damaged.

(D) The researchers found some radioactive material from spent fuel rods as well as some material that was ejected into the atmosphere directly from the plant's core.

(E) Spent fuel rods do not contain heavy isotopes in significant quantities.

25. If ecology and the physical sciences were evaluated by the same criteria, ecology would fail to be a successful science because it cannot be captured by a set of simple laws. But ecology is a successful science, although of a different sort from the physical sciences. Therefore, it clearly is not being evaluated by means of the criteria used to evaluate the physical sciences.

Which one of the following arguments is most similar in its reasoning to the argument above?

(A) If sales taxes are increased, then either the price of woodchips will go up and the consumer will have to pay more for them, or the woodchip industry will disappear. But the market cannot bear an increase in the price of woodchips, so the woodchip industry will disappear.

(B) If this gallery could borrow some of Matisse's early works, then, together with its own permanent collection of Matisse, the gallery could have the largest exhibition of Matisse ever. But there is no demand for larger exhibitions of Matisse's work. Therefore, no gallery will be inclined to lend their early Matisses to this gallery.

(C) If cars of the future are made of lighter and stronger materials, then the number of fatalities due to driving accidents will be drastically reduced. It is obvious that cars will be made of lighter and stronger materials in the future. Therefore, the number of fatalities due to driving accidents will be drastically reduced.

(D) If physicists attempted research in the social sciences, they would probably be as successful in those areas as researchers who restrict their concentration to the social sciences. However, physicists rarely attempt social science research. Therefore, physicists are not among the most successful researchers in the social sciences.

(E) If any economic theory were an adequate description of the principles according to which economies operate, then it would be possible to make accurate economic forecasts. But accurate economic forecasts cannot be made. Therefore, no economic theory is an adequate description of the principles according to which economies operate.

S T O P

IF YOU FINISH BEFORE TIME IS CALLED, YOU MAY CHECK YOUR WORK ON THIS SECTION ONLY.
DO NOT WORK ON ANY OTHER SECTION IN THE TEST.

Acknowledgment is made to the following sources from which material has been adapted for use in this test:

Aaron Bernstein, "A Minimum-Wage Argument You Haven't Heard Before." ©1996 by the McGraw-Hill Companies.

William J. Broad, "Theory of Plate Movement Marks Zones That Breed Frequent Quakes." ©1995 by The New York Times.

Norbert Juergens, "The Biological Underpinnings of Namib Desert Fairy Circles" in *Science*. ©2013 by American Association for the Advancement of Science.

Mark D. Rosen, "Was *Shelley v. Kraemer* Incorrectly Decided? Some New Answers" in *California Law Review*. ©2007 by California Law Review, Inc.

William Speed Weed, "First to Ride." ©March 2002 by the Walt Disney Company.

Computing Your Score

Directions:

1. Use the Answer Key on the next page to check your answers.

2. Use the Scoring Worksheet below to compute your raw score.

3. Use the Score Conversion Chart to convert your raw score into the 120–180 scale.*

Scoring Worksheet

1. Enter the number of questions you answered correctly in each section.

	Number Correct
SECTION I	_____
SECTION II	_____
SECTION III	_____
SECTION IV	Unscored

2. Enter the sum here: _____
   This is your Raw Score.

Score Conversion Chart

Use the table below to convert your raw score to the corresponding 120–180 scaled score for PrepTest 151.

Raw Score	Scaled Score	Raw Score	Scaled Score
78	180	38	146
77	180	37	145
76	180	36	144
75	178	35	143
74	176	34	143
73	175	33	142
72	173	32	141
71	172	31	140
70	171	30	140
69	170	29	139
68	169	28	138
67	168	27	137
66	167	26	136
65	166	25	135
64	165	24	134
63	164	23	133
62	163	22	132
61	162	21	131
60	162	20	130
59	161	19	129
58	160	18	128
57	159	17	126
56	159	16	125
55	158	15	123
54	157	14	122
53	156	13	121
52	156	12	120
51	155	11	120
50	154	10	120
49	154	9	120
48	153	8	120
47	152	7	120
46	152	6	120
45	151	5	120
44	150	4	120
43	149	3	120
42	149	2	120
41	148	1	120
40	147	0	120
39	146		

*Scores are reported on a 120–180 score scale, with 120 being the lowest possible score and 180 being the highest possible score.

Answer Key

Question	Section I	Section II	Section III	Section IV*
1	A	A	B	E
2	B	B	A	C
3	E	D	B	A
4	C	C	B	E
5	B	B	D	D
6	D	B	A	E
7	C	E	E	B
8	B	C	A	B
9	E	A	C	B
10	C	A	C	B
11	D	D	C	A
12	A	B	B	A
13	D	E	A	B
14	A	C	D	A
15	D	E	C	A
16	C	A	E	C
17	E	C	C	D
18	D	A	E	D
19	A	B	E	C
20	E	B	D	E
21	B	A	E	C
22	B	B	E	D
23	D	C	A	B
24	C	A	B	B
25	E	D	C	E
26	C	D		
27	E			

*Section IV is unscored. The number of items answered correctly in Section IV should not be added to the raw score.

What You Need for Your Journey, from Prelaw Through Practice

At LSAC, we believe everyone should have the support they need to succeed on their journey to law school and beyond.

Tens of thousands of law school candidates already **rely on LawHub** and its growing portfolio of information and resources to support that journey from prelaw to practice. From LSAT preparation in the authentic test interface to education programs designed to prepare you for the modern law practice, discover what LawHub has to offer to help you develop the confidence and skills needed to achieve your academic and professional goals.

Sign up today at **LSAC.org**.

Connect with Us

 @LawSchoolAdmissionCouncil

 @LSAC_Official

 @official_lsac

 Law School Admission Council

 Law School Admission Council

General Directions for the LSAT Answer Sheet

This test consists of four multiple-choice sections. The proctor will tell you when to begin and end each section. If you finish a section before time is called, you may check your work on that section **only**; do not turn to any other section of the test book and do not work on any other section either in the test book or on the answer sheet.

Answer spaces for each question are lettered to correspond with the letters of the potential answers to each question in the test book. After you have decided which of the answers is correct, mark the corresponding letter on the answer sheet. Give only one answer to each question. If you change an answer, be sure that all previous marks are **erased completely**. Incomplete erasures may be interpreted as intended answers. **All your answers must be marked on the answer sheet unless you have been specifically approved by Accommodated Testing to mark your answers in your test book.**

There may be more question numbers on the answer sheet than there are questions in a section. Do not be concerned, but be certain that the section and number of the question you are answering matches the answer sheet section and question number. Additional answer spaces in any answer sheet section should be left blank. Begin your next section in the number one answer space for that section.

MARKING INSTRUCTIONS

MARK ONE AND ONLY ONE ANSWER CHOICE TO EACH QUESTION. BE SURE TO FILL IN COMPLETELY THE SPACE FOR YOUR INTENDED ANSWER CHOICE USING A NO. 2 OR HB PENCIL. FAILURE TO DO SO INCREASES THE POSSIBILITY OF INACCURATE MACHINE SCORING. IF YOU ERASE, DO SO COMPLETELY. MAKE NO STRAY MARKS. EXAMPLES OF VALID AND INVALID MARKS ARE GIVEN BELOW.

VALID MARK	Ⓐ Ⓑ ● Ⓓ Ⓔ	STRAY MARKS	◖✓ Ⓑ Ⓒ Ⓓ Ⓔ
TOO LIGHT	Ⓐ Ⓑ Ⓒ Ⓓ Ⓔ	MULTIPLE MARKS	Ⓐ Ⓑ ● ● Ⓔ
INCOMPLETE	Ⓐ Ⓑ ◖ Ⓓ Ⓔ		

YOU MAY FIND MORE ANSWER SPACES THAN YOU NEED; LEAVE THE EXTRA SPACES BLANK.

LSAT Answer Sheet

Instructions for completing these items are at the back of your LSAT test book.

1. Name (Print)

Last   First   MI

2. LSAC Account Number L ⬚⬚⬚⬚⬚⬚⬚⬚

Section 1	Section 2	Section 3	Section 4
1 (A)(B)(C)(D)(E)	1 (A)(B)(C)(D)(E)	1 (A)(B)(C)(D)(E)	1 (A)(B)(C)(D)(E)
2 (A)(B)(C)(D)(E)	2 (A)(B)(C)(D)(E)	2 (A)(B)(C)(D)(E)	2 (A)(B)(C)(D)(E)
3 (A)(B)(C)(D)(E)	3 (A)(B)(C)(D)(E)	3 (A)(B)(C)(D)(E)	3 (A)(B)(C)(D)(E)
4 (A)(B)(C)(D)(E)	4 (A)(B)(C)(D)(E)	4 (A)(B)(C)(D)(E)	4 (A)(B)(C)(D)(E)
5 (A)(B)(C)(D)(E)	5 (A)(B)(C)(D)(E)	5 (A)(B)(C)(D)(E)	5 (A)(B)(C)(D)(E)
6 (A)(B)(C)(D)(E)	6 (A)(B)(C)(D)(E)	6 (A)(B)(C)(D)(E)	6 (A)(B)(C)(D)(E)
7 (A)(B)(C)(D)(E)	7 (A)(B)(C)(D)(E)	7 (A)(B)(C)(D)(E)	7 (A)(B)(C)(D)(E)
8 (A)(B)(C)(D)(E)	8 (A)(B)(C)(D)(E)	8 (A)(B)(C)(D)(E)	8 (A)(B)(C)(D)(E)
9 (A)(B)(C)(D)(E)	9 (A)(B)(C)(D)(E)	9 (A)(B)(C)(D)(E)	9 (A)(B)(C)(D)(E)
10 (A)(B)(C)(D)(E)	10 (A)(B)(C)(D)(E)	10 (A)(B)(C)(D)(E)	10 (A)(B)(C)(D)(E)
11 (A)(B)(C)(D)(E)	11 (A)(B)(C)(D)(E)	11 (A)(B)(C)(D)(E)	11 (A)(B)(C)(D)(E)
12 (A)(B)(C)(D)(E)	12 (A)(B)(C)(D)(E)	12 (A)(B)(C)(D)(E)	12 (A)(B)(C)(D)(E)
13 (A)(B)(C)(D)(E)	13 (A)(B)(C)(D)(E)	13 (A)(B)(C)(D)(E)	13 (A)(B)(C)(D)(E)
14 (A)(B)(C)(D)(E)	14 (A)(B)(C)(D)(E)	14 (A)(B)(C)(D)(E)	14 (A)(B)(C)(D)(E)
15 (A)(B)(C)(D)(E)	15 (A)(B)(C)(D)(E)	15 (A)(B)(C)(D)(E)	15 (A)(B)(C)(D)(E)
16 (A)(B)(C)(D)(E)	16 (A)(B)(C)(D)(E)	16 (A)(B)(C)(D)(E)	16 (A)(B)(C)(D)(E)
17 (A)(B)(C)(D)(E)	17 (A)(B)(C)(D)(E)	17 (A)(B)(C)(D)(E)	17 (A)(B)(C)(D)(E)
18 (A)(B)(C)(D)(E)	18 (A)(B)(C)(D)(E)	18 (A)(B)(C)(D)(E)	18 (A)(B)(C)(D)(E)
19 (A)(B)(C)(D)(E)	19 (A)(B)(C)(D)(E)	19 (A)(B)(C)(D)(E)	19 (A)(B)(C)(D)(E)
20 (A)(B)(C)(D)(E)	20 (A)(B)(C)(D)(E)	20 (A)(B)(C)(D)(E)	20 (A)(B)(C)(D)(E)
21 (A)(B)(C)(D)(E)	21 (A)(B)(C)(D)(E)	21 (A)(B)(C)(D)(E)	21 (A)(B)(C)(D)(E)
22 (A)(B)(C)(D)(E)	22 (A)(B)(C)(D)(E)	22 (A)(B)(C)(D)(E)	22 (A)(B)(C)(D)(E)
23 (A)(B)(C)(D)(E)	23 (A)(B)(C)(D)(E)	23 (A)(B)(C)(D)(E)	23 (A)(B)(C)(D)(E)
24 (A)(B)(C)(D)(E)	24 (A)(B)(C)(D)(E)	24 (A)(B)(C)(D)(E)	24 (A)(B)(C)(D)(E)
25 (A)(B)(C)(D)(E)	25 (A)(B)(C)(D)(E)	25 (A)(B)(C)(D)(E)	25 (A)(B)(C)(D)(E)
26 (A)(B)(C)(D)(E)	26 (A)(B)(C)(D)(E)	26 (A)(B)(C)(D)(E)	26 (A)(B)(C)(D)(E)
27 (A)(B)(C)(D)(E)	27 (A)(B)(C)(D)(E)	27 (A)(B)(C)(D)(E)	27 (A)(B)(C)(D)(E)
28 (A)(B)(C)(D)(E)	28 (A)(B)(C)(D)(E)	28 (A)(B)(C)(D)(E)	28 (A)(B)(C)(D)(E)
29 (A)(B)(C)(D)(E)	29 (A)(B)(C)(D)(E)	29 (A)(B)(C)(D)(E)	29 (A)(B)(C)(D)(E)
30 (A)(B)(C)(D)(E)	30 (A)(B)(C)(D)(E)	30 (A)(B)(C)(D)(E)	30 (A)(B)(C)(D)(E)

LSAT Answer Sheet

Instructions for completing these items are at the back of your LSAT test book.

1. Name (Print)

Last   First   MI

2. LSAC Account Number L

Section 1	Section 2	Section 3	Section 4
1 (A)(B)(C)(D)(E)	1 (A)(B)(C)(D)(E)	1 (A)(B)(C)(D)(E)	1 (A)(B)(C)(D)(E)
2 (A)(B)(C)(D)(E)	2 (A)(B)(C)(D)(E)	2 (A)(B)(C)(D)(E)	2 (A)(B)(C)(D)(E)
3 (A)(B)(C)(D)(E)	3 (A)(B)(C)(D)(E)	3 (A)(B)(C)(D)(E)	3 (A)(B)(C)(D)(E)
4 (A)(B)(C)(D)(E)	4 (A)(B)(C)(D)(E)	4 (A)(B)(C)(D)(E)	4 (A)(B)(C)(D)(E)
5 (A)(B)(C)(D)(E)	5 (A)(B)(C)(D)(E)	5 (A)(B)(C)(D)(E)	5 (A)(B)(C)(D)(E)
6 (A)(B)(C)(D)(E)	6 (A)(B)(C)(D)(E)	6 (A)(B)(C)(D)(E)	6 (A)(B)(C)(D)(E)
7 (A)(B)(C)(D)(E)	7 (A)(B)(C)(D)(E)	7 (A)(B)(C)(D)(E)	7 (A)(B)(C)(D)(E)
8 (A)(B)(C)(D)(E)	8 (A)(B)(C)(D)(E)	8 (A)(B)(C)(D)(E)	8 (A)(B)(C)(D)(E)
9 (A)(B)(C)(D)(E)	9 (A)(B)(C)(D)(E)	9 (A)(B)(C)(D)(E)	9 (A)(B)(C)(D)(E)
10 (A)(B)(C)(D)(E)	10 (A)(B)(C)(D)(E)	10 (A)(B)(C)(D)(E)	10 (A)(B)(C)(D)(E)
11 (A)(B)(C)(D)(E)	11 (A)(B)(C)(D)(E)	11 (A)(B)(C)(D)(E)	11 (A)(B)(C)(D)(E)
12 (A)(B)(C)(D)(E)	12 (A)(B)(C)(D)(E)	12 (A)(B)(C)(D)(E)	12 (A)(B)(C)(D)(E)
13 (A)(B)(C)(D)(E)	13 (A)(B)(C)(D)(E)	13 (A)(B)(C)(D)(E)	13 (A)(B)(C)(D)(E)
14 (A)(B)(C)(D)(E)	14 (A)(B)(C)(D)(E)	14 (A)(B)(C)(D)(E)	14 (A)(B)(C)(D)(E)
15 (A)(B)(C)(D)(E)	15 (A)(B)(C)(D)(E)	15 (A)(B)(C)(D)(E)	15 (A)(B)(C)(D)(E)
16 (A)(B)(C)(D)(E)	16 (A)(B)(C)(D)(E)	16 (A)(B)(C)(D)(E)	16 (A)(B)(C)(D)(E)
17 (A)(B)(C)(D)(E)	17 (A)(B)(C)(D)(E)	17 (A)(B)(C)(D)(E)	17 (A)(B)(C)(D)(E)
18 (A)(B)(C)(D)(E)	18 (A)(B)(C)(D)(E)	18 (A)(B)(C)(D)(E)	18 (A)(B)(C)(D)(E)
19 (A)(B)(C)(D)(E)	19 (A)(B)(C)(D)(E)	19 (A)(B)(C)(D)(E)	19 (A)(B)(C)(D)(E)
20 (A)(B)(C)(D)(E)	20 (A)(B)(C)(D)(E)	20 (A)(B)(C)(D)(E)	20 (A)(B)(C)(D)(E)
21 (A)(B)(C)(D)(E)	21 (A)(B)(C)(D)(E)	21 (A)(B)(C)(D)(E)	21 (A)(B)(C)(D)(E)
22 (A)(B)(C)(D)(E)	22 (A)(B)(C)(D)(E)	22 (A)(B)(C)(D)(E)	22 (A)(B)(C)(D)(E)
23 (A)(B)(C)(D)(E)	23 (A)(B)(C)(D)(E)	23 (A)(B)(C)(D)(E)	23 (A)(B)(C)(D)(E)
24 (A)(B)(C)(D)(E)	24 (A)(B)(C)(D)(E)	24 (A)(B)(C)(D)(E)	24 (A)(B)(C)(D)(E)
25 (A)(B)(C)(D)(E)	25 (A)(B)(C)(D)(E)	25 (A)(B)(C)(D)(E)	25 (A)(B)(C)(D)(E)
26 (A)(B)(C)(D)(E)	26 (A)(B)(C)(D)(E)	26 (A)(B)(C)(D)(E)	26 (A)(B)(C)(D)(E)
27 (A)(B)(C)(D)(E)	27 (A)(B)(C)(D)(E)	27 (A)(B)(C)(D)(E)	27 (A)(B)(C)(D)(E)
28 (A)(B)(C)(D)(E)	28 (A)(B)(C)(D)(E)	28 (A)(B)(C)(D)(E)	28 (A)(B)(C)(D)(E)
29 (A)(B)(C)(D)(E)	29 (A)(B)(C)(D)(E)	29 (A)(B)(C)(D)(E)	29 (A)(B)(C)(D)(E)
30 (A)(B)(C)(D)(E)	30 (A)(B)(C)(D)(E)	30 (A)(B)(C)(D)(E)	30 (A)(B)(C)(D)(E)

LSAT Answer Sheet

Instructions for completing these items are at the back of your LSAT test book.

1. Name (Print)

Last   First   MI

2. LSAC Account Number L ☐☐☐☐☐☐☐

Section 1	Section 2	Section 3	Section 4
1 Ⓐ Ⓑ Ⓒ Ⓓ Ⓔ	1 Ⓐ Ⓑ Ⓒ Ⓓ Ⓔ	1 Ⓐ Ⓑ Ⓒ Ⓓ Ⓔ	1 Ⓐ Ⓑ Ⓒ Ⓓ Ⓔ
2 Ⓐ Ⓑ Ⓒ Ⓓ Ⓔ	2 Ⓐ Ⓑ Ⓒ Ⓓ Ⓔ	2 Ⓐ Ⓑ Ⓒ Ⓓ Ⓔ	2 Ⓐ Ⓑ Ⓒ Ⓓ Ⓔ
3 Ⓐ Ⓑ Ⓒ Ⓓ Ⓔ	3 Ⓐ Ⓑ Ⓒ Ⓓ Ⓔ	3 Ⓐ Ⓑ Ⓒ Ⓓ Ⓔ	3 Ⓐ Ⓑ Ⓒ Ⓓ Ⓔ
4 Ⓐ Ⓑ Ⓒ Ⓓ Ⓔ	4 Ⓐ Ⓑ Ⓒ Ⓓ Ⓔ	4 Ⓐ Ⓑ Ⓒ Ⓓ Ⓔ	4 Ⓐ Ⓑ Ⓒ Ⓓ Ⓔ
5 Ⓐ Ⓑ Ⓒ Ⓓ Ⓔ	5 Ⓐ Ⓑ Ⓒ Ⓓ Ⓔ	5 Ⓐ Ⓑ Ⓒ Ⓓ Ⓔ	5 Ⓐ Ⓑ Ⓒ Ⓓ Ⓔ
6 Ⓐ Ⓑ Ⓒ Ⓓ Ⓔ	6 Ⓐ Ⓑ Ⓒ Ⓓ Ⓔ	6 Ⓐ Ⓑ Ⓒ Ⓓ Ⓔ	6 Ⓐ Ⓑ Ⓒ Ⓓ Ⓔ
7 Ⓐ Ⓑ Ⓒ Ⓓ Ⓔ	7 Ⓐ Ⓑ Ⓒ Ⓓ Ⓔ	7 Ⓐ Ⓑ Ⓒ Ⓓ Ⓔ	7 Ⓐ Ⓑ Ⓒ Ⓓ Ⓔ
8 Ⓐ Ⓑ Ⓒ Ⓓ Ⓔ	8 Ⓐ Ⓑ Ⓒ Ⓓ Ⓔ	8 Ⓐ Ⓑ Ⓒ Ⓓ Ⓔ	8 Ⓐ Ⓑ Ⓒ Ⓓ Ⓔ
9 Ⓐ Ⓑ Ⓒ Ⓓ Ⓔ	9 Ⓐ Ⓑ Ⓒ Ⓓ Ⓔ	9 Ⓐ Ⓑ Ⓒ Ⓓ Ⓔ	9 Ⓐ Ⓑ Ⓒ Ⓓ Ⓔ
10 Ⓐ Ⓑ Ⓒ Ⓓ Ⓔ	10 Ⓐ Ⓑ Ⓒ Ⓓ Ⓔ	10 Ⓐ Ⓑ Ⓒ Ⓓ Ⓔ	10 Ⓐ Ⓑ Ⓒ Ⓓ Ⓔ
11 Ⓐ Ⓑ Ⓒ Ⓓ Ⓔ	11 Ⓐ Ⓑ Ⓒ Ⓓ Ⓔ	11 Ⓐ Ⓑ Ⓒ Ⓓ Ⓔ	11 Ⓐ Ⓑ Ⓒ Ⓓ Ⓔ
12 Ⓐ Ⓑ Ⓒ Ⓓ Ⓔ	12 Ⓐ Ⓑ Ⓒ Ⓓ Ⓔ	12 Ⓐ Ⓑ Ⓒ Ⓓ Ⓔ	12 Ⓐ Ⓑ Ⓒ Ⓓ Ⓔ
13 Ⓐ Ⓑ Ⓒ Ⓓ Ⓔ	13 Ⓐ Ⓑ Ⓒ Ⓓ Ⓔ	13 Ⓐ Ⓑ Ⓒ Ⓓ Ⓔ	13 Ⓐ Ⓑ Ⓒ Ⓓ Ⓔ
14 Ⓐ Ⓑ Ⓒ Ⓓ Ⓔ	14 Ⓐ Ⓑ Ⓒ Ⓓ Ⓔ	14 Ⓐ Ⓑ Ⓒ Ⓓ Ⓔ	14 Ⓐ Ⓑ Ⓒ Ⓓ Ⓔ
15 Ⓐ Ⓑ Ⓒ Ⓓ Ⓔ	15 Ⓐ Ⓑ Ⓒ Ⓓ Ⓔ	15 Ⓐ Ⓑ Ⓒ Ⓓ Ⓔ	15 Ⓐ Ⓑ Ⓒ Ⓓ Ⓔ
16 Ⓐ Ⓑ Ⓒ Ⓓ Ⓔ	16 Ⓐ Ⓑ Ⓒ Ⓓ Ⓔ	16 Ⓐ Ⓑ Ⓒ Ⓓ Ⓔ	16 Ⓐ Ⓑ Ⓒ Ⓓ Ⓔ
17 Ⓐ Ⓑ Ⓒ Ⓓ Ⓔ	17 Ⓐ Ⓑ Ⓒ Ⓓ Ⓔ	17 Ⓐ Ⓑ Ⓒ Ⓓ Ⓔ	17 Ⓐ Ⓑ Ⓒ Ⓓ Ⓔ
18 Ⓐ Ⓑ Ⓒ Ⓓ Ⓔ	18 Ⓐ Ⓑ Ⓒ Ⓓ Ⓔ	18 Ⓐ Ⓑ Ⓒ Ⓓ Ⓔ	18 Ⓐ Ⓑ Ⓒ Ⓓ Ⓔ
19 Ⓐ Ⓑ Ⓒ Ⓓ Ⓔ	19 Ⓐ Ⓑ Ⓒ Ⓓ Ⓔ	19 Ⓐ Ⓑ Ⓒ Ⓓ Ⓔ	19 Ⓐ Ⓑ Ⓒ Ⓓ Ⓔ
20 Ⓐ Ⓑ Ⓒ Ⓓ Ⓔ	20 Ⓐ Ⓑ Ⓒ Ⓓ Ⓔ	20 Ⓐ Ⓑ Ⓒ Ⓓ Ⓔ	20 Ⓐ Ⓑ Ⓒ Ⓓ Ⓔ
21 Ⓐ Ⓑ Ⓒ Ⓓ Ⓔ	21 Ⓐ Ⓑ Ⓒ Ⓓ Ⓔ	21 Ⓐ Ⓑ Ⓒ Ⓓ Ⓔ	21 Ⓐ Ⓑ Ⓒ Ⓓ Ⓔ
22 Ⓐ Ⓑ Ⓒ Ⓓ Ⓔ	22 Ⓐ Ⓑ Ⓒ Ⓓ Ⓔ	22 Ⓐ Ⓑ Ⓒ Ⓓ Ⓔ	22 Ⓐ Ⓑ Ⓒ Ⓓ Ⓔ
23 Ⓐ Ⓑ Ⓒ Ⓓ Ⓔ	23 Ⓐ Ⓑ Ⓒ Ⓓ Ⓔ	23 Ⓐ Ⓑ Ⓒ Ⓓ Ⓔ	23 Ⓐ Ⓑ Ⓒ Ⓓ Ⓔ
24 Ⓐ Ⓑ Ⓒ Ⓓ Ⓔ	24 Ⓐ Ⓑ Ⓒ Ⓓ Ⓔ	24 Ⓐ Ⓑ Ⓒ Ⓓ Ⓔ	24 Ⓐ Ⓑ Ⓒ Ⓓ Ⓔ
25 Ⓐ Ⓑ Ⓒ Ⓓ Ⓔ	25 Ⓐ Ⓑ Ⓒ Ⓓ Ⓔ	25 Ⓐ Ⓑ Ⓒ Ⓓ Ⓔ	25 Ⓐ Ⓑ Ⓒ Ⓓ Ⓔ
26 Ⓐ Ⓑ Ⓒ Ⓓ Ⓔ	26 Ⓐ Ⓑ Ⓒ Ⓓ Ⓔ	26 Ⓐ Ⓑ Ⓒ Ⓓ Ⓔ	26 Ⓐ Ⓑ Ⓒ Ⓓ Ⓔ
27 Ⓐ Ⓑ Ⓒ Ⓓ Ⓔ	27 Ⓐ Ⓑ Ⓒ Ⓓ Ⓔ	27 Ⓐ Ⓑ Ⓒ Ⓓ Ⓔ	27 Ⓐ Ⓑ Ⓒ Ⓓ Ⓔ
28 Ⓐ Ⓑ Ⓒ Ⓓ Ⓔ	28 Ⓐ Ⓑ Ⓒ Ⓓ Ⓔ	28 Ⓐ Ⓑ Ⓒ Ⓓ Ⓔ	28 Ⓐ Ⓑ Ⓒ Ⓓ Ⓔ
29 Ⓐ Ⓑ Ⓒ Ⓓ Ⓔ	29 Ⓐ Ⓑ Ⓒ Ⓓ Ⓔ	29 Ⓐ Ⓑ Ⓒ Ⓓ Ⓔ	29 Ⓐ Ⓑ Ⓒ Ⓓ Ⓔ
30 Ⓐ Ⓑ Ⓒ Ⓓ Ⓔ	30 Ⓐ Ⓑ Ⓒ Ⓓ Ⓔ	30 Ⓐ Ⓑ Ⓒ Ⓓ Ⓔ	30 Ⓐ Ⓑ Ⓒ Ⓓ Ⓔ

LSAT Answer Sheet

Instructions for completing these items are at the back of your LSAT test book.

1. Name (Print)

Last   First   MI

2. LSAC Account Number   L ☐☐☐☐☐☐☐☐

Section 1	Section 2	Section 3	Section 4
1 Ⓐ Ⓑ Ⓒ Ⓓ Ⓔ	1 Ⓐ Ⓑ Ⓒ Ⓓ Ⓔ	1 Ⓐ Ⓑ Ⓒ Ⓓ Ⓔ	1 Ⓐ Ⓑ Ⓒ Ⓓ Ⓔ
2 Ⓐ Ⓑ Ⓒ Ⓓ Ⓔ	2 Ⓐ Ⓑ Ⓒ Ⓓ Ⓔ	2 Ⓐ Ⓑ Ⓒ Ⓓ Ⓔ	2 Ⓐ Ⓑ Ⓒ Ⓓ Ⓔ
3 Ⓐ Ⓑ Ⓒ Ⓓ Ⓔ	3 Ⓐ Ⓑ Ⓒ Ⓓ Ⓔ	3 Ⓐ Ⓑ Ⓒ Ⓓ Ⓔ	3 Ⓐ Ⓑ Ⓒ Ⓓ Ⓔ
4 Ⓐ Ⓑ Ⓒ Ⓓ Ⓔ	4 Ⓐ Ⓑ Ⓒ Ⓓ Ⓔ	4 Ⓐ Ⓑ Ⓒ Ⓓ Ⓔ	4 Ⓐ Ⓑ Ⓒ Ⓓ Ⓔ
5 Ⓐ Ⓑ Ⓒ Ⓓ Ⓔ	5 Ⓐ Ⓑ Ⓒ Ⓓ Ⓔ	5 Ⓐ Ⓑ Ⓒ Ⓓ Ⓔ	5 Ⓐ Ⓑ Ⓒ Ⓓ Ⓔ
6 Ⓐ Ⓑ Ⓒ Ⓓ Ⓔ	6 Ⓐ Ⓑ Ⓒ Ⓓ Ⓔ	6 Ⓐ Ⓑ Ⓒ Ⓓ Ⓔ	6 Ⓐ Ⓑ Ⓒ Ⓓ Ⓔ
7 Ⓐ Ⓑ Ⓒ Ⓓ Ⓔ	7 Ⓐ Ⓑ Ⓒ Ⓓ Ⓔ	7 Ⓐ Ⓑ Ⓒ Ⓓ Ⓔ	7 Ⓐ Ⓑ Ⓒ Ⓓ Ⓔ
8 Ⓐ Ⓑ Ⓒ Ⓓ Ⓔ	8 Ⓐ Ⓑ Ⓒ Ⓓ Ⓔ	8 Ⓐ Ⓑ Ⓒ Ⓓ Ⓔ	8 Ⓐ Ⓑ Ⓒ Ⓓ Ⓔ
9 Ⓐ Ⓑ Ⓒ Ⓓ Ⓔ	9 Ⓐ Ⓑ Ⓒ Ⓓ Ⓔ	9 Ⓐ Ⓑ Ⓒ Ⓓ Ⓔ	9 Ⓐ Ⓑ Ⓒ Ⓓ Ⓔ
10 Ⓐ Ⓑ Ⓒ Ⓓ Ⓔ	10 Ⓐ Ⓑ Ⓒ Ⓓ Ⓔ	10 Ⓐ Ⓑ Ⓒ Ⓓ Ⓔ	10 Ⓐ Ⓑ Ⓒ Ⓓ Ⓔ
11 Ⓐ Ⓑ Ⓒ Ⓓ Ⓔ	11 Ⓐ Ⓑ Ⓒ Ⓓ Ⓔ	11 Ⓐ Ⓑ Ⓒ Ⓓ Ⓔ	11 Ⓐ Ⓑ Ⓒ Ⓓ Ⓔ
12 Ⓐ Ⓑ Ⓒ Ⓓ Ⓔ	12 Ⓐ Ⓑ Ⓒ Ⓓ Ⓔ	12 Ⓐ Ⓑ Ⓒ Ⓓ Ⓔ	12 Ⓐ Ⓑ Ⓒ Ⓓ Ⓔ
13 Ⓐ Ⓑ Ⓒ Ⓓ Ⓔ	13 Ⓐ Ⓑ Ⓒ Ⓓ Ⓔ	13 Ⓐ Ⓑ Ⓒ Ⓓ Ⓔ	13 Ⓐ Ⓑ Ⓒ Ⓓ Ⓔ
14 Ⓐ Ⓑ Ⓒ Ⓓ Ⓔ	14 Ⓐ Ⓑ Ⓒ Ⓓ Ⓔ	14 Ⓐ Ⓑ Ⓒ Ⓓ Ⓔ	14 Ⓐ Ⓑ Ⓒ Ⓓ Ⓔ
15 Ⓐ Ⓑ Ⓒ Ⓓ Ⓔ	15 Ⓐ Ⓑ Ⓒ Ⓓ Ⓔ	15 Ⓐ Ⓑ Ⓒ Ⓓ Ⓔ	15 Ⓐ Ⓑ Ⓒ Ⓓ Ⓔ
16 Ⓐ Ⓑ Ⓒ Ⓓ Ⓔ	16 Ⓐ Ⓑ Ⓒ Ⓓ Ⓔ	16 Ⓐ Ⓑ Ⓒ Ⓓ Ⓔ	16 Ⓐ Ⓑ Ⓒ Ⓓ Ⓔ
17 Ⓐ Ⓑ Ⓒ Ⓓ Ⓔ	17 Ⓐ Ⓑ Ⓒ Ⓓ Ⓔ	17 Ⓐ Ⓑ Ⓒ Ⓓ Ⓔ	17 Ⓐ Ⓑ Ⓒ Ⓓ Ⓔ
18 Ⓐ Ⓑ Ⓒ Ⓓ Ⓔ	18 Ⓐ Ⓑ Ⓒ Ⓓ Ⓔ	18 Ⓐ Ⓑ Ⓒ Ⓓ Ⓔ	18 Ⓐ Ⓑ Ⓒ Ⓓ Ⓔ
19 Ⓐ Ⓑ Ⓒ Ⓓ Ⓔ	19 Ⓐ Ⓑ Ⓒ Ⓓ Ⓔ	19 Ⓐ Ⓑ Ⓒ Ⓓ Ⓔ	19 Ⓐ Ⓑ Ⓒ Ⓓ Ⓔ
20 Ⓐ Ⓑ Ⓒ Ⓓ Ⓔ	20 Ⓐ Ⓑ Ⓒ Ⓓ Ⓔ	20 Ⓐ Ⓑ Ⓒ Ⓓ Ⓔ	20 Ⓐ Ⓑ Ⓒ Ⓓ Ⓔ
21 Ⓐ Ⓑ Ⓒ Ⓓ Ⓔ	21 Ⓐ Ⓑ Ⓒ Ⓓ Ⓔ	21 Ⓐ Ⓑ Ⓒ Ⓓ Ⓔ	21 Ⓐ Ⓑ Ⓒ Ⓓ Ⓔ
22 Ⓐ Ⓑ Ⓒ Ⓓ Ⓔ	22 Ⓐ Ⓑ Ⓒ Ⓓ Ⓔ	22 Ⓐ Ⓑ Ⓒ Ⓓ Ⓔ	22 Ⓐ Ⓑ Ⓒ Ⓓ Ⓔ
23 Ⓐ Ⓑ Ⓒ Ⓓ Ⓔ	23 Ⓐ Ⓑ Ⓒ Ⓓ Ⓔ	23 Ⓐ Ⓑ Ⓒ Ⓓ Ⓔ	23 Ⓐ Ⓑ Ⓒ Ⓓ Ⓔ
24 Ⓐ Ⓑ Ⓒ Ⓓ Ⓔ	24 Ⓐ Ⓑ Ⓒ Ⓓ Ⓔ	24 Ⓐ Ⓑ Ⓒ Ⓓ Ⓔ	24 Ⓐ Ⓑ Ⓒ Ⓓ Ⓔ
25 Ⓐ Ⓑ Ⓒ Ⓓ Ⓔ	25 Ⓐ Ⓑ Ⓒ Ⓓ Ⓔ	25 Ⓐ Ⓑ Ⓒ Ⓓ Ⓔ	25 Ⓐ Ⓑ Ⓒ Ⓓ Ⓔ
26 Ⓐ Ⓑ Ⓒ Ⓓ Ⓔ	26 Ⓐ Ⓑ Ⓒ Ⓓ Ⓔ	26 Ⓐ Ⓑ Ⓒ Ⓓ Ⓔ	26 Ⓐ Ⓑ Ⓒ Ⓓ Ⓔ
27 Ⓐ Ⓑ Ⓒ Ⓓ Ⓔ	27 Ⓐ Ⓑ Ⓒ Ⓓ Ⓔ	27 Ⓐ Ⓑ Ⓒ Ⓓ Ⓔ	27 Ⓐ Ⓑ Ⓒ Ⓓ Ⓔ
28 Ⓐ Ⓑ Ⓒ Ⓓ Ⓔ	28 Ⓐ Ⓑ Ⓒ Ⓓ Ⓔ	28 Ⓐ Ⓑ Ⓒ Ⓓ Ⓔ	28 Ⓐ Ⓑ Ⓒ Ⓓ Ⓔ
29 Ⓐ Ⓑ Ⓒ Ⓓ Ⓔ	29 Ⓐ Ⓑ Ⓒ Ⓓ Ⓔ	29 Ⓐ Ⓑ Ⓒ Ⓓ Ⓔ	29 Ⓐ Ⓑ Ⓒ Ⓓ Ⓔ
30 Ⓐ Ⓑ Ⓒ Ⓓ Ⓔ	30 Ⓐ Ⓑ Ⓒ Ⓓ Ⓔ	30 Ⓐ Ⓑ Ⓒ Ⓓ Ⓔ	30 Ⓐ Ⓑ Ⓒ Ⓓ Ⓔ

LSAT Answer Sheet

Instructions for completing these items are at the back of your LSAT test book.

1. Name (Print)

Last   First   MI

2. LSAC Account Number   L

Section 1	Section 2	Section 3	Section 4
1 Ⓐ Ⓑ Ⓒ Ⓓ Ⓔ	1 Ⓐ Ⓑ Ⓒ Ⓓ Ⓔ	1 Ⓐ Ⓑ Ⓒ Ⓓ Ⓔ	1 Ⓐ Ⓑ Ⓒ Ⓓ Ⓔ
2 Ⓐ Ⓑ Ⓒ Ⓓ Ⓔ	2 Ⓐ Ⓑ Ⓒ Ⓓ Ⓔ	2 Ⓐ Ⓑ Ⓒ Ⓓ Ⓔ	2 Ⓐ Ⓑ Ⓒ Ⓓ Ⓔ
3 Ⓐ Ⓑ Ⓒ Ⓓ Ⓔ	3 Ⓐ Ⓑ Ⓒ Ⓓ Ⓔ	3 Ⓐ Ⓑ Ⓒ Ⓓ Ⓔ	3 Ⓐ Ⓑ Ⓒ Ⓓ Ⓔ
4 Ⓐ Ⓑ Ⓒ Ⓓ Ⓔ	4 Ⓐ Ⓑ Ⓒ Ⓓ Ⓔ	4 Ⓐ Ⓑ Ⓒ Ⓓ Ⓔ	4 Ⓐ Ⓑ Ⓒ Ⓓ Ⓔ
5 Ⓐ Ⓑ Ⓒ Ⓓ Ⓔ	5 Ⓐ Ⓑ Ⓒ Ⓓ Ⓔ	5 Ⓐ Ⓑ Ⓒ Ⓓ Ⓔ	5 Ⓐ Ⓑ Ⓒ Ⓓ Ⓔ
6 Ⓐ Ⓑ Ⓒ Ⓓ Ⓔ	6 Ⓐ Ⓑ Ⓒ Ⓓ Ⓔ	6 Ⓐ Ⓑ Ⓒ Ⓓ Ⓔ	6 Ⓐ Ⓑ Ⓒ Ⓓ Ⓔ
7 Ⓐ Ⓑ Ⓒ Ⓓ Ⓔ	7 Ⓐ Ⓑ Ⓒ Ⓓ Ⓔ	7 Ⓐ Ⓑ Ⓒ Ⓓ Ⓔ	7 Ⓐ Ⓑ Ⓒ Ⓓ Ⓔ
8 Ⓐ Ⓑ Ⓒ Ⓓ Ⓔ	8 Ⓐ Ⓑ Ⓒ Ⓓ Ⓔ	8 Ⓐ Ⓑ Ⓒ Ⓓ Ⓔ	8 Ⓐ Ⓑ Ⓒ Ⓓ Ⓔ
9 Ⓐ Ⓑ Ⓒ Ⓓ Ⓔ	9 Ⓐ Ⓑ Ⓒ Ⓓ Ⓔ	9 Ⓐ Ⓑ Ⓒ Ⓓ Ⓔ	9 Ⓐ Ⓑ Ⓒ Ⓓ Ⓔ
10 Ⓐ Ⓑ Ⓒ Ⓓ Ⓔ	10 Ⓐ Ⓑ Ⓒ Ⓓ Ⓔ	10 Ⓐ Ⓑ Ⓒ Ⓓ Ⓔ	10 Ⓐ Ⓑ Ⓒ Ⓓ Ⓔ
11 Ⓐ Ⓑ Ⓒ Ⓓ Ⓔ	11 Ⓐ Ⓑ Ⓒ Ⓓ Ⓔ	11 Ⓐ Ⓑ Ⓒ Ⓓ Ⓔ	11 Ⓐ Ⓑ Ⓒ Ⓓ Ⓔ
12 Ⓐ Ⓑ Ⓒ Ⓓ Ⓔ	12 Ⓐ Ⓑ Ⓒ Ⓓ Ⓔ	12 Ⓐ Ⓑ Ⓒ Ⓓ Ⓔ	12 Ⓐ Ⓑ Ⓒ Ⓓ Ⓔ
13 Ⓐ Ⓑ Ⓒ Ⓓ Ⓔ	13 Ⓐ Ⓑ Ⓒ Ⓓ Ⓔ	13 Ⓐ Ⓑ Ⓒ Ⓓ Ⓔ	13 Ⓐ Ⓑ Ⓒ Ⓓ Ⓔ
14 Ⓐ Ⓑ Ⓒ Ⓓ Ⓔ	14 Ⓐ Ⓑ Ⓒ Ⓓ Ⓔ	14 Ⓐ Ⓑ Ⓒ Ⓓ Ⓔ	14 Ⓐ Ⓑ Ⓒ Ⓓ Ⓔ
15 Ⓐ Ⓑ Ⓒ Ⓓ Ⓔ	15 Ⓐ Ⓑ Ⓒ Ⓓ Ⓔ	15 Ⓐ Ⓑ Ⓒ Ⓓ Ⓔ	15 Ⓐ Ⓑ Ⓒ Ⓓ Ⓔ
16 Ⓐ Ⓑ Ⓒ Ⓓ Ⓔ	16 Ⓐ Ⓑ Ⓒ Ⓓ Ⓔ	16 Ⓐ Ⓑ Ⓒ Ⓓ Ⓔ	16 Ⓐ Ⓑ Ⓒ Ⓓ Ⓔ
17 Ⓐ Ⓑ Ⓒ Ⓓ Ⓔ	17 Ⓐ Ⓑ Ⓒ Ⓓ Ⓔ	17 Ⓐ Ⓑ Ⓒ Ⓓ Ⓔ	17 Ⓐ Ⓑ Ⓒ Ⓓ Ⓔ
18 Ⓐ Ⓑ Ⓒ Ⓓ Ⓔ	18 Ⓐ Ⓑ Ⓒ Ⓓ Ⓔ	18 Ⓐ Ⓑ Ⓒ Ⓓ Ⓔ	18 Ⓐ Ⓑ Ⓒ Ⓓ Ⓔ
19 Ⓐ Ⓑ Ⓒ Ⓓ Ⓔ	19 Ⓐ Ⓑ Ⓒ Ⓓ Ⓔ	19 Ⓐ Ⓑ Ⓒ Ⓓ Ⓔ	19 Ⓐ Ⓑ Ⓒ Ⓓ Ⓔ
20 Ⓐ Ⓑ Ⓒ Ⓓ Ⓔ	20 Ⓐ Ⓑ Ⓒ Ⓓ Ⓔ	20 Ⓐ Ⓑ Ⓒ Ⓓ Ⓔ	20 Ⓐ Ⓑ Ⓒ Ⓓ Ⓔ
21 Ⓐ Ⓑ Ⓒ Ⓓ Ⓔ	21 Ⓐ Ⓑ Ⓒ Ⓓ Ⓔ	21 Ⓐ Ⓑ Ⓒ Ⓓ Ⓔ	21 Ⓐ Ⓑ Ⓒ Ⓓ Ⓔ
22 Ⓐ Ⓑ Ⓒ Ⓓ Ⓔ	22 Ⓐ Ⓑ Ⓒ Ⓓ Ⓔ	22 Ⓐ Ⓑ Ⓒ Ⓓ Ⓔ	22 Ⓐ Ⓑ Ⓒ Ⓓ Ⓔ
23 Ⓐ Ⓑ Ⓒ Ⓓ Ⓔ	23 Ⓐ Ⓑ Ⓒ Ⓓ Ⓔ	23 Ⓐ Ⓑ Ⓒ Ⓓ Ⓔ	23 Ⓐ Ⓑ Ⓒ Ⓓ Ⓔ
24 Ⓐ Ⓑ Ⓒ Ⓓ Ⓔ	24 Ⓐ Ⓑ Ⓒ Ⓓ Ⓔ	24 Ⓐ Ⓑ Ⓒ Ⓓ Ⓔ	24 Ⓐ Ⓑ Ⓒ Ⓓ Ⓔ
25 Ⓐ Ⓑ Ⓒ Ⓓ Ⓔ	25 Ⓐ Ⓑ Ⓒ Ⓓ Ⓔ	25 Ⓐ Ⓑ Ⓒ Ⓓ Ⓔ	25 Ⓐ Ⓑ Ⓒ Ⓓ Ⓔ
26 Ⓐ Ⓑ Ⓒ Ⓓ Ⓔ	26 Ⓐ Ⓑ Ⓒ Ⓓ Ⓔ	26 Ⓐ Ⓑ Ⓒ Ⓓ Ⓔ	26 Ⓐ Ⓑ Ⓒ Ⓓ Ⓔ
27 Ⓐ Ⓑ Ⓒ Ⓓ Ⓔ	27 Ⓐ Ⓑ Ⓒ Ⓓ Ⓔ	27 Ⓐ Ⓑ Ⓒ Ⓓ Ⓔ	27 Ⓐ Ⓑ Ⓒ Ⓓ Ⓔ
28 Ⓐ Ⓑ Ⓒ Ⓓ Ⓔ	28 Ⓐ Ⓑ Ⓒ Ⓓ Ⓔ	28 Ⓐ Ⓑ Ⓒ Ⓓ Ⓔ	28 Ⓐ Ⓑ Ⓒ Ⓓ Ⓔ
29 Ⓐ Ⓑ Ⓒ Ⓓ Ⓔ	29 Ⓐ Ⓑ Ⓒ Ⓓ Ⓔ	29 Ⓐ Ⓑ Ⓒ Ⓓ Ⓔ	29 Ⓐ Ⓑ Ⓒ Ⓓ Ⓔ
30 Ⓐ Ⓑ Ⓒ Ⓓ Ⓔ	30 Ⓐ Ⓑ Ⓒ Ⓓ Ⓔ	30 Ⓐ Ⓑ Ⓒ Ⓓ Ⓔ	30 Ⓐ Ⓑ Ⓒ Ⓓ Ⓔ

LSAT Answer Sheet

Instructions for completing these items are at the back of your LSAT test book.

1. Name (Print)

Last   First   MI

2. LSAC Account Number L ☐☐☐☐☐☐☐☐

Section 1	Section 2	Section 3	Section 4
1 Ⓐ Ⓑ Ⓒ Ⓓ Ⓔ	1 Ⓐ Ⓑ Ⓒ Ⓓ Ⓔ	1 Ⓐ Ⓑ Ⓒ Ⓓ Ⓔ	1 Ⓐ Ⓑ Ⓒ Ⓓ Ⓔ
2 Ⓐ Ⓑ Ⓒ Ⓓ Ⓔ	2 Ⓐ Ⓑ Ⓒ Ⓓ Ⓔ	2 Ⓐ Ⓑ Ⓒ Ⓓ Ⓔ	2 Ⓐ Ⓑ Ⓒ Ⓓ Ⓔ
3 Ⓐ Ⓑ Ⓒ Ⓓ Ⓔ	3 Ⓐ Ⓑ Ⓒ Ⓓ Ⓔ	3 Ⓐ Ⓑ Ⓒ Ⓓ Ⓔ	3 Ⓐ Ⓑ Ⓒ Ⓓ Ⓔ
4 Ⓐ Ⓑ Ⓒ Ⓓ Ⓔ	4 Ⓐ Ⓑ Ⓒ Ⓓ Ⓔ	4 Ⓐ Ⓑ Ⓒ Ⓓ Ⓔ	4 Ⓐ Ⓑ Ⓒ Ⓓ Ⓔ
5 Ⓐ Ⓑ Ⓒ Ⓓ Ⓔ	5 Ⓐ Ⓑ Ⓒ Ⓓ Ⓔ	5 Ⓐ Ⓑ Ⓒ Ⓓ Ⓔ	5 Ⓐ Ⓑ Ⓒ Ⓓ Ⓔ
6 Ⓐ Ⓑ Ⓒ Ⓓ Ⓔ	6 Ⓐ Ⓑ Ⓒ Ⓓ Ⓔ	6 Ⓐ Ⓑ Ⓒ Ⓓ Ⓔ	6 Ⓐ Ⓑ Ⓒ Ⓓ Ⓔ
7 Ⓐ Ⓑ Ⓒ Ⓓ Ⓔ	7 Ⓐ Ⓑ Ⓒ Ⓓ Ⓔ	7 Ⓐ Ⓑ Ⓒ Ⓓ Ⓔ	7 Ⓐ Ⓑ Ⓒ Ⓓ Ⓔ
8 Ⓐ Ⓑ Ⓒ Ⓓ Ⓔ	8 Ⓐ Ⓑ Ⓒ Ⓓ Ⓔ	8 Ⓐ Ⓑ Ⓒ Ⓓ Ⓔ	8 Ⓐ Ⓑ Ⓒ Ⓓ Ⓔ
9 Ⓐ Ⓑ Ⓒ Ⓓ Ⓔ	9 Ⓐ Ⓑ Ⓒ Ⓓ Ⓔ	9 Ⓐ Ⓑ Ⓒ Ⓓ Ⓔ	9 Ⓐ Ⓑ Ⓒ Ⓓ Ⓔ
10 Ⓐ Ⓑ Ⓒ Ⓓ Ⓔ	10 Ⓐ Ⓑ Ⓒ Ⓓ Ⓔ	10 Ⓐ Ⓑ Ⓒ Ⓓ Ⓔ	10 Ⓐ Ⓑ Ⓒ Ⓓ Ⓔ
11 Ⓐ Ⓑ Ⓒ Ⓓ Ⓔ	11 Ⓐ Ⓑ Ⓒ Ⓓ Ⓔ	11 Ⓐ Ⓑ Ⓒ Ⓓ Ⓔ	11 Ⓐ Ⓑ Ⓒ Ⓓ Ⓔ
12 Ⓐ Ⓑ Ⓒ Ⓓ Ⓔ	12 Ⓐ Ⓑ Ⓒ Ⓓ Ⓔ	12 Ⓐ Ⓑ Ⓒ Ⓓ Ⓔ	12 Ⓐ Ⓑ Ⓒ Ⓓ Ⓔ
13 Ⓐ Ⓑ Ⓒ Ⓓ Ⓔ	13 Ⓐ Ⓑ Ⓒ Ⓓ Ⓔ	13 Ⓐ Ⓑ Ⓒ Ⓓ Ⓔ	13 Ⓐ Ⓑ Ⓒ Ⓓ Ⓔ
14 Ⓐ Ⓑ Ⓒ Ⓓ Ⓔ	14 Ⓐ Ⓑ Ⓒ Ⓓ Ⓔ	14 Ⓐ Ⓑ Ⓒ Ⓓ Ⓔ	14 Ⓐ Ⓑ Ⓒ Ⓓ Ⓔ
15 Ⓐ Ⓑ Ⓒ Ⓓ Ⓔ	15 Ⓐ Ⓑ Ⓒ Ⓓ Ⓔ	15 Ⓐ Ⓑ Ⓒ Ⓓ Ⓔ	15 Ⓐ Ⓑ Ⓒ Ⓓ Ⓔ
16 Ⓐ Ⓑ Ⓒ Ⓓ Ⓔ	16 Ⓐ Ⓑ Ⓒ Ⓓ Ⓔ	16 Ⓐ Ⓑ Ⓒ Ⓓ Ⓔ	16 Ⓐ Ⓑ Ⓒ Ⓓ Ⓔ
17 Ⓐ Ⓑ Ⓒ Ⓓ Ⓔ	17 Ⓐ Ⓑ Ⓒ Ⓓ Ⓔ	17 Ⓐ Ⓑ Ⓒ Ⓓ Ⓔ	17 Ⓐ Ⓑ Ⓒ Ⓓ Ⓔ
18 Ⓐ Ⓑ Ⓒ Ⓓ Ⓔ	18 Ⓐ Ⓑ Ⓒ Ⓓ Ⓔ	18 Ⓐ Ⓑ Ⓒ Ⓓ Ⓔ	18 Ⓐ Ⓑ Ⓒ Ⓓ Ⓔ
19 Ⓐ Ⓑ Ⓒ Ⓓ Ⓔ	19 Ⓐ Ⓑ Ⓒ Ⓓ Ⓔ	19 Ⓐ Ⓑ Ⓒ Ⓓ Ⓔ	19 Ⓐ Ⓑ Ⓒ Ⓓ Ⓔ
20 Ⓐ Ⓑ Ⓒ Ⓓ Ⓔ	20 Ⓐ Ⓑ Ⓒ Ⓓ Ⓔ	20 Ⓐ Ⓑ Ⓒ Ⓓ Ⓔ	20 Ⓐ Ⓑ Ⓒ Ⓓ Ⓔ
21 Ⓐ Ⓑ Ⓒ Ⓓ Ⓔ	21 Ⓐ Ⓑ Ⓒ Ⓓ Ⓔ	21 Ⓐ Ⓑ Ⓒ Ⓓ Ⓔ	21 Ⓐ Ⓑ Ⓒ Ⓓ Ⓔ
22 Ⓐ Ⓑ Ⓒ Ⓓ Ⓔ	22 Ⓐ Ⓑ Ⓒ Ⓓ Ⓔ	22 Ⓐ Ⓑ Ⓒ Ⓓ Ⓔ	22 Ⓐ Ⓑ Ⓒ Ⓓ Ⓔ
23 Ⓐ Ⓑ Ⓒ Ⓓ Ⓔ	23 Ⓐ Ⓑ Ⓒ Ⓓ Ⓔ	23 Ⓐ Ⓑ Ⓒ Ⓓ Ⓔ	23 Ⓐ Ⓑ Ⓒ Ⓓ Ⓔ
24 Ⓐ Ⓑ Ⓒ Ⓓ Ⓔ	24 Ⓐ Ⓑ Ⓒ Ⓓ Ⓔ	24 Ⓐ Ⓑ Ⓒ Ⓓ Ⓔ	24 Ⓐ Ⓑ Ⓒ Ⓓ Ⓔ
25 Ⓐ Ⓑ Ⓒ Ⓓ Ⓔ	25 Ⓐ Ⓑ Ⓒ Ⓓ Ⓔ	25 Ⓐ Ⓑ Ⓒ Ⓓ Ⓔ	25 Ⓐ Ⓑ Ⓒ Ⓓ Ⓔ
26 Ⓐ Ⓑ Ⓒ Ⓓ Ⓔ	26 Ⓐ Ⓑ Ⓒ Ⓓ Ⓔ	26 Ⓐ Ⓑ Ⓒ Ⓓ Ⓔ	26 Ⓐ Ⓑ Ⓒ Ⓓ Ⓔ
27 Ⓐ Ⓑ Ⓒ Ⓓ Ⓔ	27 Ⓐ Ⓑ Ⓒ Ⓓ Ⓔ	27 Ⓐ Ⓑ Ⓒ Ⓓ Ⓔ	27 Ⓐ Ⓑ Ⓒ Ⓓ Ⓔ
28 Ⓐ Ⓑ Ⓒ Ⓓ Ⓔ	28 Ⓐ Ⓑ Ⓒ Ⓓ Ⓔ	28 Ⓐ Ⓑ Ⓒ Ⓓ Ⓔ	28 Ⓐ Ⓑ Ⓒ Ⓓ Ⓔ
29 Ⓐ Ⓑ Ⓒ Ⓓ Ⓔ	29 Ⓐ Ⓑ Ⓒ Ⓓ Ⓔ	29 Ⓐ Ⓑ Ⓒ Ⓓ Ⓔ	29 Ⓐ Ⓑ Ⓒ Ⓓ Ⓔ
30 Ⓐ Ⓑ Ⓒ Ⓓ Ⓔ	30 Ⓐ Ⓑ Ⓒ Ⓓ Ⓔ	30 Ⓐ Ⓑ Ⓒ Ⓓ Ⓔ	30 Ⓐ Ⓑ Ⓒ Ⓓ Ⓔ

LSAT Answer Sheet

Instructions for completing these items are at the back of your LSAT test book.

1. Name (Print)

Last　　　　　　　　　　　　　First　　　　　　　　　　　MI

2. LSAC Account Number　L ☐☐☐☐☐☐☐☐

Section 1	Section 2	Section 3	Section 4
1 Ⓐ Ⓑ Ⓒ Ⓓ Ⓔ	1 Ⓐ Ⓑ Ⓒ Ⓓ Ⓔ	1 Ⓐ Ⓑ Ⓒ Ⓓ Ⓔ	1 Ⓐ Ⓑ Ⓒ Ⓓ Ⓔ
2 Ⓐ Ⓑ Ⓒ Ⓓ Ⓔ	2 Ⓐ Ⓑ Ⓒ Ⓓ Ⓔ	2 Ⓐ Ⓑ Ⓒ Ⓓ Ⓔ	2 Ⓐ Ⓑ Ⓒ Ⓓ Ⓔ
3 Ⓐ Ⓑ Ⓒ Ⓓ Ⓔ	3 Ⓐ Ⓑ Ⓒ Ⓓ Ⓔ	3 Ⓐ Ⓑ Ⓒ Ⓓ Ⓔ	3 Ⓐ Ⓑ Ⓒ Ⓓ Ⓔ
4 Ⓐ Ⓑ Ⓒ Ⓓ Ⓔ	4 Ⓐ Ⓑ Ⓒ Ⓓ Ⓔ	4 Ⓐ Ⓑ Ⓒ Ⓓ Ⓔ	4 Ⓐ Ⓑ Ⓒ Ⓓ Ⓔ
5 Ⓐ Ⓑ Ⓒ Ⓓ Ⓔ	5 Ⓐ Ⓑ Ⓒ Ⓓ Ⓔ	5 Ⓐ Ⓑ Ⓒ Ⓓ Ⓔ	5 Ⓐ Ⓑ Ⓒ Ⓓ Ⓔ
6 Ⓐ Ⓑ Ⓒ Ⓓ Ⓔ	6 Ⓐ Ⓑ Ⓒ Ⓓ Ⓔ	6 Ⓐ Ⓑ Ⓒ Ⓓ Ⓔ	6 Ⓐ Ⓑ Ⓒ Ⓓ Ⓔ
7 Ⓐ Ⓑ Ⓒ Ⓓ Ⓔ	7 Ⓐ Ⓑ Ⓒ Ⓓ Ⓔ	7 Ⓐ Ⓑ Ⓒ Ⓓ Ⓔ	7 Ⓐ Ⓑ Ⓒ Ⓓ Ⓔ
8 Ⓐ Ⓑ Ⓒ Ⓓ Ⓔ	8 Ⓐ Ⓑ Ⓒ Ⓓ Ⓔ	8 Ⓐ Ⓑ Ⓒ Ⓓ Ⓔ	8 Ⓐ Ⓑ Ⓒ Ⓓ Ⓔ
9 Ⓐ Ⓑ Ⓒ Ⓓ Ⓔ	9 Ⓐ Ⓑ Ⓒ Ⓓ Ⓔ	9 Ⓐ Ⓑ Ⓒ Ⓓ Ⓔ	9 Ⓐ Ⓑ Ⓒ Ⓓ Ⓔ
10 Ⓐ Ⓑ Ⓒ Ⓓ Ⓔ	10 Ⓐ Ⓑ Ⓒ Ⓓ Ⓔ	10 Ⓐ Ⓑ Ⓒ Ⓓ Ⓔ	10 Ⓐ Ⓑ Ⓒ Ⓓ Ⓔ
11 Ⓐ Ⓑ Ⓒ Ⓓ Ⓔ	11 Ⓐ Ⓑ Ⓒ Ⓓ Ⓔ	11 Ⓐ Ⓑ Ⓒ Ⓓ Ⓔ	11 Ⓐ Ⓑ Ⓒ Ⓓ Ⓔ
12 Ⓐ Ⓑ Ⓒ Ⓓ Ⓔ	12 Ⓐ Ⓑ Ⓒ Ⓓ Ⓔ	12 Ⓐ Ⓑ Ⓒ Ⓓ Ⓔ	12 Ⓐ Ⓑ Ⓒ Ⓓ Ⓔ
13 Ⓐ Ⓑ Ⓒ Ⓓ Ⓔ	13 Ⓐ Ⓑ Ⓒ Ⓓ Ⓔ	13 Ⓐ Ⓑ Ⓒ Ⓓ Ⓔ	13 Ⓐ Ⓑ Ⓒ Ⓓ Ⓔ
14 Ⓐ Ⓑ Ⓒ Ⓓ Ⓔ	14 Ⓐ Ⓑ Ⓒ Ⓓ Ⓔ	14 Ⓐ Ⓑ Ⓒ Ⓓ Ⓔ	14 Ⓐ Ⓑ Ⓒ Ⓓ Ⓔ
15 Ⓐ Ⓑ Ⓒ Ⓓ Ⓔ	15 Ⓐ Ⓑ Ⓒ Ⓓ Ⓔ	15 Ⓐ Ⓑ Ⓒ Ⓓ Ⓔ	15 Ⓐ Ⓑ Ⓒ Ⓓ Ⓔ
16 Ⓐ Ⓑ Ⓒ Ⓓ Ⓔ	16 Ⓐ Ⓑ Ⓒ Ⓓ Ⓔ	16 Ⓐ Ⓑ Ⓒ Ⓓ Ⓔ	16 Ⓐ Ⓑ Ⓒ Ⓓ Ⓔ
17 Ⓐ Ⓑ Ⓒ Ⓓ Ⓔ	17 Ⓐ Ⓑ Ⓒ Ⓓ Ⓔ	17 Ⓐ Ⓑ Ⓒ Ⓓ Ⓔ	17 Ⓐ Ⓑ Ⓒ Ⓓ Ⓔ
18 Ⓐ Ⓑ Ⓒ Ⓓ Ⓔ	18 Ⓐ Ⓑ Ⓒ Ⓓ Ⓔ	18 Ⓐ Ⓑ Ⓒ Ⓓ Ⓔ	18 Ⓐ Ⓑ Ⓒ Ⓓ Ⓔ
19 Ⓐ Ⓑ Ⓒ Ⓓ Ⓔ	19 Ⓐ Ⓑ Ⓒ Ⓓ Ⓔ	19 Ⓐ Ⓑ Ⓒ Ⓓ Ⓔ	19 Ⓐ Ⓑ Ⓒ Ⓓ Ⓔ
20 Ⓐ Ⓑ Ⓒ Ⓓ Ⓔ	20 Ⓐ Ⓑ Ⓒ Ⓓ Ⓔ	20 Ⓐ Ⓑ Ⓒ Ⓓ Ⓔ	20 Ⓐ Ⓑ Ⓒ Ⓓ Ⓔ
21 Ⓐ Ⓑ Ⓒ Ⓓ Ⓔ	21 Ⓐ Ⓑ Ⓒ Ⓓ Ⓔ	21 Ⓐ Ⓑ Ⓒ Ⓓ Ⓔ	21 Ⓐ Ⓑ Ⓒ Ⓓ Ⓔ
22 Ⓐ Ⓑ Ⓒ Ⓓ Ⓔ	22 Ⓐ Ⓑ Ⓒ Ⓓ Ⓔ	22 Ⓐ Ⓑ Ⓒ Ⓓ Ⓔ	22 Ⓐ Ⓑ Ⓒ Ⓓ Ⓔ
23 Ⓐ Ⓑ Ⓒ Ⓓ Ⓔ	23 Ⓐ Ⓑ Ⓒ Ⓓ Ⓔ	23 Ⓐ Ⓑ Ⓒ Ⓓ Ⓔ	23 Ⓐ Ⓑ Ⓒ Ⓓ Ⓔ
24 Ⓐ Ⓑ Ⓒ Ⓓ Ⓔ	24 Ⓐ Ⓑ Ⓒ Ⓓ Ⓔ	24 Ⓐ Ⓑ Ⓒ Ⓓ Ⓔ	24 Ⓐ Ⓑ Ⓒ Ⓓ Ⓔ
25 Ⓐ Ⓑ Ⓒ Ⓓ Ⓔ	25 Ⓐ Ⓑ Ⓒ Ⓓ Ⓔ	25 Ⓐ Ⓑ Ⓒ Ⓓ Ⓔ	25 Ⓐ Ⓑ Ⓒ Ⓓ Ⓔ
26 Ⓐ Ⓑ Ⓒ Ⓓ Ⓔ	26 Ⓐ Ⓑ Ⓒ Ⓓ Ⓔ	26 Ⓐ Ⓑ Ⓒ Ⓓ Ⓔ	26 Ⓐ Ⓑ Ⓒ Ⓓ Ⓔ
27 Ⓐ Ⓑ Ⓒ Ⓓ Ⓔ	27 Ⓐ Ⓑ Ⓒ Ⓓ Ⓔ	27 Ⓐ Ⓑ Ⓒ Ⓓ Ⓔ	27 Ⓐ Ⓑ Ⓒ Ⓓ Ⓔ
28 Ⓐ Ⓑ Ⓒ Ⓓ Ⓔ	28 Ⓐ Ⓑ Ⓒ Ⓓ Ⓔ	28 Ⓐ Ⓑ Ⓒ Ⓓ Ⓔ	28 Ⓐ Ⓑ Ⓒ Ⓓ Ⓔ
29 Ⓐ Ⓑ Ⓒ Ⓓ Ⓔ	29 Ⓐ Ⓑ Ⓒ Ⓓ Ⓔ	29 Ⓐ Ⓑ Ⓒ Ⓓ Ⓔ	29 Ⓐ Ⓑ Ⓒ Ⓓ Ⓔ
30 Ⓐ Ⓑ Ⓒ Ⓓ Ⓔ	30 Ⓐ Ⓑ Ⓒ Ⓓ Ⓔ	30 Ⓐ Ⓑ Ⓒ Ⓓ Ⓔ	30 Ⓐ Ⓑ Ⓒ Ⓓ Ⓔ

LSAT Answer Sheet

Instructions for completing these items are at the back of your LSAT test book.

1. Name (Print)

Last   First   MI

2. LSAC Account Number L ☐☐☐☐☐☐☐

Section 1	Section 2	Section 3	Section 4
1 Ⓐ Ⓑ Ⓒ Ⓓ Ⓔ	1 Ⓐ Ⓑ Ⓒ Ⓓ Ⓔ	1 Ⓐ Ⓑ Ⓒ Ⓓ Ⓔ	1 Ⓐ Ⓑ Ⓒ Ⓓ Ⓔ
2 Ⓐ Ⓑ Ⓒ Ⓓ Ⓔ	2 Ⓐ Ⓑ Ⓒ Ⓓ Ⓔ	2 Ⓐ Ⓑ Ⓒ Ⓓ Ⓔ	2 Ⓐ Ⓑ Ⓒ Ⓓ Ⓔ
3 Ⓐ Ⓑ Ⓒ Ⓓ Ⓔ	3 Ⓐ Ⓑ Ⓒ Ⓓ Ⓔ	3 Ⓐ Ⓑ Ⓒ Ⓓ Ⓔ	3 Ⓐ Ⓑ Ⓒ Ⓓ Ⓔ
4 Ⓐ Ⓑ Ⓒ Ⓓ Ⓔ	4 Ⓐ Ⓑ Ⓒ Ⓓ Ⓔ	4 Ⓐ Ⓑ Ⓒ Ⓓ Ⓔ	4 Ⓐ Ⓑ Ⓒ Ⓓ Ⓔ
5 Ⓐ Ⓑ Ⓒ Ⓓ Ⓔ	5 Ⓐ Ⓑ Ⓒ Ⓓ Ⓔ	5 Ⓐ Ⓑ Ⓒ Ⓓ Ⓔ	5 Ⓐ Ⓑ Ⓒ Ⓓ Ⓔ
6 Ⓐ Ⓑ Ⓒ Ⓓ Ⓔ	6 Ⓐ Ⓑ Ⓒ Ⓓ Ⓔ	6 Ⓐ Ⓑ Ⓒ Ⓓ Ⓔ	6 Ⓐ Ⓑ Ⓒ Ⓓ Ⓔ
7 Ⓐ Ⓑ Ⓒ Ⓓ Ⓔ	7 Ⓐ Ⓑ Ⓒ Ⓓ Ⓔ	7 Ⓐ Ⓑ Ⓒ Ⓓ Ⓔ	7 Ⓐ Ⓑ Ⓒ Ⓓ Ⓔ
8 Ⓐ Ⓑ Ⓒ Ⓓ Ⓔ	8 Ⓐ Ⓑ Ⓒ Ⓓ Ⓔ	8 Ⓐ Ⓑ Ⓒ Ⓓ Ⓔ	8 Ⓐ Ⓑ Ⓒ Ⓓ Ⓔ
9 Ⓐ Ⓑ Ⓒ Ⓓ Ⓔ	9 Ⓐ Ⓑ Ⓒ Ⓓ Ⓔ	9 Ⓐ Ⓑ Ⓒ Ⓓ Ⓔ	9 Ⓐ Ⓑ Ⓒ Ⓓ Ⓔ
10 Ⓐ Ⓑ Ⓒ Ⓓ Ⓔ	10 Ⓐ Ⓑ Ⓒ Ⓓ Ⓔ	10 Ⓐ Ⓑ Ⓒ Ⓓ Ⓔ	10 Ⓐ Ⓑ Ⓒ Ⓓ Ⓔ
11 Ⓐ Ⓑ Ⓒ Ⓓ Ⓔ	11 Ⓐ Ⓑ Ⓒ Ⓓ Ⓔ	11 Ⓐ Ⓑ Ⓒ Ⓓ Ⓔ	11 Ⓐ Ⓑ Ⓒ Ⓓ Ⓔ
12 Ⓐ Ⓑ Ⓒ Ⓓ Ⓔ	12 Ⓐ Ⓑ Ⓒ Ⓓ Ⓔ	12 Ⓐ Ⓑ Ⓒ Ⓓ Ⓔ	12 Ⓐ Ⓑ Ⓒ Ⓓ Ⓔ
13 Ⓐ Ⓑ Ⓒ Ⓓ Ⓔ	13 Ⓐ Ⓑ Ⓒ Ⓓ Ⓔ	13 Ⓐ Ⓑ Ⓒ Ⓓ Ⓔ	13 Ⓐ Ⓑ Ⓒ Ⓓ Ⓔ
14 Ⓐ Ⓑ Ⓒ Ⓓ Ⓔ	14 Ⓐ Ⓑ Ⓒ Ⓓ Ⓔ	14 Ⓐ Ⓑ Ⓒ Ⓓ Ⓔ	14 Ⓐ Ⓑ Ⓒ Ⓓ Ⓔ
15 Ⓐ Ⓑ Ⓒ Ⓓ Ⓔ	15 Ⓐ Ⓑ Ⓒ Ⓓ Ⓔ	15 Ⓐ Ⓑ Ⓒ Ⓓ Ⓔ	15 Ⓐ Ⓑ Ⓒ Ⓓ Ⓔ
16 Ⓐ Ⓑ Ⓒ Ⓓ Ⓔ	16 Ⓐ Ⓑ Ⓒ Ⓓ Ⓔ	16 Ⓐ Ⓑ Ⓒ Ⓓ Ⓔ	16 Ⓐ Ⓑ Ⓒ Ⓓ Ⓔ
17 Ⓐ Ⓑ Ⓒ Ⓓ Ⓔ	17 Ⓐ Ⓑ Ⓒ Ⓓ Ⓔ	17 Ⓐ Ⓑ Ⓒ Ⓓ Ⓔ	17 Ⓐ Ⓑ Ⓒ Ⓓ Ⓔ
18 Ⓐ Ⓑ Ⓒ Ⓓ Ⓔ	18 Ⓐ Ⓑ Ⓒ Ⓓ Ⓔ	18 Ⓐ Ⓑ Ⓒ Ⓓ Ⓔ	18 Ⓐ Ⓑ Ⓒ Ⓓ Ⓔ
19 Ⓐ Ⓑ Ⓒ Ⓓ Ⓔ	19 Ⓐ Ⓑ Ⓒ Ⓓ Ⓔ	19 Ⓐ Ⓑ Ⓒ Ⓓ Ⓔ	19 Ⓐ Ⓑ Ⓒ Ⓓ Ⓔ
20 Ⓐ Ⓑ Ⓒ Ⓓ Ⓔ	20 Ⓐ Ⓑ Ⓒ Ⓓ Ⓔ	20 Ⓐ Ⓑ Ⓒ Ⓓ Ⓔ	20 Ⓐ Ⓑ Ⓒ Ⓓ Ⓔ
21 Ⓐ Ⓑ Ⓒ Ⓓ Ⓔ	21 Ⓐ Ⓑ Ⓒ Ⓓ Ⓔ	21 Ⓐ Ⓑ Ⓒ Ⓓ Ⓔ	21 Ⓐ Ⓑ Ⓒ Ⓓ Ⓔ
22 Ⓐ Ⓑ Ⓒ Ⓓ Ⓔ	22 Ⓐ Ⓑ Ⓒ Ⓓ Ⓔ	22 Ⓐ Ⓑ Ⓒ Ⓓ Ⓔ	22 Ⓐ Ⓑ Ⓒ Ⓓ Ⓔ
23 Ⓐ Ⓑ Ⓒ Ⓓ Ⓔ	23 Ⓐ Ⓑ Ⓒ Ⓓ Ⓔ	23 Ⓐ Ⓑ Ⓒ Ⓓ Ⓔ	23 Ⓐ Ⓑ Ⓒ Ⓓ Ⓔ
24 Ⓐ Ⓑ Ⓒ Ⓓ Ⓔ	24 Ⓐ Ⓑ Ⓒ Ⓓ Ⓔ	24 Ⓐ Ⓑ Ⓒ Ⓓ Ⓔ	24 Ⓐ Ⓑ Ⓒ Ⓓ Ⓔ
25 Ⓐ Ⓑ Ⓒ Ⓓ Ⓔ	25 Ⓐ Ⓑ Ⓒ Ⓓ Ⓔ	25 Ⓐ Ⓑ Ⓒ Ⓓ Ⓔ	25 Ⓐ Ⓑ Ⓒ Ⓓ Ⓔ
26 Ⓐ Ⓑ Ⓒ Ⓓ Ⓔ	26 Ⓐ Ⓑ Ⓒ Ⓓ Ⓔ	26 Ⓐ Ⓑ Ⓒ Ⓓ Ⓔ	26 Ⓐ Ⓑ Ⓒ Ⓓ Ⓔ
27 Ⓐ Ⓑ Ⓒ Ⓓ Ⓔ	27 Ⓐ Ⓑ Ⓒ Ⓓ Ⓔ	27 Ⓐ Ⓑ Ⓒ Ⓓ Ⓔ	27 Ⓐ Ⓑ Ⓒ Ⓓ Ⓔ
28 Ⓐ Ⓑ Ⓒ Ⓓ Ⓔ	28 Ⓐ Ⓑ Ⓒ Ⓓ Ⓔ	28 Ⓐ Ⓑ Ⓒ Ⓓ Ⓔ	28 Ⓐ Ⓑ Ⓒ Ⓓ Ⓔ
29 Ⓐ Ⓑ Ⓒ Ⓓ Ⓔ	29 Ⓐ Ⓑ Ⓒ Ⓓ Ⓔ	29 Ⓐ Ⓑ Ⓒ Ⓓ Ⓔ	29 Ⓐ Ⓑ Ⓒ Ⓓ Ⓔ
30 Ⓐ Ⓑ Ⓒ Ⓓ Ⓔ	30 Ⓐ Ⓑ Ⓒ Ⓓ Ⓔ	30 Ⓐ Ⓑ Ⓒ Ⓓ Ⓔ	30 Ⓐ Ⓑ Ⓒ Ⓓ Ⓔ